# Tax List of Chester County Pennsylvania 1768

Reprinted from the
*Pennsylvania Archives*
Third Series

F. Edward Wright

HERITAGE BOOKS
2012

# HERITAGE BOOKS
*AN IMPRINT OF HERITAGE BOOKS, INC.*

## Books, CDs, and more—Worldwide

For our listing of thousands of titles see our website at
www.HeritageBooks.com

Published 2012 by
HERITAGE BOOKS, INC.
Publishing Division
100 Railroad Ave. #104
Westminster, Maryland 21157

Copyright © 1989 F. Edward Wright

All rights reserved. No part of this book may be reproduced or transmitted in any form or by any means, electronic or mechanical, including photocopying, recording or by any information storage and retrieval system without written permission from the author, except for the inclusion of brief quotations in a review.

International Standard Book Numbers
Paperbound: 978-1-58549-130-8
Clothbound: 978-0-7884-9408-6

## CONTENTS

| | |
|---|---|
| Introduction | v |
| Upper Darby Township | 1 |
| Chester Township | 2 |
| Middletown Township | 5 |
| West Town Township | 6 |
| Thornbury Township | 7 |
| East Bradford Township | 9 |
| New Garden Township | 11 |
| West Whiteland Township | 12 |
| East Followfield Township | 14 |
| Sadsbury Township | 15 |
| New London Township | 17 |
| Kennett Township | 19 |
| Newlinton Township | 22 |
| West Nottingham Township | 23 |
| East Nottingham Township | 26 |
| Astown Township | 30 |
| West Marlborough Township | 32 |
| Uwchland Township | 33 |
| Upper Providence Township | 35 |
| Lower Darby | 37 |
| Coventry Township | 38 |
| Pikeland Township | 41 |
| Nether Providence Township | 43 |
| Haverford Township | 44 |
| Upper Chichester Township | 45 |
| Bethel Township | 47 |
| Springfield Township | 48 |
| Edgement Township | 49 |
| Concord Township | 50 |
| Marple Township | 52 |
| Ridley Township | 53 |
| Lower Chichester Township | 55 |
| Charles Town Township | 57 |
| Birmingham Township | 60 |
| London Britain Township | 61 |
| London Grove Township | 63 |
| East Marlborough Township | 64 |
| West Bradford Township | 66 |
| West Nantmill Township | 69 |
| Oxford Township | 72 |
| London Derry Township | 74 |
| West Fallowfield Township | 76 |
| East Caln Township | 78 |
| West Caln Township | 81 |
| East Nantmill Township | 83 |
| Vincent Township | 85 |
| Tredyffrin Township | 88 |
| East Town Township | 90 |
| Radnor Township | 92 |
| East Whiteland Township | 94 |
| Newtown Township | 95 |
| Goshen Township | 96 |
| Willis Town Township | 99 |
| Index | 103 |

## INTRODUCTION

The following persons were taxed:
(1) Householders or landholders including land owners and tenants - no distinction was made between the two.
(2) Inmates, meaning residents in the household of another (not a renter) who worked for the landowner.
(3) Freemen, who were single men over the age of 21. They appear at the end of the listing of the township and were always assessed the same amount.
(4) Non-residents, unseated landowners (unoccupied land).

This listing was taken exactly as written in the published Third Series of Pennsylvania Archives. The spelling of names has not been changed.

Abbreviations have the following meanings.

| | |
|---|---|
| f. - ferry, forge or furnace | s. - still |
| f.m. - fulling mill | s.f. - steel forge |
| g.m. - grist mill | s.m. - saw mill |
| h.m. - hemp mill | s.q. - stone quarry |
| m. - miller | t.k. - tavern keeper |
| m.h. - malt house | w.s.q. - whetstone quarry |
| p.m. - paper mill | |

F. Edward Wright
Westminster, Maryland

## CHESTER COUNTY RATES - 1768

### Upper Darby Rate

| | Acres | Horses | Cattle | Sheep | Servants |
|---|---|---|---|---|---|
| Joshua Ash | 300 | 5 | 10 | 20 | 1 |
| Joshua Ash, Jun'r | 50 | 1 | -- | -- | -- |
| Isaac Grent, shoemaker | -- | -- | -- | -- | -- |
| William Alexander | 50 | 2 | 3 | -- | -- |
| Abraham Bonsall | 196 | 5 | 8 | 8 | -- |
| John Brennan | 147 | 3 | 6 | 6 | -- |
| John Ball | 100 | 2 | 3 | 8 | -- |
| Benjamin Bonsall | 150 | 3 | 5 | -- | -- |
| John Brookes | 55 | 3 | 3 | 6 | -- |
| Eno'ch Bonsall, Jun'r, cordwainer | 50 | 1 | 3 | -- | -- |
| Joseph Bonsall, s.m. | 130 | 3 | 3 | 6 | -- |
| Joshua Bonsall | 119 1/2 | 4 | 5 | 6 | -- |
| Jonathan Bonsall | 100 | 3 | 6 | 8 | -- |
| Adam Bowle | 94 | 2 | 5 | 6 | -- |
| William Booth | -- | -- | -- | -- | -- |
| Tho's Brooke, miller | -- | -- | 1 | -- | -- |
| John Broady | -- | -- | -- | -- | -- |
| John Barr | -- | -- | -- | -- | -- |
| Robert Crozier, carpenter | 16 | -- | 2 | -- | -- |
| William Davis | 100 | 2 | -- | 6 | -- |
| John Davis, weaver | 190 | 5 | 4 | 10 | -- |
| Peter David | 140 | 3 | 9 | -- | -- |
| Thomas Davis | 12 | 2 | 1 | -- | -- |
| Jno. Davis, England | 10 | -- | 1 | 2 | -- |
| John Dunbarr | -- | -- | -- | -- | -- |
| James Hewing | 125 | 3 | 10 | 20 | -- |
| Evan Evans, taylor | -- | -- | -- | -- | -- |
| Jonathan Evans, carpenter | -- | -- | -- | -- | -- |
| William Farrier | -- | -- | -- | -- | -- |
| Nathan Garrett, weaver | 200 | 6 | 6 | 8 | 1 |
| John Garrett | 120 | 4 | 5 | 20 | -- |
| William Garrett, 1. m., b. m. | 60 | 3 | 3 | -- | -- |
| Isaac Hibberd | 190 | 4 | 6 | 10 | -- |
| John Hibberd | 76 | 1 | 1 | -- | -- |
| John Hayes, millwright | -- | 1 | 2 | -- | -- |
| Elizabeth Horn | 41 | -- | 1 | -- | -- |
| William Hoskins, weaver | -- | -- | 1 | -- | -- |
| Abraham Johnson, s.m. | 25 | 3 | 4 | -- | -- |
| Isaac Kirk | 86 | 2 | 8 | 8 | -- |
| John Kirk | 150 | 4 | 2 | -- | -- |
| Samuel Kirk | 50 | 1 | 3 | 4 | -- |
| Benjamin Lobb, cooper | 100 | 3 | 3 | 6 | -- |
| Isaac Lobb | 350 | 3 | 6 | 12 | -- |
| Abraham Lewes | 50 | 2 | 5 | 9 | -- |
| Abraham Lewes, Jun'r | 100 | 3 | 3 | 5 | -- |
| Anthony Lewes | 50 | 1 | 5 | -- | -- |
| Abel Lodge, taylor | 50 | 1 | 2 | -- | -- |
| Thomas Lewis | 40 | 1 | 2 | -- | -- |
| Samuel Levis | 50 | -- | -- | -- | -- |
| Joseph Levis | 30 | -- | 1 | -- | -- |
| Abraham Musgrove | 229 | 4 | 9 | -- | -- |

| Upper Darby | Acres | Horses | Cattle | Sheep | Servants |
|---|---|---|---|---|---|
| William McClenan | 100 | 3 | 3 | 8 | -- |
| John Moore, weaver | 50 | 3 | 3 | -- | -- |
| James Moore | 22 | -- | -- | -- | -- |
| Thomas Marshall, f.m. | 9 | 2 | 1 | -- | -- |
| John Marshall, g.m., miller | 2 | 1 | 1 | -- | -- |
| Michael Overly | 50 | 2 | 4 | 6 | -- |
| James Pyatt | 130 | 4 | 7 | 2 | -- |
| Eliz'th Phillips | 200 | 4 | 6 | 18 | -- |
| John Pawlin | 15 | 1 | 2 | 2 | -- |
| Tho's Roberts | -- | 1 | 1 | -- | -- |
| Samuel Sellers | 100 | 1 | 2 | 2 | -- |
| John Sellers, weaver | 170 | 4 | 5 | 8 | 2 |
| Samuel Smith | 340 | 5 | 4 | -- | 1 |
| William Smith | 10 | -- | 2 | -- | -- |
| George Smith | 160 | 2 | 4 | 10 | -- |
| John Smith | 15 | -- | -- | -- | -- |
| John Sorrell, carpenter | -- | -- | 1 | -- | -- |
| James Steel, g.m., miller | -- | 1 | 1 | -- | -- |
| Seth Thomas | 50 | 2 | 2 | 3 | -- |
| John Thomas | -- | -- | 1 | -- | -- |
| Thomas Vaughan | 30 | 2 | 3 | 3 | -- |
| William West, cooper | 35 3/4 | 3 | 6 | 7 | -- |
| Wm. Linville | 12 | -- | -- | -- | -- |

### Freemen

David Bonsall
Wm. Cameron
Jam's Crozier
Charles Donalson
James Davis
Assa Davis
Nathan Garrett
John Hawes
Will'm Lindsey

Samuel Lewes
Sam'l Levis, Jun'r
Benjamin Lobb
Abra'm Musgrove, Jun'r
Caleb Maris
Thomas Rudolph
James Russell
Griffith Phillips

### Inmates

Enoch Bonsall
Randal Croxen
Joseph Hayes
Joseph Kirk
John Wright, weaver
Benjamin Simcocks

Chargable Child
Joshua Thompson
Thomas Warner
William Pattin
Job Cooper
Benjamin Brannan

### Chester Township Rate

| | Acres | Horses | Cattle | Sheep | Servants |
|---|---|---|---|---|---|
| Joseph Ashbridge, shalloping | 44 | 1 | 2 | -- | -- |
| Davis Beven, t.k. | -- | 1 | 2 | 2 | -- |
| Jam's Barton, blacksmith | 117 | 3 | 5 | 5 | 1 |
| Jane Bezor, shopkeeper | -- | -- | -- | -- | -- |

| Chester Township | Acres | Horses | Cattle | Sheep | Servants |
|---|---|---|---|---|---|
| Jam's Beatty, quarryman | 50 | 1 | 2 | -- | -- |
| Patrick Burns | 48 | 1 | 4 | 4 | -- |
| Samuel Shaw | 22 | 1 | 2 | -- | -- |
| David Cowpland, innholder | 2 | 1 | 2 | 10 | 2 |
| Dav'd Cowpland, Jun'r | 200 | 1 | 2 | -- | -- |
| Jam's Claxton, shop | 145 | 2 | 5 | 15 | 1 |
| John Cox, g.m., s.m., miller | 50 | 5 | 5 | 6 | -- |
| Caleb Coburn | 113 | 3 | 3 | 6 | 1 |
| Edward Carter | 100 | 2 | 2 | -- | -- |
| Abra'm Carter, weaver | 100 | 1 | 5 | 12 | -- |
| John Caldwell, joyner | 20 | 1 | 1 | -- | -- |
| Joseph Cobourn | 20 | 2 | 2 | -- | -- |
| Joshua Cowpland, shallopman | -- | 1 | 1 | -- | 1 |
| Alice Cummings | -- | -- | -- | -- | -- |
| Robert Cobourn, hatter | -- | 1 | 1 | -- | -- |
| Josiah Campbell | 100 | 2 | 2 | -- | -- |
| George Craige | -- | 3 | -- | -- | -- |
| Mich'l Coyle | -- | -- | -- | -- | -- |
| John Cooke | -- | -- | -- | -- | -- |
| Robert Cherrey | -- | -- | -- | -- | -- |
| James Day | 97 | 3 | 3 | -- | 1 |
| Ann David | -- | -- | -- | -- | -- |
| Isaac Eyre, tanner | 8 | 1 | 2 | 7 | 1 |
| John Eyres, taylor | 12 | -- | 1 | -- | -- |
| Will'm Evans | 88 | 4 | 3 | 6 | -- |
| William Elliott | -- | -- | -- | -- | -- |
| John File | 145 | 3 | 2 | 8 | -- |
| Henry H. Graham, Prothonotary Clerk | 21 | 1 | 2 | -- | 1 |
| Adam Grubb | -- | 1 | 1 | -- | -- |
| Elea'r Graham, shopkeeper | -- | -- | -- | -- | -- |
| Mich'l Gill, quarryman | -- | -- | -- | -- | -- |
| Jacob Howell | 26 | 2 | 2 | -- | -- |
| Joseph Hoskins | 206 | 5 | 19 | 25 | -- |
| John Hanley, beer house | 95 | 3 | 7 | 20 | 1 |
| Benj'n Hance, mason | -- | -- | 1 | -- | -- |
| Samuel Shaw, as executor to Burgess and Thomas Horssfall, brew house | -- | -- | -- | -- | -- |
| Hiram Hancock | -- | -- | -- | -- | -- |
| Humphrey Johnson | 50 | 2 | 2 | -- | -- |
| George Keith, cooper | -- | -- | -- | -- | -- |
| Samuel Lightfoot | 35 | 2 | -- | 1 | -- |
| Wm. Lane, coppersmith | -- | -- | -- | -- | -- |
| John Mather, shopkeeper | 170 | 1 | 1 | -- | -- |
| James Mather, t.k. | 107 | 3 | 30 | 20 | 3 |
| Erasmus Moreton | 61 | 2 | 4 | 5 | -- |
| Will & Joseph Marloe | 148 | 4 | 5 | 6 | -- |
| John Mitchel | -- | 2 | 2 | -- | -- |
| David Ogden, carpenter | 5 | -- | 2 | -- | -- |
| Tho's Oliver | -- | -- | -- | -- | -- |
| John Oliver | 10 | -- | 1 | -- | -- |
| William Owen, painter | -- | -- | -- | -- | -- |
| Jonas Preston | 200 | 3 | 6 | -- | 4 |
| Elisha Price, attorney | 2 1/2 | 1 | 1 | -- | -- |

| Chester Township | Acres | Horses | Cattle | Sheep | Servants |
|---|---|---|---|---|---|
| Tho's Pedrick, tanner | 7 | 1 | 1 | -- | -- |
| Thomas Parsons, shipwright | -- | -- | -- | -- | -- |
| Mary Pennell | -- | -- | -- | -- | -- |
| Thomas Pedrick, shoemaker | -- | -- | -- | -- | -- |
| Edward Russell | 32 | 1 | 5 | -- | -- |
| Job Ridgway | 202 | 5 | 10 | 9 | -- |
| Jacob Rummond | 60 | 1 | 3 | -- | -- |
| Francis Ruth, carpenter | -- | -- | -- | -- | -- |
| John Rogers | 3 | -- | 1 | -- | -- |
| Samuel Robinson, labourer | -- | -- | -- | -- | -- |
| Samuel Shaw, g.m., miller | 150 | 4 | 6 | 15 | 4 |
| John Salkield | 210 | 8 | 7 | 20 | 2 |
| Nath'l Squib, shoemaker | 125 | 3 | 3 | 5 | -- |
| George Speer, blacksmith | 2 1/2 | -- | 1 | -- | -- |
| Rob't Squib, Jun'r | 50 | 3 | 3 | 5 | -- |
| Joseph Swaffer | 100 | 3 | 3 | 5 | -- |
| Thomas Sharpless, wheelwright | 12 | 1 | 2 | -- | -- |
| Peter Steell, wheelwright | 18 | 1 | -- | -- | -- |
| Mary Shaw | -- | -- | -- | -- | -- |
| John Smith, chairmaker | -- | 1 | 1 | -- | -- |
| Jeremiah Starr | 200 | 4 | 4 | 10 | -- |
| William Starr, mill | 9 | -- | -- | -- | -- |
| Isaac Salkield, innkeeper | 22 | 1 | -- | -- | 1 |
| Wm. Swaffer | 37 | 2 | 2 | -- | -- |
| George Syng, carpenter | -- | -- | -- | -- | -- |
| Jno. Scantling, barber | -- | -- | -- | -- | -- |
| Jno. Sketchley, labourer | -- | -- | -- | -- | -- |
| John Taylor, shoemaker | -- | -- | 2 | -- | -- |
| Joseph Thomas, sub-sheriff | 7 | 2 | 1 | -- | -- |
| Tho's Taylor | -- | -- | -- | -- | -- |
| Branson Vanleer, physician | -- | 2 | 1 | -- | 2 |
| Mary Whitey, innkeeper | 20 | 3 | 2 | -- | 1 |
| Valentine Weaver, innkeeper | -- | 1 | 2 | -- | 1 |
| Black Sam | -- | -- | 2 | -- | -- |
| Black Mary | -- | 1 | 1 | -- | -- |
| Fra's Richardson | 12 | -- | -- | -- | -- |
| Jonathan Cowpland | 10 | -- | -- | -- | -- |
| Mary Norris | 200 | -- | -- | -- | -- |
| John Sharpless | 4 | -- | -- | -- | -- |
| Dan'l Sharpless | 48 | -- | -- | -- | -- |
| Jesse Maris | 3 | -- | -- | -- | -- |
| Jno. Power | 20 | -- | -- | -- | -- |
| Tho's Felton, stone quarry | -- | -- | -- | -- | -- |
| John Smith | 160 | -- | -- | -- | -- |
| John Coppock | 140 | -- | -- | -- | -- |
| Wm. Salkeld | 8 | -- | -- | -- | -- |
| Henry Plat | -- | -- | -- | -- | -- |

Inmates

Joseph Cunningham  
Rob''t Crawford  
Jno. Morrisson  

Dav'd Cobourn  
Geo. Mumford  
Jno. Whithead

Inmates

Jam's McCallion
Jam's Ruth, joyner
Jacob Howell, Jun'r
John Mitchel
Wm. Norris
Rob't Rogers

Nehemiah Davis
Rowland Burk
John Purnell
Jam's Rood
John Mileman

Freeman

Zedekiah Graham
Caleb Squibb
Lodowick Stone
John Green
Edw'd Carter, Jun'r
Trustrum Smith
Sam'l Carpenter
Wm. Downing
Lewis Farrel
Rich'd Panter
Rich'd Oliver
Fra's Gollingher

Jam's Downing
Jno. Swaffer
John Chism
Jacob Hopperget
John Watson
Will'm Watson
Barnabas Cunningham
Dennis Voley
David Jackson
Jam's Graves
Rob't File

Middletown Township Rate

|  | Acres | Horses | Cattle | Sheep | Servants |
|---|---|---|---|---|---|
| Mary Bennett, s.m. | -- | -- | -- | -- | -- |
| Jam's Black | 70 | 4 | 4 | -- | -- |
| John Baker | 110 | 2 | 2 | 6 | -- |
| Rich'd Baker | 100 | 3 | 5 | 4 | -- |
| Timothy Bullock, weaver | 3 | -- | 1 | -- | -- |
| Jno. Cunningham | 140 | 2 | 3 | 8 | -- |
| Sam'l Crosby | -- | -- | 1 | -- | -- |
| David Dutton, smith | 50 | 3 | 3 | 1 | -- |
| Jam's Day | 170 | 2 | 3 | -- | -- |
| Fredirick Engle, tan yard, tanner and shoemaker | 120 | 2 | 3 | -- | -- |
| Nathan Edwards, shoemaker, t.k. | 114 | 3 | 6 | 8 | -- |
| Joseph Edwards | 130 | 2 | 7 | 6 | -- |
| John Essy | -- | -- | -- | -- | -- |
| Nicholas Fairlamb | 200 | 2 | 6 | 11 | -- |
| Fred'k Fairlamb | 180 | 1 | -- | -- | -- |
| Hary Grubb | 250 | -- | -- | -- | -- |
| Jno. Haversack, labourer | -- | -- | 1 | -- | -- |
| Caleb Harrison | 200 | 4 | 5 | 6 | -- |
| Moses Hill, labourer | -- | -- | -- | -- | -- |
| Joseph Collens, cooper | -- | -- | 1 | -- | -- |
| Jno. Hill, t.k. | 170 | 4 | 5 | 12 | 1 |
| Jno. Heacock, joyner | 100 | 3 | 3 | 6 | -- |
| Joseph Jones, blacksmith | -- | 1 | 1 | -- | -- |
| Jno. Ingram | 119 | -- | -- | -- | -- |
| Caleb James, g.m., miller | 45 | 2 | 2 | -- | -- |
| Jam's Lindsy, labourer | -- | -- | 1 | 6 | -- |
| Tho's Minshall | 200 | 5 | 6 | 10 | -- |

| Middletown Township | Acres | Horses | Cattle | Sheep | Servants |
|---|---|---|---|---|---|
| Jno. Minshall | 369 | 4 | 8 | 10 | -- |
| Jonathan Martin | 350 | 3 | 8 | 10 | -- |
| Jam's McCleland | 290 | 5 | 5 | 6 | -- |
| Rob't McCleland | 90 | 2 | 4 | 7 | 1 |
| Wm. Miller, taylor | 80 | 1 | 3 | -- | -- |
| Jno. Noblit, shoemaker | 150 | -- | 1 | -- | -- |
| Jno. Norry, cooper | -- | -- | -- | -- | -- |
| Rob't Pennell | 290 | 3 | 8 | 10 | -- |
| Tho's Pilkerton, whitesmith | 50 | 3 | 2 | 4 | -- |
| Wm. Pennell, Jun'r | 300 | 4 | 5 | 8 | -- |
| Wm. Pennell, g.m., s.m. | 500 | 8 | 16 | 16 | 4 |
| Rob't Rogers, miller | -- | 1 | 2 | -- | -- |
| Tho's Ryan | 100 | 3 | 3 | 7 | -- |
| Joseph Sharpless | 138 | 4 | 5 | 10 | -- |
| Benj'n Sharpless | 150 | 6 | 8 | 18 | -- |
| Sam'l Sharpless, weaver | 217 | 4 | 11 | 15 | -- |
| Eliz'th Smedley | 190 | 2 | 3 | 6 | -- |
| Jno. Slaughter, cooper | -- | -- | 1 | -- | -- |
| Rich'd Sill, mason | 6 | -- | 1 | -- | -- |
| Mich'l Sill | 100 | 2 | 2 | -- | -- |
| Ambrose Smedly | 190 | 2 | 1 | -- | -- |
| Bartho'w Sutton, storekeeper | 30 | 1 | 2 | -- | -- |
| Frederick Taylor, labourer | -- | -- | 1 | -- | -- |
| Tho's Trimble | 100 | 1 | 3 | 5 | -- |
| Sam'l Trimble | 100 | 3 | 4 | 6 | -- |
| Joseph Talbot | 150 | 4 | 7 | 10 | -- |
| Joseph Talbot, Jun'r. g.m., miller | 30 | 1 | 2 | 4 | -- |
| Tho's Wills | 240 | 2 | 7 | 8 | 1 |
| Peter Worral | 200 | 5 | 5 | 14 | -- |
| Tho's Worrall | 214 | 3 | 5 | -- | 1 |
| Jno. Worrall | 100 | 2 | 1 | -- | -- |
| Nathan Yarnal | 25 | -- | -- | -- | -- |
| Will'm Mollon | 100 | -- | -- | -- | -- |

Freemen

Jacob Minshall
Joseph Baker
Joseph Sharpless
Dan'l Sharpless
Tho's Sharpless
Rob't Farrier
Wm. Miller
Tho's Smedley
Joshua Smedley
Nathan Haycock

John Edwards
Rob't Miller
Wm. Noblet, Jun'r
Sam'l Noblet
Levy Pilkerton
Joseph Pilkerton
Charles King
Tho's James
Tho's Slater

West Town Rate

| | Acres | Horses | Cattle | Sheep | Servants |
|---|---|---|---|---|---|
| Wm. Chamberin | 140 | 4 | 2 | -- | -- |
| Eliz'th Ebison | 150 | -- | -- | -- | -- |

## West Town

| | Acres | Horses | Cattle | Sheep | Servants |
|---|---|---|---|---|---|
| Joseph Gibbons, g.m. | 292 | 4 | 13 | 18 | 1 |
| Jam's Gibbons, mill | 380 | 3 | 14 | 18 | 3 |
| Joshua Hoops | 340 | 6 | 6 | 10 | -- |
| Joseph Hunt | 60 | -- | -- | -- | 1 |
| Wm. Hunt | 132 | 3 | 6 | 6 | -- |
| John Hunt | 235 | 5 | 9 | 10 | -- |
| Facis Hickman | 150 | 4 | 7 | 10 | -- |
| Abra'm Hoops | 390 | 3 | 4 | 4 | -- |
| Jno. Hibbin | 100 | 4 | 3 | 12 | -- |
| Joseph Hibbard | 46 | -- | -- | -- | -- |
| Jam's Hughs | 125 | 3 | 3 | -- | -- |
| Joseph James | 222 | 8 | 7 | 20 | -- |
| Jacob James | 71 | 4 | 3 | -- | -- |
| Isaac James | 46 | 2 | 1 | -- | -- |
| Wm. Jones | 44 | -- | -- | -- | -- |
| Thomas Mercer | 268 | 6 | 15 | 13 | 1 |
| Mary Norris | 475 | -- | -- | -- | -- |
| Sam'l Osborn | 180 | 4 | 8 | 12 | 1 |
| Wm. Plustead | 400 | -- | -- | -- | -- |
| John Sharpless | 148 | 2 | 8 | 10 | -- |
| John Poles, Sale | 94 | 3 | 3 | 12 | 1 |
| Tho's Taylor | 150 | 5 | 7 | 5 | -- |
| Rich'd Thornbery, taylor | 50 | 3 | 2 | -- | -- |
| Nicolas Thasher | 30 | -- | 1 | -- | -- |
| John Walter | 50 | 2 | 4 | 3 | -- |
| Joseph White | 90 | 2 | 4 | -- | -- |
| Tho's Yearsly, s.m. | 150 | 4 | 5 | 15 | -- |
| Sam'l Enterkin | 40 | -- | -- | -- | -- |

Inmates

Cornelius Wood
Edw'd Thornbery
Joshua Smith
Joseph James
Amos Hoops
Joseph Hickman

Rich'd Jefferis
Peter Osborn
Joseph Burnit
Jam's Hayney
Simon Forster

## Thornbury Township Rate

| | Acres | Horses | Cattle | Sheep | Servants |
|---|---|---|---|---|---|
| Geo'e Brinton | 225 | 4 | 6 | 9 | 1 |
| John Brinton | 58 | 4 | 3 | 18 | -- |
| John Briggs | 115 | 4 | 6 | 6 | -- |
| Caleb Brinton | 190 | -- | -- | -- | -- |
| John Buker | 18 | 2 | 1 | -- | -- |
| Nehemiah Baker | 30 | -- | -- | -- | -- |
| Jacob Bobb, collier | 10 | 1 | 1 | -- | -- |
| Wm. Beaumons, shoemaker | -- | 1 | 1 | -- | -- |
| Benj'n Cock | 180 | 4 | 4 | 5 | -- |
| Benj'n Cock, Jun'r | 50 | 3 | 1 | -- | -- |

| Thornbury | Acres | Horses | Cattle | Sheep | Servants |
|---|---|---|---|---|---|
| Moses Cock | -- | 3 | 1 | -- | -- |
| Tho's Cheyney | 150 | 3 | 4 | 11 | 1 |
| John Cheyney | 286 | 4 | 6 | 11 | -- |
| Joseph Cheyney, cooper | 150 | 5 | 4 | 10 | -- |
| Rich'd Cheyney, s.m. | 282 | 5 | 4 | 12 | -- |
| Ann Cheyney | -- | 1 | 1 | -- | -- |
| Isaac Davis | 150 | 4 | 4 | 8 | -- |
| Rich'd Everson | 200 | 6 | 6 | 8 | -- |
| Eliz'th Eavenson | 130 | 5 | 7 | -- | -- |
| Geo. Evenson | 203 | 4 | 5 | 6 | -- |
| Seth Eavenson | 91 | 3 | 3 | 9 | -- |
| Persifor Frazier | -- | 2 | 2 | -- | 2 |
| Geo'e Frier, weaver | -- | 1 | 2 | -- | -- |
| Tho's Frier, weaver | 2 | -- | 1 | -- | -- |
| Edward Green | 100 | 2 | 2 | 3 | -- |
| Henry Guest | 165 | 3 | 4 | 6 | -- |
| Will'm Gibbons | 175 | 5 | 6 | 9 | 1 |
| Edw'd Grissell, labourer | 4 | -- | 1 | -- | -- |
| Tho's Hunter | 200 | 3 | 4 | 6 | -- |
| John Harper | 88 | 5 | 2 | 6 | -- |
| Wm. Harden, shoemaker | -- | -- | -- | -- | -- |
| John Hemphill | 140 | 3 | 2 | 6 | -- |
| Simon Hampton | 138 | 3 | 2 | 6 | -- |
| George Hunter | 49 | -- | -- | -- | -- |
| Joshua Hoops | 160 | 3 | 5 | 6 | -- |
| Wm. Johnson, joyner | -- | 1 | 1 | -- | -- |
| David Lewis, mason | 41 | 1 | 2 | -- | -- |
| Dennis McCoy | 150 | 3 | 4 | -- | -- |
| Edw'd McBride | -- | -- | 1 | -- | -- |
| Joseph Mercer | -- | 2 | 1 | -- | -- |
| Joseph McDevor, cooper | -- | 1 | 1 | -- | -- |
| Geo'e Mire | -- | 1 | 1 | -- | -- |
| Tho's Marshall, stave maker | -- | -- | -- | -- | -- |
| John Maese, shoemaker | -- | -- | -- | -- | -- |
| Josiah McNease, weaver | -- | -- | 1 | -- | -- |
| Isaac Moore | -- | 1 | 1 | -- | -- |
| Cornelius McDaniel | -- | -- | -- | -- | -- |
| John Norry, brewer | -- | -- | -- | -- | -- |
| Christopher Nufer, labourer | -- | -- | -- | -- | -- |
| John Peirce | 566 | -- | -- | 35 | -- |
| Rich'd Parks | 290 | 6 | 5 | 12 | -- |
| Caleb Peirce | 297 | 6 | 7 | 7 | 1 |
| Wm. Pyle | -- | 1 | 1 | -- | -- |
| Jacob Pyle, weaver | 15 | 1 | 1 | -- | -- |
| John Perkins | -- | -- | -- | -- | -- |
| Will'm Proad | 300 | 5 | 4 | 10 | -- |
| Rob't Wright | -- | 1 | 1 | -- | -- |
| Jacob Sharpless | 260 | 6 | 6 | 15 | 1 |
| Wm. Shanklin | -- | -- | 1 | -- | -- |
| Tho's Taylor, carpenter | 147 | 4 | 3 | 2 | -- |
| Tho's Thatcher | 111 | 3 | 3 | -- | -- |
| Isaac Taylor, carpenter | 90 | 2 | 2 | 4 | -- |
| Step'n Taylor, Jun'r | 200 | 4 | 5 | 8 | -- |
| Eliz'th Taylor | 50 | 1 | -- | -- | -- |
| Wm. Trimble | 20 | -- | -- | -- | -- |

| Thornbury | Acres | Horses | Cattle | Sheep | Servants |
|---|---|---|---|---|---|
| Isaac Taylor | -- | -- | 1 | -- | -- |
| Eliz'th Vernon | 224 | 4 | 2 | 10 | -- |
| Jno. Woodward | 170 | 5 | 6 | 10 | 1 |
| Isaac Yearsley | 118 | 4 | 3 | 6 | -- |
| Susan'h Yearsley | -- | 1 | 2 | 2 | -- |
| Tho's Young | -- | -- | -- | -- | -- |

## Inmates

James Cook
Daniel Bailiff
Jacob Hallbright
Jesse Baker
Will'm Conner
Stephen Taylor, Jun'r
Nathan Mendenhall
Thos's Hickman
Benjamin Jones
Jacob Vernon
Dan'l McKinley
Joseph Curtain
Allen Key
Israel Pyle
Walter Hampton
Tho's Green
William England

Charles Daily
Levy Pyle
Mich'l Ponward
John Muhaic, tanyard
Gabril Walker
Tho's Howell
Fredirick Camp
Benjamin Johnson
John Davis
Dan'l Davis
John Cock
Tho's Evenson
Isaac Frank
Simon Forster
John Hickman
Jam's Taylor

## East Bradford Township Rate

| | Acres | Horses | Cattle | Sheep | Servants |
|---|---|---|---|---|---|
| Abiah Taylor, miller, g.m., s.m. | 250 | 3 | 5 | 15 | -- |
| Abel Bogue | 250 | 4 | 4 | 8 | -- |
| Abraham Taylor | 100 | 2 | 1 | 6 | -- |
| Abigail Fling | 95 | -- | 2 | -- | -- |
| Benj'n Townsend | 80 | 3 | 3 | -- | -- |
| Benj'n Hawley | 100 | 3 | 4 | 8 | -- |
| Caleb Stroud | 160 | 4 | 5 | -- | -- |
| Daniel Guest, tanyard, tanner | 193 | 3 | 4 | 4 | 1 |
| Deborah Taylor | 20 | 1 | 3 | -- | -- |
| Dennis McLoy | 100 | -- | 2 | -- | -- |
| Amer Jefferis | 290 | 5 | 7 | 12 | 1 |
| Ezekil Boggs | -- | 2 | 3 | 6 | -- |
| Evan Jones | 160 | 3 | 9 | 6 | -- |
| Alex'r Foreman, painter | 100 | 2 | 2 | -- | -- |
| Fran's Townsend, f.m., s.m., fuller | 95 | 2 | 2 | 4 | -- |
| George Stroud | 400 | 4 | 6 | -- | 1 |
| Geo'e Entrekin, miller, g.m. | 250 | 5 | 6 | 4 | -- |
| George Carter | 260 | 4 | 4 | 8 | -- |
| Hannah Burgsign | 113 | 1 | 1 | -- | -- |
| Henry Woodward | 32 | 2 | 2 | -- | -- |

East Bradford Township

| | Acres | Horses | Cattle | Sheep | Servants |
|---|---|---|---|---|---|
| James Davis | 150 | 5 | 5 | 6 | -- |
| John Davis, sawyer, s.m. | 210 | 4 | 3 | 10 | -- |
| John Carter | 130 | 5 | 6 | 7 | -- |
| Jam's Jefferis | 250 | 5 | 6 | 12 | 2 |
| Joseph Cope | 70 | 1 | -- | -- | -- |
| John Jones, miller, g.m., s.m. | 25 | 1 | 2 | -- | -- |
| Joseph Parks | 200 | 5 | 6 | 10 | -- |
| John Hannum, s.m. | 380 | 3 | 3 | -- | -- |
| John Lawrence | -- | 4 | 2 | -- | -- |
| Joshua Hoopes | 200 | 4 | 7 | 10 | -- |
| Jam's Wollerton | 100 | 2 | 3 | 6 | -- |
| Jno. Wollerton | 80 | 2 | 2 | 4 | -- |
| Jam's Starr | 150 | 2 | 2 | 4 | -- |
| John Townsend | 200 | 4 | 6 | 20 | 1 |
| James Kenney, storekeeper | 46 | 2 | 2 | -- | -- |
| James Bogle | 100 | 1 | -- | -- | -- |
| John Grey | 99 | 1 | 2 | -- | -- |
| James Clark | 30 | -- | -- | -- | -- |
| James Few | 50 | -- | -- | -- | -- |
| Jonathan Eldridge | 140 | -- | -- | -- | -- |
| John Darlinton, blacksmith | 150 | 4 | 6 | 10 | -- |
| Lidia Jefferis | 100 | -- | -- | -- | -- |
| Mary Grubb | 15 | 1 | 1 | -- | -- |
| Michael Farrill | -- | 1 | 1 | -- | -- |
| Michael Righter | 100 | 3 | 4 | -- | -- |
| Nathaniel Jefferis, joyner | 50 | 2 | 3 | 4 | -- |
| Nathan Cope, lime burner | 100 | 3 | 6 | 6 | -- |
| Nathan Hoopes, weaver | 100 | 2 | 2 | -- | -- |
| Richard Jones | 30 | 1 | 2 | 4 | -- |
| Rich'd Woodward | 200 | 5 | 4 | -- | -- |
| Sam'l Painter | 400 | 4 | 7 | 10 | 1 |
| Samuel Osbourn | 50 | -- | -- | -- | -- |
| Samuel Cope | 400 | 3 | 6 | 12 | -- |
| John Cope, malthouse | -- | -- | -- | -- | -- |
| Susannah Davis | 8 | -- | 1 | -- | -- |
| Thomas Worth | 350 | 4 | 8 | 20 | -- |
| Thomas Johnson, carpenter | 70 | 1 | 3 | -- | -- |
| Tho's Darlinton, joyner | 150 | 4 | 7 | 6 | -- |
| Tho's Speakeman, miller, g.m. | -- | 1 | 2 | 3 | -- |
| Timothy Dailey | 500 | -- | -- | -- | -- |
| Will'm Jefferis | 200 | 4 | 6 | 12 | -- |
| William Mercer | -- | 1 | 2 | 3 | -- |
| William Pearson, saddle tree maker | 100 | 1 | -- | -- | -- |
| William Jefferis | -- | 1 | 2 | 3 | -- |
| Tho's Gibbons | 250 | 3 | 4 | -- | -- |
| Abraham Pyle | 200 | 4 | 4 | 10 | -- |
| Jam's Robinson | 150 | 2 | 2 | -- | -- |
| Francis Townsend | 80 | -- | -- | -- | -- |

Freemen

| | |
|---|---|
| Joseph Buffinton | Jos. McCormack |
| Ebenezer Worth | Jam's Master |
| James Painter | John Neal |
| James Simcock | Thomas Stephens |
| Nathan Jefferis | Jno. Harrack |
| John Weston | Gilbert Bradley |
| John Cummins | George Effibit |
| Jacob Walts | Edward Lawrence |
| Lethrim Ingram | John Stinson |
| Isaac Chapman | Phillip Halyard |
| Matthew Forrester | Jno. McCarty |

Inmates

| | |
|---|---|
| Edward Jones | Jam's Rammage |
| John Strowd | John Brison |
| Amos Woodward | Enoch Gray |
| Sam'l Enterkin | William Boyle |
| Will'm Cullepher | William Read |
| Tho's Jefferis | David Jenkins |
| William Taylor | Daniel Davis |
| Sam'l Simcock | William Patterson |
| Jno. McGuire | William Boyde |
| Isaac Stephens | Abram Davis |

New Garden Rate

| | Acres | Horses | Cattle | Sheep | Servants |
|---|---|---|---|---|---|
| Will'm Miller, miller, g.m., s.m. | 1,200 | 7 | 9 | 16 | 1 |
| Jam's Miller | 290 | 5 | 5 | 10 | 1 |
| Will Miller, Jun'r | 317 | 1 | -- | -- | -- |
| Samuel Miller | 300 | 4 | 4 | 6 | 1 |
| John Miller | 150 | 4 | 4 | 7 | -- |
| Isaac Miller | 200 | 4 | 4 | -- | 1 |
| Jesse Miller | 150 | -- | -- | -- | -- |
| Jno. Hurford | 160 | 3 | 3 | 4 | -- |
| Sam'l Hulford | 100 | 3 | 1 | -- | -- |
| Joseph Hulford | 80 | 2 | 3 | -- | -- |
| Tho's Hutton | 120 | 4 | 3 | 5 | -- |
| Benj'n Hutton | 120 | 3 | 5 | 7 | -- |
| Joseph Hobson | 200 | 3 | 2 | -- | 1 |
| Cha's Hall | 23 | 4 | 3 | 8 | -- |
| Joseph Fread | 200 | 2 | 4 | 6 | -- |
| Isaac Jackson | 200 | 2 | 3 | -- | 1 |
| Jam's Jackson | 190 | 4 | 4 | 6 | -- |
| Isaac Jackson, farmer | 180 | 3 | 3 | -- | -- |
| William Row | 120 | -- | 2 | 5 | -- |
| Will'm Richards | 250 | 2 | 3 | -- | 1 |
| Nath'l Richards | 110 | 1 | 3 | -- | -- |
| Isaac Richards | 220 | 3 | 5 | 15 | 1 |
| Jam's Rowan | 200 | 3 | 3 | -- | 1 |
| John Rankin, shopkeeper | 50 | 1 | 1 | -- | -- |

| New Garden | Acres | Horses | Cattle | Sheep | Servants |
|---|---|---|---|---|---|
| Sam'l Riddle | 38 | 2 | 1 | -- | -- |
| Nath'l Scarlet | 200 | 1 | 3 | 7 | -- |
| John Scarlet | 160 | 3 | 2 | 6 | -- |
| Moses Star | 124 | 2 | 2 | 5 | -- |
| Benj'n Sharp | 100 | 1 | 1 | -- | -- |
| Rob't Shields, cooper | 75 | 1 | 2 | 2 | -- |
| George Sharp | 100 | 1 | -- | -- | -- |
| And'w McEntire | 300 | 2 | 4 | 6 | 1 |
| Stephen McAferson, blacksmith | 120 | 3 | 4 | 8 | -- |
| Isaac Allen, tavernkeeper | 150 | 5 | 3 | 10 | -- |
| Will'm Allen, miller, g.m. | -- | 2 | 2 | 6 | -- |
| And'w McCoy | 300 | 3 | 4 | 6 | -- |
| Wm. Dixson | 170 | 4 | 4 | 3 | -- |
| Rebecca Dixson | 150 | 4 | 4 | 10 | -- |
| Allen Cuningham | 180 | 2 | 2 | -- | -- |
| George Chandler | 200 | 2 | 5 | 10 | -- |
| Tho's Carpenter, shoemaker | -- | 1 | 2 | 5 | -- |
| Sarah Baldwin | 200 | -- | -- | -- | -- |
| Tho's Barrett | 100 | 1 | -- | -- | -- |
| Wm. Knight | 40 | -- | -- | -- | -- |
| Enoch Grigg | 100 | 1 | 2 | 4 | -- |
| Geo'e Doherty, blacksmith | -- | -- | 2 | -- | -- |
| Micha'l Plaister | 10 | 2 | 2 | 6 | -- |
| Wm. Elliott, labourer | -- | 1 | 2 | -- | -- |
| James Ellis, labourer | -- | -- | 2 | -- | -- |
| William Ross, weaver | -- | -- | 1 | -- | -- |
| Joshua Jackson, labourer | 75 | 2 | 1 | -- | -- |
| Will'm Murphy, labourer | -- | 1 | 3 | 8 | -- |
| Wm. Griffith, shoemaker | -- | -- | 1 | -- | -- |
| Wm. Cays, labourer | -- | -- | 1 | -- | -- |
| Jno. Wilson, weaver | -- | -- | 1 | -- | -- |
| John Curl, cooper | -- | -- | 1 | -- | -- |
| Sarah Baldwin, tavern | 50 | 1 | 1 | 6 | -- |
| Joseph Musgrove | 100 | -- | -- | -- | -- |
| Sarah Black | 100 | -- | -- | -- | -- |
| Jam's Millhouse | 180 | 2 | 2 | -- | -- |

Freemen

Samuel Cherry
Joseph Scarlet
John Elliot
Moses Rowan
Sam'l McClure

John Doherty
John Goodloop
Joseph Hutton
Wm. McConnell

Inmate: Samuel Logan

West Whiteland Rate

| | Acres | Horses | Cattle | Sheep | Servants |
|---|---|---|---|---|---|
| Will'm Beal, store and shop-keeper | 250 | 4 | 10 | 15 | -- |

West Whiteland

| | Acres | Horses | Cattle | Sheep | Servants |
|---|---|---|---|---|---|
| Sam'l Bond | 394 | 4 | 8 | 14 | -- |
| Joseph Morris | 250 | 4 | 6 | 6 | -- |
| Richard Thomas, miller | 93 | 1 | -- | -- | -- |
| John Cuthbert | 200 | 4 | 5 | 10 | 1 |
| Will'm Trimble, Senior, miller, g.m., s.m. | 100 | 4 | 6 | 12 | 1 |
| George Thomas | 250 | -- | -- | 10 | -- |
| John Clark | 200 | 1 | 2 | -- | -- |
| Garret Berry | 100 | 3 | 4 | 7 | -- |
| James Brown, hatter | 140 | 3 | 5 | 13 | -- |
| John Carr | 150 | 5 | 5 | 12 | -- |
| John Jacobs | 574 | 5 | 8 | 20 | -- |
| Jonathan Eldridge | 150 | 2 | 4 | -- | -- |
| Jacob Bower | 135 | 3 | 3 | -- | -- |
| Joseph Downing | 231 | -- | -- | -- | -- |
| Richard Bull | 240 | 4 | 6 | 15 | 1 |
| John Merideth | 180 | 2 | 2 | 5 | -- |
| Samuel Lewis | 128 | 3 | 3 | 4 | -- |
| Dan'l Evans | 140 | 3 | 5 | 5 | 1 |
| Jam's Richardson, mason | 180 | 3 | 4 | -- | -- |
| John Harper | 160 | 2 | 4 | 7 | 2 |
| John Smith | 146 | 4 | 5 | 4 | -- |
| John Jones | 100 | 2 | 3 | -- | 1 |
| David Dunwoodey | 200 | 4 | 4 | 4 | -- |
| Ellis Haines | 200 | 3 | 3 | 6 | -- |
| John Newlin | 50 | 2 | 1 | -- | -- |
| Thomas Evans, cordwainer | 4 | -- | 2 | -- | -- |
| Evan Anderson, blacksmith | 30 | 1 | 1 | -- | -- |
| John Garret | 80 | 2 | 3 | 6 | -- |
| Walter Lilley | 129 | 2 | 2 | 6 | -- |
| Will Ingram, blacksmith | 130 | 3 | 1 | -- | -- |
| Manasah McLees | 78 | -- | -- | -- | -- |
| Will'm Iles, cordwainer | 10 | 1 | 1 | -- | -- |
| Henry Tims | 19 | -- | 2 | -- | 1 |
| Will'm Trimble, miller | -- | -- | -- | -- | -- |

Freemen

Thomas Bull                Dan'l Trimble
Tho's Cuthbert             Mathias Finger
John Cuthbert              David Bail
David Howel                John Dillen
Sam'l Hodge                John Reece
Samuel Ray                 John Jolly
Jam's Dunwoody

Inmates

Sam'l Fear                 Jno. McEntire
Wm. Ring                   Aresiah Evans
Neal McCarty               Henry Huffman
Wm. Atherton               Rich'd Hutson
Rob't Morrel               Darby McDaniel

Inmates

Barth'w Tims                    Phillip Nullard
Barnabas Swagger                Jno. Turk

East Followfield Rate

|  | Acres | Horses | Cattle | Sheep | Servants |
|---|---|---|---|---|---|
| Jo's Arthurs, labourer | 150 | 2 | 3 | 4 | -- |
| Rob't Allen | 60 | -- | 1 | -- | -- |
| Jeffery Bentley | 125 | 2 | 3 | 6 | -- |
| John Bentley | 120 | 3 | 3 | 12 | -- |
| Sam'l Bealey | 80 | 1 | 2 | 2 | -- |
| David Bealey | 80 | 2 | 2 | 1 | -- |
| Jam's Blettock | 150 | 3 | 4 | 4 | -- |
| Fra's Boggs | 100 | 2 | 1 | -- | -- |
| Pat'k Carson | 100 | 2 | 3 | 6 | -- |
| Jno. Carson | 100 | -- | -- | -- | -- |
| Charles Carl | 70 | 1 | 1 | -- | -- |
| Alex'r Duncan | 50 | 1 | 1 | -- | -- |
| Cha's Ackles | 100 | 2 | 3 | 3 | -- |
| John Elliot | 100 | 1 | 2 | 2 | -- |
| Davidson Filson | 150 | 2 | 3 | 6 | -- |
| Robert Filson | 100 | 2 | 1 | -- | -- |
| Davidson Filson, gardian | 100 | -- | -- | -- | -- |
| Jam's Gray | 100 | 2 | 4 | 7 | -- |
| Rob't Greer | 100 | 2 | 2 | 6 | -- |
| Jam's Gray, weaver | 70 | -- | 1 | -- | -- |
| Jno. McClenaughen, labourer | 70 | 1 | 2 | 3 | -- |
| Wm. Grant, weaver | 125 | 2 | 2 | -- | -- |
| Mary Hayes | 300 | 3 | 8 | 10 | 1 |
| Jam's Hambleton | 90 | 2 | 2 | 2 | -- |
| John Hannah | 70 | 1 | 2 | 2 | -- |
| Will'm Hannah | 70 | 1 | 1 | 2 | -- |
| Tho's Keslip | 150 | 2 | 3 | 4 | -- |
| Thomas Hayes | 150 | 1 | 2 | 4 | -- |
| Robert Carr, g.m. | 300 | 2 | 4 | 7 | -- |
| Duncan McCalister | 100 | 2 | 3 | 3 | -- |
| James McKim | 90 | 1 | 2 | -- | -- |
| Will'm Moad, f.m. | 100 | 2 | 2 | 4 | -- |
| Will'm Mackey | 100 | 2 | 3 | 6 | -- |
| Will'm McKim | 70 | -- | -- | -- | -- |
| Will'm McFerson | 60 | 1 | 3 | 3 | -- |
| Will'm McIlvain, taylor | 100 | 2 | 2 | -- | -- |
| Jno. Montgomery | 200 | 3 | 4 | 6 | 1 |
| Wm. Harlan | 50 | -- | -- | -- | -- |
| And'w Oliphant | -- | -- | -- | -- | -- |
| Dav'd Powel | 150 | 3 | 4 | 10 | -- |
| Wm. Peoples | 80 | 1 | 2 | 6 | -- |
| Israel Pemberton | 1,000 | -- | -- | -- | -- |
| Arch'd Quay, cordwainer | 50 | 1 | 1 | 6 | -- |
| Rob't Rusk | 150 | 2 | 2 | 5 | -- |
| And'w Scott | 100 | 3 | 4 | 6 | -- |
| Jam's Shields | 65 | 2 | 2 | 4 | -- |
| Tho's Scott | 130 | 2 | 5 | 5 | -- |

| East Followfield | Acres | Horses | Cattle | Sheep | Servants |
|---|---|---|---|---|---|
| Price Travalley | 260 | 2 | 2 | 1 | -- |
| Josh. Thomas | 25 | -- | -- | -- | -- |
| John Whiley, weaver | 60 | 1 | 2 | -- | 1 |
| Abra'm Wolfinton | 50 | 2 | 2 | 2 | -- |
| Jno. Walker | 50 | 1 | 1 | 3 | -- |
| Elenor Young | 100 | 2 | 3 | 6 | -- |
| Will'm Parkhill, weaver | 3 | 1 | 1 | -- | -- |
| Jam's McIlroy, labourer | 32 | -- | -- | -- | -- |
| Josh. Wilson, labourer | 3 | -- | -- | -- | -- |

Inmates

Nath'l Ackles                David McKim
Jam's Bennett                Joseph Powel
Wm. Leonard                  John Boyd
Cha's Posley

Freeman

William Wiley                John Stephenson
Geratt Gevoad                Fra's Heslip
Will'm Blettock              Alex'r Clendenen
Will'm Peterson              Pet'r Burgett
Will'm Arthurs

Sadsbury Rate

| | Acres | Horses | Cattle | Sheep | Servants |
|---|---|---|---|---|---|
| Will'm Armstrong | 100 | 2 | 4 | 5 | -- |
| Rob't Armstrong | 100 | 2 | 2 | 4 | -- |
| Matthew Boyd | 150 | 2 | 2 | 4 | -- |
| George Boyd | 150 | 2 | 2 | 4 | -- |
| Tho's Bulla | 200 | 3 | 3 | 5 | -- |
| Jam's Boyd, stiller | 125 | 2 | 2 | -- | -- |
| And'w Boyd | 250 | 2 | 4 | 10 | -- |
| Tho's Boyd | 190 | 2 | 3 | 10 | 1 |
| Jam's Blettock | 200 | -- | -- | -- | -- |
| Sam'l Brenemon | 170 | 1 | 1 | 5 | -- |
| Joshua Chamberlin | 200 | -- | -- | -- | -- |
| Rob't Cowen | 200 | 3 | 4 | 12 | -- |
| Hugh Cowen | 170 | 4 | 3 | 6 | -- |
| Joseph Cowan, blacksmith | 170 | 3 | 3 | 10 | -- |
| Wm. Cowen | 60 | 2 | 2 | -- | -- |
| Rob't Cooper | 166 | 2 | 3 | 4 | -- |
| Tho's Climson | 40 | -- | -- | -- | -- |
| Tho's Davis | 200 | 2 | 3 | 6 | -- |
| Tho's Dunn, g.m., miller | 150 | 4 | 4 | 10 | -- |
| John Dickey | 190 | 2 | 2 | 6 | 1 |
| Wm. Dickey | 150 | 2 | 3 | 6 | -- |
| Jam's Fleming, wheelwright | 150 | 2 | 3 | 6 | -- |
| Jona's Gilkey | 200 | 4 | 2 | 10 | -- |

| Sadsbury | Acres | Horses | Cattle | Sheep | Servants |
|---|---|---|---|---|---|
| Wm. Clendenen, labourer | 50 | -- | 1 | -- | -- |
| Dan'l Henderson | 200 | 2 | 4 | 10 | -- |
| John Henry | 150 | 2 | 3 | -- | -- |
| Thomas Hope | 100 | 3 | 3 | 3 | 1 |
| Robert Hope | 150 | 1 | 3 | 4 | -- |
| Sam'l Jenkins | 100 | 2 | 2 | 6 | -- |
| Godson Ervin | 150 | 4 | -- | -- | -- |
| Josiah Ervin, g.m., s.m. | 150 | -- | -- | -- | -- |
| Cha's Kinkead | 200 | 4 | 4 | 12 | -- |
| Wm. Marsh | 150 | 2 | 4 | 10 | -- |
| Sam'l McCleland, carpenter | 200 | 2 | 4 | 5 | -- |
| Jam's Miller | 280 | 4 | 5 | -- | -- |
| Henry Marsh | 200 | 3 | 4 | 5 | -- |
| John Moor, g.m., miller | 300 | 3 | 3 | 15 | -- |
| William Moor | 266 | 4 | 6 | 10 | -- |
| John Maxfield | 50 | 1 | 1 | -- | -- |
| Sam'l Martin | 180 | 2 | 4 | 3 | 1 |
| Will'm Marshall | 332 | 4 | 7 | 6 | -- |
| Will'm Marshall | 50 | -- | -- | -- | -- |
| Robert Moodey | 60 | -- | -- | -- | -- |
| Alex'r McFerson | 200 | 4 | 4 | 10 | -- |
| Robert McFerson | 194 | 4 | 6 | 5 | -- |
| David McClure | 100 | 2 | 2 | 3 | 1 |
| William Powell, s.m. | 200 | 4 | 3 | 5 | -- |
| Abraham Patton | 100 | 1 | 1 | -- | -- |
| George Robeson | 50 | 2 | 2 | -- | -- |
| Anthony Robeson, labourer | 21 | 1 | -- | -- | -- |
| William Simmonds | 100 | 2 | 4 | 5 | -- |
| John Sharp, stiller | 200 | 3 | 5 | 6 | 1 |
| James Sharp | 250 | 3 | 3 | 5 | 1 |
| A'drew Stuart | 200 | 2 | 2 | 6 | -- |
| Alex'r Simerall | 200 | 4 | 4 | 10 | -- |
| John Simerall | 100 | 2 | 2 | -- | -- |
| James Simerall, mill, miller | 22 | 2 | 1 | -- | -- |
| John Scott | 150 | 2 | 3 | 6 | -- |
| Tho's Trueman | 150 | 3 | 3 | 9 | -- |
| John Trueman, g.m., miller | 218 | 2 | 6 | 6 | -- |
| John Turner | 50 | 2 | 1 | -- | -- |
| Joseph Williams | 250 | 2 | 4 | 10 | -- |
| Jam's Williams | 300 | 2 | 3 | 6 | -- |
| Wm. Wilkins | 125 | 3 | 4 | 6 | -- |
| Thomas White | 100 | 1 | 1 | -- | -- |

Inmates

Barney Smith
Samuel Cooper
Charles Kilkey
James Williams
James Bigam
James Henon
John Clark

Charles Shaw
Tho's Law
William Henderson
Henry Neal
James Bogg
Jam's Alleson

Freemen

Patrick Dougherty
Phillip Dougherty
Andrew Walker
John Dermond
John Cooper
John Armstrong
Benjamin Breneman
Joseph Henderson
James Stuart
Wm. Cooper

John Wilkin
Sam'l Kilpatrick
John Donaughey
Matthew Cowen
Francis Armstrong
George Richmond
David Cowen
Jam's Kinkead
Thomas Simeral

New London Rate

|  | Acres | Horses | Cattle | Sheep | Servants |
|---|---|---|---|---|---|
| Alexander Johnson, shopkeeper | 460 | 4 | 6 | -- | 2 |
| Jacob Bundle, t.k. | 10 | 1 | 1 | -- | -- |
| David Mackey, t.k. | 30 | 1 | 1 | -- | -- |
| Mich'l Montgomery | 100 | -- | -- | -- | -- |
| Thomas Minard | 200 | 2 | 2 | 7 | 1 |
| Robert Finney | 190 | 2 | 2 | 6 | -- |
| Widow Finney | 80 | 2 | 2 | -- | -- |
| Jam's Hedleston | 100 | 2 | 3 | -- | -- |
| Jam's Hutchenson | 100 | 1 | 1 | 3 | -- |
| Robert Finney | 200 | 1 | 3 | 6 | -- |
| James Hughes | 150 | 2 | 2 | 6 | -- |
| And'w Gambell | 150 | 2 | 2 | 5 | -- |
| Thomas Gilmore | 100 | 1 | 1 | -- | -- |
| Robert Gilmore, Jun'r | 100 | 1 | 1 | -- | -- |
| Andrew McBath | 120 | 1 | 2 | -- | -- |
| Tho's Finney | 100 | 1 | 2 | 6 | -- |
| John Scott | 200 | -- | -- | -- | -- |
| David Curry | 200 | 3 | 3 | 6 | -- |
| George Cambell | 60 | 1 | 2 | -- | -- |
| John Monough | 130 | 2 | 5 | 6 | -- |
| George McDowel | 130 | 1 | 1 | -- | -- |
| And'w Scott | 50 | 1 | 2 | -- | -- |
| Elizabeth Furry, t.k. | 100 | 1 | 4 | 6 | 1 |
| William Beatty | 130 | 2 | 3 | 6 | -- |
| John Fleming | 100 | 2 | 3 | 10 | 1 |
| Arthur McCluer | 30 | 1 | 2 | 2 | -- |
| John Galespy | 60 | 1 | 2 | -- | -- |
| And'w Galespy | 60 | 1 | 2 | -- | -- |
| Robert Wilkin, g.m., miller | 300 | 4 | 4 | 20 | -- |
| Joseph Young | 80 | 2 | 3 | 6 | -- |
| John Robeson | 100 | 2 | 2 | -- | -- |
| Joseph Furry | 60 | 1 | 1 | -- | -- |
| Matthew Wilson | 70 | 2 | -- | -- | -- |
| Alex'r Morrison | 70 | 1 | 1 | -- | -- |
| John Hutchenson | 40 | 1 | 1 | -- | -- |
| Tho's Donaldson | 100 | 2 | 2 | -- | -- |
| Humphrey Rusk | 120 | -- | -- | -- | -- |
| David Steward | 30 | 1 | 2 | -- | -- |
| John Peoples | 70 | 2 | 2 | -- | -- |
| Joseph Smith | 70 | 1 | 1 | 2 | -- |

| New London | Acres | Horses | Cattle | Sheep | Servants |
|---|---|---|---|---|---|
| Widow Gottas | 60 | 1 | 2 | 4 | -- |
| Daniel Baily | 90 | 2 | 2 | 1 | -- |
| Widow Mountgomery | 50 | -- | -- | -- | -- |
| Peter Gubby | 50 | 2 | 2 | 6 | -- |
| Samuel Mairs | 100 | 2 | -- | -- | -- |
| James Reed, g.m., s.m., miller | 300 | 4 | 4 | 10 | -- |
| Wm. Hutchenson | 150 | 2 | 3 | 6 | -- |
| John Lemman | 140 | 1 | 1 | -- | -- |
| Rob't Giffin | 150 | 2 | 3 | 6 | -- |
| Wm. Morrison | 60 | 1 | 1 | -- | -- |
| John Sturgeon | 60 | 1 | 2 | 4 | -- |
| John Small | 130 | 2 | 2 | 6 | -- |
| Jam's Whitecraft | 60 | 1 | 2 | -- | -- |
| George Lashley | 60 | 1 | 2 | 4 | -- |
| Will'm Cummins | 100 | 1 | 3 | 6 | -- |
| George Currey | 180 | 3 | 4 | 6 | 1 |
| John Whitton | 90 | -- | -- | -- | -- |
| Rob't Gilmore | 80 | 2 | 2 | 4 | -- |
| Jeremiah Starr | 180 | 3 | 2 | 4 | -- |
| Jam's Harbison | 80 | 3 | 3 | -- | -- |
| David Viley | 90 | -- | -- | -- | -- |
| Joseph Cook | 70 | 1 | 2 | 4 | -- |
| James Moss | 40 | 1 | 1 | -- | -- |
| John Henderson, Senior, g.m. | 200 | 2 | 3 | 4 | -- |
| Rob't Mountgomery | 40 | -- | 1 | -- | -- |
| Isaac Mountgomery | 60 | 1 | 1 | -- | -- |
| Will'm Steel | 60 | 1 | 1 | 4 | -- |
| Sam'l Floyd | 100 | 2 | 2 | 6 | -- |
| Tho's Fulton | 70 | 2 | 2 | 2 | -- |
| John Todd | 150 | 2 | 2 | 4 | -- |
| James Purtle | 13 | 1 | 1 | -- | -- |
| Arch'd Woodside | 130 | 2 | 4 | 3 | -- |
| Hugh Cambell | 100 | 2 | 3 | 7 | -- |
| John Cambell | 60 | 1 | 1 | -- | -- |
| Joseph Moor | 150 | 2 | 3 | 6 | -- |
| Widow Henderson | 120 | -- | 2 | -- | -- |
| Robert Allison | 100 | 2 | 3 | -- | -- |
| John Smith | 150 | 2 | 4 | -- | -- |
| John Smith, Jun'r | 100 | 1 | -- | -- | -- |
| David Steward | 100 | -- | -- | -- | -- |
| Wm. McDowell | 40 | -- | 1 | -- | -- |

Inmates

John Bowman  
Dan'l McAnally  
Thomas Scott  
Andrew Oliver  

Timothy Hughes  
Robert Norris  
George Bond

## Freemen

Will'm Sherer
Sam'l Hutchenson
John Finney
Will'm Galaspey
Hugh Morrison
John Moore

Will Reed
Robert Elder
James Hogg
Ephraim Morrison
David Hutchenson
Joseph Morrison

## Kennett Rate

|  | Acres | Horses | Cattle | Sheep | Servants |
|---|---|---|---|---|---|
| George Brown, millwright | 150 | 4 | 3 | 10 | -- |
| Wm. Baldwin, taylor | 110 | 3 | 3 | 4 | 1 |
| Rob't Brown | 150 | 4 | 5 | 8 | -- |
| James Brinton | 330 | 4 | 7 | 10 | 1 |
| Benj'n Oran, carpenter | 2 | -- | 1 | -- | -- |
| Rob't Herrege, labourer | 3 | 1 | 1 | -- | -- |
| John Brinton | 195 | 3 | 4 | 11 | -- |
| James Bennett | 327 | 4 | 6 | 25 | 1 |
| Robert Barr | 200 | 4 | 5 | 3 | -- |
| Joseph Bonsall | 125 | 2 | 2 | 7 | -- |
| Robert Cooper, f.m. | 100 | 3 | 4 | 6 | -- |
| Wm. Cloud | 110 | -- | -- | -- | -- |
| John Clark, weaver | 180 | 4 | 3 | 5 | -- |
| Joseph Chandler, blacksmith | 75 | 2 | 4 | -- | -- |
| Tho's Carlinton | 200 | 4 | 4 | 10 | -- |
| Walter Crage | 200 | 4 | 7 | 8 | -- |
| Jeremiah Cloud | 139 | 2 | -- | -- | -- |
| Walter Crage | 200 | -- | -- | -- | -- |
| Will'm Campbell, fuller | 34 | -- | -- | -- | -- |
| Enock Dixson | 112 | 3 | 2 | 6 | -- |
| Henry Dixson | 147 | 4 | 3 | 10 | -- |
| Jno. Edwards | 100 | 4 | 6 | 8 | -- |
| John Eaves | 100 | 3 | 4 | 10 | 1 |
| John Fred | 50 | 1 | 1 | -- | -- |
| Jno. Fitzgarral | 172 | 4 | 3 | 10 | -- |
| Samuel Grubb | 142 | 5 | 7 | 16 | -- |
| Tho's Gibson | 300 | 4 | 5 | 20 | 1 |
| Israel Gilpin, tanner | 3 | 1 | 1 | -- | -- |
| Michael Grigg | 150 | 4 | 8 | 10 | -- |
| Joseph Grigg | 100 | 3 | 4 | 6 | -- |
| Benjamin Grigg | 100 | 2 | 2 | 6 | 1 |
| Sam'l Harlin | 120 | 3 | 2 | 10 | -- |
| Joseph Harlin, s.m., g.m. | 180 | 5 | 7 | -- | -- |
| Joseph Henry | 120 | 3 | 2 | -- | -- |
| James Hance | 150 | 2 | 1 | -- | -- |
| Wm. Harvey, malster | 290 | 4 | 7 | 12 | -- |
| Amos Hope | 350 | 4 | 4 | 5 | -- |
| James Harvey | 170 | 1 | -- | -- | -- |
| Evan Harry | 140 | 3 | 3 | -- | -- |
| Amos Harry, taylor | 130 | 4 | 4 | 13 | -- |
| Stephen Hayes | 40 | 2 | 2 | 4 | -- |
| Tho's Hope, taylor | 50 | 1 | 3 | -- | -- |
| John Heald | 150 | 3 | 4 | 6 | -- |

## Kennett

| | Acres | Horses | Cattle | Sheep | Servants |
|---|---|---|---|---|---|
| Sam'l Heald | 200 | 3 | 3 | 9 | -- |
| Joshua Harlan | 180 | 2 | 6 | 2 | -- |
| Amos House | 96 | -- | -- | -- | -- |
| Enoch Hollinsworth, miller | 100 | 2 | 2 | -- | -- |
| Joseph Hines | 45 | 3 | 3 | 10 | -- |
| Zacchus Kay | 100 | 2 | 1 | -- | -- |
| Sam'l Leavis | 380 | 5 | 8 | 10 | -- |
| John Lamburn | 175 | 3 | 6 | 12 | 2 |
| Will'm Leavis, g.m., miller | 220 | 3 | 6 | 15 | -- |
| Robert Lamborn | 76 | 4 | 3 | 14 | 1 |
| Wm. Lamborn, sadler | 100 | 1 | 3 | 6 | -- |
| Aaron Musgrove, shopkeeper | 81 | 2 | 2 | -- | 1 |
| Jesse Miller | 250 | 5 | 7 | 20 | -- |
| Sam'l McCooll | 130 | 4 | 4 | 10 | -- |
| Joseph Milner | 100 | 1 | 2 | -- | -- |
| Isaac Mendenhall | 300 | 4 | 6 | 20 | -- |
| Benj'n Mendenhall | 200 | 3 | 10 | 10 | -- |
| Jam's Mountgomery | 180 | 3 | 4 | 4 | -- |
| And'w Mitchel | 250 | -- | -- | -- | -- |
| Jesse Mendenhall | 200 | 3 | 7 | 12 | -- |
| Dav'd Mercer | 120 | 5 | 6 | 10 | -- |
| Mat'w McConnall | 146 | 3 | 3 | 10 | -- |
| Benj'n Mendenhall | 138 | -- | -- | -- | -- |
| Moses Mendenhall | 112 | 3 | 5 | 12 | -- |
| Jos. Musgrove | 9 | 3 | 2 | 20 | -- |
| Jno. Nubrough, smith | 30 | 1 | 2 | -- | -- |
| Estate of John Nichols, deceas'd | 119 | -- | -- | -- | -- |
| Will'm Pew | 150 | 4 | 3 | 4 | -- |
| Tho's McConnall, taylor | 4 | 1 | 2 | -- | -- |
| Enoch Pasmore | 210 | 5 | 5 | 4 | -- |
| Geo'e Pasmore | 100 | 4 | 4 | 11 | -- |
| Jno. Pyle, | 73 | 2 | 2 | 3 | -- |
| Jno. Pyle, Jun'r | 150 | 4 | 4 | 6 | 1 |
| Jno. Richardson, carpenter | 250 | 5 | 12 | 7 | -- |
| Joshua Scott, t.k. | 75 | 2 | 2 | 7 | -- |
| Tho's Suit | 150 | 3 | 5 | 10 | -- |
| Dennis Sullavan | 200 | 5 | 3 | 6 | -- |
| Fran's Swain | -- | 4 | 2 | -- | -- |
| Abra'm Taylor | 110 | 2 | 4 | 5 | -- |
| Tho's Temple | 190 | 4 | 6 | 3 | 1 |
| Benj'n Taylor, g.m., s.m. | 340 | 4 | 46 | 6 | 1 |
| John Taylor, tanner | 100 | 3 | 2 | 8 | 1 |
| Benj'n Taylor, Jun'r, stiller | 140 | 3 | 2 | 8 | 1 |
| Joseph Taylor | 100 | 2 | 2 | 4 | -- |
| Wm. Temple | 200 | 3 | 5 | 10 | -- |
| Jno. Thomson, weaver | 133 | 3 | 3 | -- | -- |
| Isaac Taylor | 250 | 3 | 6 | 10 | -- |
| Caleb Taylor | 50 | 1 | -- | -- | -- |
| Tho's Welsh, t.k. | 5 | 1 | 2 | -- | -- |
| Will'm Webb | 230 | 4 | 6 | 6 | 1 |
| Stephen Webb, s.m. | 327 | 5 | 7 | 15 | -- |
| Daniel Webb | 188 | 4 | 4 | 3 | -- |
| Joseph Walter | 150 | 4 | 6 | 18 | -- |
| Jno. & Jacob Way | 200 | 3 | 8 | 10 | -- |
| William White | 150 | 2 | 5 | 12 | 1 |

| Kennett | Acres | Horses | Cattle | Sheep | Servants |
|---|---|---|---|---|---|
| Jacob Way | 150 | 5 | 7 | -- | -- |
| Elinor Wickersham | 130 | -- | -- | -- | -- |
| Wm. West | 300 | 5 | 4 | -- | -- |
| Caleb Wiley | 200 | 4 | 8 | 10 | -- |
| Rob't Way | 200 | -- | -- | -- | -- |
| Isaac & Jos. Woodrow, sawyers | 180 | 5 | 2 | -- | -- |
| Jacob Zimpher | 12 | -- | -- | -- | -- |
| Jno. Wilston, wool comber | 10 | -- | -- | -- | -- |
| And'w Read | 100 | 2 | 3 | -- | -- |
| Eliz'th Ring | 166 | -- | -- | -- | -- |

## Freemen

Jacob Brown
Jno. Brown
Titus Bennett
Jno. Boker
Sam'l Chandler
Will'm Dimson
Andrew Crator
Joseph Acoff
Silvenes Day
Will'm Erwin
Robert Fisher
Jam's Gormingly
Stephen Grigg
Tho's Harry
Jesse Harry
Jno. Hayes
Caleb Harlan

Ezekel Leonard
James Moor
Benj'n McCowan
Jno. Morrow
Sam'l McCormack
George Gray
Jno. McCarty
John Pyle
Sam'l Pyle
Caleb Pyle
John Starr
Mich'l Shivery
John Smith
George Stearn
Moses Welden
Jam's Walter
Will'm Hague

## Inmates

Jno. Delap
Lawrence Fling
William McColough
Charles McCalley
Tho's Monke
Timothy Mahany
Jno. Nickols
George Owen
Wm. Ralph
Phillip Pyle
Eleck Stuard
Alexander Steal
Matthew Wilston
John Warner
William Wiley
Joshua Wiley
Jesse Harlan
Thomas Gormley
William Hayes

Helvert Maxfield
Jno. Marshall
Timothy Melton
Jno. McFalam
Cain McCanney
Thomas Huston
Joseph Heald
Thomas Johnson
David Jemeson
William Jemeson
Daniel Leonard
Andrew Reece
John Hatton
Tho's Boyle
Jane Culbertson
William White
Joseph Money
Benjamin Walker

## Newlinton Rate

|  | Acres | Horses | Cattle | Sheep | Servants |
|---|---|---|---|---|---|
| Will'm Atkins | 100 | 3 | 2 | -- | -- |
| Tho's Baldwin, carpenter | 60 | 2 | 2 | 5 | -- |
| Jonathan Buffington, g.m., s.m., miller | 150 | 2 | 2 | 6 | -- |
| Robert Bentley, s.m. | 270 | 1 | 2 | 6 | -- |
| John Bailey | 160 | 3 | 4 | 10 | -- |
| George Bentley | 100 | 1 | -- | -- | -- |
| John Bullar | 200 | 4 | 5 | -- | -- |
| John Bullar, as adm'r to Rich'd Bullar | 140 | -- | -- | -- | -- |
| Isaac Bailey | 327 | -- | -- | -- | -- |
| Richard Barnett | 370 | 8 | 10 | 10 | 1 |
| John Brown, sadler | 22 | 1 | 2 | -- | -- |
| Tho's Buffington | 200 | 4 | 4 | 8 | -- |
| Rob't Chalfant | 90 | 4 | 3 | -- | -- |
| Robert Cowen | 100 | 2 | 2 | 3 | -- |
| David Drennon | 200 | 2 | 3 | 5 | -- |
| David Acoffe, tanner | 144 | 3 | 3 | 2 | -- |
| Mich'l Acoffe | 7 1/2 | -- | -- | -- | -- |
| Joel Harlan | 160 | 5 | 5 | 9 | -- |
| Caleb Hayes | 100 | 2 | 3 | 6 | -- |
| Joseph Hayes, smith | 90 | 4 | 3 | -- | -- |
| Henry Hayes, shoemaker | 100 | 3 | 2 | 4 | 1 |
| Francis Hannah | 120 | 2 | 2 | 4 | -- |
| Hannah Hayes | 100 | -- | -- | -- | -- |
| Will Kirgin | 200 | 3 | 3 | 4 | -- |
| John Martin | 200 | 4 | 2 | 6 | -- |
| Will'm Nichols | 125 | 3 | 3 | -- | -- |
| George Peirce | 450 | 5 | 6 | 13 | -- |
| James Smith | 200 | 4 | 4 | 10 | -- |
| Phillip Chaff | 140 | 3 | 3 | -- | 1 |
| Jam's Shields | 250 | 5 | 4 | 10 | 2 |
| Ebenezer Spikeman | 170 | 3 | 2 | -- | 1 |
| Will'm Thompson, weaver | 12 | 1 | 2 | -- | -- |
| Jesse Taylor | 180 | 3 | 5 | 9 | -- |
| John Taylor | 30 | 2 | 2 | 3 | -- |
| Isaac Williams | 100 | 3 | 3 | 4 | -- |
| Tho's Wilson | 116 | 2 | 3 | -- | -- |
| Caleb Wilson | 100 | 2 | 2 | -- | 1 |
| Will'm Wickersham | 150 | 3 | 4 | 8 | -- |
| Peter Wickersham | 100 | 1 | -- | -- | -- |
| Wm. Wickersham, Jun'r | 100 | 2 | 1 | -- | -- |
| Cha's Wilson, blacksmith | 150 | 3 | 3 | 6 | -- |
| John Watson | 200 | 3 | 4 | 6 | -- |

### Freemen

Jesse Bentley  
Rob't Chalfant  
Peter Myers  
Rob't Nelson  
Will'm Nickols  
Tho's Wilson  
Joshua Pierce  
Joseph Kearns  
John York  
Jam's Brown  
Jno. Smith  
Wm. McFarlan

Inmates

Frederick Carpenter
Mark Cuningham
Wm. Eachoff
Jno. Gray
Jno. Harvey
Jno. Hailey
Jno. Holden
Wm. Hannah, storekeeper
James Lynch

Christopher Myers
Jam's Powel
John Sample
Will'm Walker
Anthony Baldwin, carpenter
Simon Kearns
John Griest
Rich'd Ladly

West Nottingham Rate

|  | Acres | Horses | Cattle | Sheep | Servants |
|---|---|---|---|---|---|
| Will'm Allen, blacksmith | 100 | 4 | 4 | 10 | -- |
| John Alexander | 200 | 3 | 9 | 18 | -- |
| James Aken | 150 | 2 | 6 | -- | 1 |
| James Allen | 150 | 4 | 4 | -- | -- |
| Henry Anderson | 200 | 3 | 4 | 10 | 1 |
| Jno. Beard | 130 | 3 | 4 | 8 | 1 |
| Thomas Brown | 80 | 2 | 2 | 6 | -- |
| Sam'l Brown | 150 | 2 | 2 | 3 | -- |
| Joseph Brown | 100 | 1 | -- | -- | -- |
| James Barclay | 150 | 2 | 4 | 4 | -- |
| Mary Brown | -- | 2 | 3 | 4 | -- |
| Fra's Boyde | 50 | 3 | 4 | 10 | -- |
| John Brown | 70 | 2 | 4 | 5 | -- |
| Isaac Brown | 150 | 2 | 4 | 5 | -- |
| Jane Blair | 40 | 2 | 1 | -- | -- |
| Mary Blackburn | 100 | 2 | 4 | 10 | -- |
| Wm. Buckanan | 170 | 2 | 4 | 10 | 1 |
| Jacob Brown | 100 | 2 | 4 | 2 | -- |
| Jacob Brown | 150 | 1 | -- | -- | -- |
| Jam's Barns | 200 | 3 | 6 | 18 | 1 |
| Elnor Brown | 100 | -- | -- | -- | -- |
| John Borland | 130 | 3 | 4 | 16 | 1 |
| John Butterfield | 140 | 2 | 4 | 6 | -- |
| Joseph Brown, Senior | 150 | 3 | 6 | 15 | -- |
| William Brown | 100 | -- | -- | -- | -- |
| Jacob Clark, cooper | 25 | -- | 1 | -- | -- |
| Rob't McNutt, jobber | 25 | -- | 1 | -- | -- |
| Elisha Brown, cooper | 100 | 2 | 4 | 6 | 1 |
| Jam's Cowden | 90 | 2 | 2 | 6 | -- |
| Jam's Cambell | 100 | 2 | 2 | -- | -- |
| Jno. CarMichall | 70 | 2 | 2 | 5 | -- |
| Joseph Coltson | 100 | 3 | 2 | 6 | -- |
| Jno. Craford | 46 | 2 | 2 | 6 | -- |
| Tho's Collins | 150 | 1 | -- | -- | -- |
| Agnes Cummins, tavern | 55 | 1 | 3 | 6 | 1 |
| Thomas Coltson, g.m., miller | 80 | 1 | 2 | 3 | -- |
| Wm. Cole | 100 | 2 | 2 | 6 | -- |
| Jno. Crosgrove, weaver | 113 | 1 | 3 | -- | 1 |
| Rob't Croswell | 150 | 2 | 3 | 6 | -- |
| John Coltson | 150 | 3 | 4 | 6 | -- |

West Nottingham

| | Acres | Horses | Cattle | Sheep | Servants |
|---|---|---|---|---|---|
| Will'm Cambell | 100 | 2 | 3 | 6 | -- |
| Jam's Dougherty | 100 | 2 | 3 | 4 | -- |
| John Dixson | 10 | 2 | 1 | -- | -- |
| John Dickey | 150 | -- | -- | -- | -- |
| Sam'l Ewing | 150 | 1 | 2 | 3 | -- |
| Jonathan Edwards | 100 | 2 | 2 | -- | -- |
| Daniel England | 10 | 1 | 1 | 2 | -- |
| Marga't Edmundson | 200 | 2 | 6 | 20 | 1 |
| James Evans | 350 | 6 | 10 | 20 | 4 |
| Dav'd Edmundson | 200 | 4 | 4 | 6 | -- |
| John Glasgow, storekeeper | 100 | 1 | 3 | -- | 2 |
| Sam'l Glasgow | 100 | 2 | 4 | 10 | -- |
| Rob't Given | 200 | 2 | 4 | 10 | -- |
| Will'm Hains, s.m. | 200 | 4 | 8 | 20 | -- |
| Joseph Hains | 100 | 3 | 6 | 15 | -- |
| Isaac Haynes | 100 | 3 | 3 | 6 | -- |
| Job Haynes | 160 | 3 | 8 | 20 | -- |
| Wm. Harris | 90 | 2 | 2 | 10 | -- |
| Johanas Huss | 80 | 1 | 1 | -- | -- |
| James Harbison | 100 | 2 | 2 | 3 | -- |
| Robert Hindman | 150 | 3 | 4 | 10 | -- |
| Jacob Haynes | 150 | 4 | 6 | 12 | -- |
| Micajah James, g.m., miller | 116 | 6 | 4 | -- | 1 |
| George James, g.m., s.m. | 70 | 1 | 3 | -- | -- |
| Daniel Job, blacksmith | 50 | 2 | 4 | 6 | 1 |
| Ruth Johnson | 100 | 1 | 1 | -- | -- |
| John Johnson | 200 | 4 | 6 | 12 | -- |
| Jno. KirkPatrick, Senior | 100 | 2 | 3 | 6 | -- |
| Jno. KirkPatrick, Junior | 200 | 3 | 3 | 6 | -- |
| Will'm Knight, tanner | 200 | 6 | 4 | 12 | -- |
| Elizabeth Kirk | 200 | 4 | 6 | 15 | 3 |
| Mary Kirk | 50 | -- | -- | -- | -- |
| Timothy Kirk | 50 | 2 | 2 | -- | -- |
| Samuel Love | 10 | 2 | 2 | 10 | -- |
| And'w Leaper | 200 | 2 | 3 | 10 | 1 |
| Jno. Lewden, g.m. | 250 | 8 | 10 | 20 | 2 |
| Wm. Maxwell | 50 | 2 | 3 | 4 | -- |
| Jam's Maxwell | 50 | 2 | 3 | 4 | -- |
| Wm. McMaster | 60 | 2 | 2 | 6 | -- |
| James Moor, blacksmith | 72 | 1 | 2 | -- | -- |
| Joseph McReynolds | 150 | 2 | 4 | 10 | -- |
| Robert Moor | 150 | 4 | 5 | 15 | 1 |
| Curtis Midkiff | 100 | 2 | 3 | 6 | -- |
| Andrew McDowell, mill, miller | 10 | 3 | 3 | -- | 1 |
| Rob't McDowell | 150 | 4 | 3 | 10 | -- |
| Adam Miller | 130 | 2 | 2 | 4 | -- |
| Tho's Morton | 70 | 2 | 2 | 4 | -- |
| David Moor | 70 | 2 | 2 | 4 | -- |
| Tho's McCartney | 40 | 2 | 2 | 6 | -- |
| Patrick McLoy | 150 | 2 | 2 | 6 | -- |
| Jno. McMullen | 150 | 2 | 4 | 4 | -- |
| Ann Morgan | 45 | -- | -- | -- | -- |
| Martha McKee | 60 | 2 | 2 | -- | -- |
| John McIntire | 80 | 2 | 2 | 6 | -- |
| Jam's Merchant | 160 | 2 | 4 | 6 | -- |

| West Nottingham | Acres | Horses | Cattle | Sheep | Servants |
|---|---|---|---|---|---|
| Joseph Niesbit | -- | -- | -- | -- | -- |
| David Poak | 150 | 2 | 4 | 10 | -- |
| Mich'l Patton | 80 | 2 | 2 | 6 | -- |
| David Patton | 100 | 2 | 3 | 6 | 1 |
| Jam's Patton | 150 | 1 | -- | -- | -- |
| Wm. Poake | 204 | 4 | 6 | 20 | 1 |
| Jam's Poake | 150 | 2 | 4 | 15 | -- |
| John Reed | 56 | 2 | 2 | 16 | -- |
| David Reece | 100 | 3 | 3 | 6 | -- |
| Wm. Reynolds, g.m., s.m., miller | 100 | 3 | 4 | 6 | 1 |
| Tho's Rogers | 100 | 3 | 5 | 10 | -- |
| Sam'l Reynolds, storekeeper | 100 | 4 | 6 | 12 | -- |
| Jacob Reynolds | 100 | 4 | 6 | 20 | -- |
| Jane Rowland | 50 | 1 | 2 | 3 | -- |
| Hugh Rowland | 100 | 2 | 3 | 6 | -- |
| Patrick Ray | 180 | 2 | 4 | 10 | -- |
| Jam's Rice | 10 | 1 | 1 | -- | -- |
| Henry Reynolds | 200 | 4 | 10 | 18 | -- |
| Benj'n Reynolds | 100 | 2 | 2 | -- | -- |
| Joseph Rich | 105 | 4 | 4 | 10 | -- |
| Henry Sidwell, distiller | 70 | 3 | 2 | 6 | -- |
| Jam's Scott | 100 | 2 | 2 | 6 | -- |
| Abra'm Sidwell | 6 | 1 | 1 | 6 | -- |
| Jacob Sidwell | 100 | 2 | 3 | 10 | -- |
| Jam's Steal | 100 | 2 | 3 | -- | -- |
| And'w Steal | 130 | 2 | 3 | 6 | -- |
| Tho's Scott | 80 | 2 | 3 | -- | -- |
| Sam'l Scott | 200 | 2 | 3 | 6 | -- |
| Elizabeth Tidball | 150 | 3 | 4 | 6 | -- |
| Will'm Tidball | 23 | 2 | 4 | 15 | -- |
| Joseph Woods, f.m. | 100 | 2 | 2 | 10 | -- |
| Tho's Wilson, weaver | 80 | 2 | 2 | 6 | -- |
| Joseph Boon, taylor | 50 | 1 | 1 | -- | -- |
| Jam's McMullen, labourer | 100 | 1 | 1 | -- | -- |
| Jam's Murphy, jobber | -- | -- | -- | -- | -- |
| Isaac McCown | -- | -- | -- | -- | -- |
| Patrick Nelson | -- | -- | -- | -- | -- |
| John Woodrow, jobber | -- | 1 | 1 | -- | -- |
| Jam's Anderson, jobber | -- | 1 | 1 | -- | -- |
| Samuel Adams, miller | -- | 1 | 1 | -- | -- |
| John Blackburn, blacksmith | -- | 1 | 1 | -- | -- |
| Joakim Breachley, nailor | -- | 1 | 1 | -- | -- |
| Dan'l Blair | -- | -- | -- | -- | -- |
| Sam'l Blackburn, taylor | -- | 1 | 1 | -- | -- |
| Walter Denny, weaver | -- | -- | 1 | -- | -- |
| Alex'r Cockran | 100 | 2 | 2 | -- | -- |
| Tho's Clendenan, weaver | -- | 1 | 1 | -- | -- |
| John Crompton | -- | -- | -- | -- | -- |
| Patrick Cannon, jobber | -- | -- | -- | -- | -- |
| Victor Creag, smith | -- | -- | -- | -- | -- |
| Will'm Calhoon, jobber | -- | -- | -- | -- | -- |
| David Edmondson, taylor | -- | -- | 1 | -- | -- |
| Timothy Ginney, jobber | -- | 1 | 1 | -- | -- |
| Jno. Marshman, shoemaker | -- | 1 | 1 | -- | -- |
| Geo'e Hutcheson, jobber | -- | -- | 1 | -- | -- |

| West Nottingham | Acres | Horses | Cattle | Sheep | Servants |
|---|---|---|---|---|---|
| John Homes, carpenter | -- | -- | -- | -- | -- |
| Cornelius Menan, jobber | -- | -- | -- | -- | -- |
| Jam's McClung | -- | -- | -- | -- | -- |
| And'w McCown, jobber | -- | -- | 1 | -- | -- |
| Tho's McCleary, carpenter | -- | 1 | 1 | -- | -- |
| Thomas Philips, labourer | -- | 1 | 1 | -- | -- |
| John Tibbs, labourer | -- | 2 | 2 | -- | -- |
| John Thompson, labourer | -- | -- | 1 | -- | -- |
| Tho's Woodward, jobber | -- | -- | 1 | -- | -- |
| Jam's Wilson, weaver | -- | -- | 1 | -- | -- |
| Richard Harris | 50 | 2 | 2 | 5 | -- |
| And'w Wilson | 30 | -- | -- | -- | -- |
| Jacob Sidwell | 100 | 2 | 2 | 5 | -- |

### Freemen

| | |
|---|---|
| Jam's Anderson | Alex'r Boyde |
| Jno. Alexander | Jam's Bullar |
| Nathan Allen | Jam's Braden |
| George Brown | Jno. Scott |
| Ephram Blackborn | Wm. Wallace |
| Wm. Buchanan | Wm. Wallar |
| Geo'e Becket | Fra'c White |
| Jam's Creswell | Jam's White |
| Jam's Creswell | Patrick Reagon |
| David Edmundson | Robert Brown |
| Flower Greenland | Tho's Pook |
| Robert Hambleton | Jno. Cambell |
| Wm. Johnson | Jam's McReynolds |
| John Jay | Jno. Cole |
| Hugh McKnight | Andrew Wilson |
| Daniel McKan | Jno. Reynolds |
| Jam's McMullan | Isaac Reynolds |
| Jam's Orr | Joseph Cummins |
| Tho's Picket | Jam's Allen |
| Tho's Patton | Wm. Leggitt |
| Joseph Rogers | Jno. Barkly |
| Jno. Wright | Andrew Reak |
| Henry Reynolds, Jun'r | Jno. Kilpatrick |
| Wm. Sims | |

### Inmates

| | |
|---|---|
| Charles Forker | Jno. Glasgow |
| Jam's Curl | |

### East Nottingham Rate

| | Acres | Horses | Cattle | Sheep | Servants |
|---|---|---|---|---|---|
| Henry Askin, carpenter | 60 | 2 | 2 | 6 | -- |
| Jam's Adams | 40 | 1 | 2 | -- | -- |

| East Nottingham | Acres | Horses | Cattle | Sheep | Servants |
|---|---|---|---|---|---|
| Jno. Boggs, shoemaker | 60 | 1 | 1 | -- | -- |
| Hannah Butcher | 100 | -- | -- | -- | -- |
| Wm. Bane | 300 | 4 | 6 | 10 | 1 |
| And'w Boyde, g.m. | 100 | 3 | 3 | 8 | -- |
| Gilbert Buchanan | 60 | 1 | 2 | 6 | -- |
| Messer Brown | 300 | 4 | 7 | 20 | 1 |
| Tho's Berrett | 180 | 3 | 7 | 7 | -- |
| Daniel Brown | 90 | 1 | 3 | 6 | -- |
| William Brown, mason | 130 | 3 | 4 | 8 | -- |
| David Brown, blacksmith | 30 | 2 | 3 | 6 | -- |
| John Bigham | 150 | -- | 2 | 10 | -- |
| Jam's Boge, taylor | 25 | 1 | 1 | -- | -- |
| Andrew Byers | 130 | 2 | 3 | 8 | -- |
| Timothy Brown, mason | 100 | 2 | 3 | 6 | -- |
| Josiah Crawford | 100 | 3 | 2 | 4 | -- |
| James Cowden | 100 | 1 | 2 | 2 | -- |
| John Churchman | 80 | 3 | 4 | 5 | -- |
| George Churchman, surveyor | 300 | 4 | 8 | 12 | -- |
| Wm. Churchman | 150 | 5 | 7 | 9 | -- |
| Robert Colven, joyner | 60 | 2 | 2 | 6 | -- |
| John Clendenon, blacksmith | 94 | 2 | 3 | 10 | -- |
| Benj'n Chandley, clockmaker | 180 | 3 | 4 | 8 | 1 |
| John Crawford | 40 | 1 | 1 | -- | -- |
| Tho's Churchman | 50 | -- | -- | -- | -- |
| Sam'l Dickey | 30 | 2 | 2 | 10 | -- |
| Andrew Dickson | 60 | 2 | 2 | 10 | -- |
| Joseph Drenon | 80 | 1 | 2 | 4 | -- |
| John Day, tanner, tan house & yard | 100 | -- | -- | -- | -- |
| George Douglass | 30 | 2 | 2 | 6 | -- |
| Hannah Dillon | 20 | -- | -- | -- | -- |
| Rob't Darragh | 50 | 2 | 2 | 6 | -- |
| Sam'l Dickey, Jun'r | 160 | 2 | 3 | 6 | -- |
| James Douglass | 60 | 1 | -- | -- | -- |
| Henry Ewing | 250 | 3 | 4 | 6 | 1 |
| Robert Ewing | 200 | 2 | 3 | 10 | 1 |
| John Erwin | 80 | 2 | 2 | 4 | -- |
| Tho's Ewing | 130 | 1 | 3 | 10 | -- |
| Samuel Elliott | 100 | 2 | 2 | 4 | -- |
| Robert Erwin | 130 | 2 | 2 | 6 | -- |
| John & Wm. Fulton, f.m. | 200 | 4 | 4 | 12 | -- |
| Joseph Gitchell | 200 | 4 | 4 | 2 | -- |
| Elisha Gitchell, s.m. | 300 | 4 | 6 | 10 | 3 |
| Ivan Greer | 40 | 1 | 1 | 2 | -- |
| John Glasco | 50 | -- | -- | -- | -- |
| Tho's Gotherp | 100 | -- | -- | -- | -- |
| James Gautt | 150 | 3 | 4 | 10 | 1 |
| Archabald Glover | 30 | 2 | 1 | -- | -- |
| Robert Graham | 80 | 2 | 2 | 3 | -- |
| William Gibson, weaver | 50 | 1 | 2 | 2 | -- |
| Matthew Grive | 90 | 1 | 1 | -- | -- |
| Robert Harvey | 100 | 2 | 1 | 4 | -- |
| Elisha Hughes, tavernkeeper, tavern | 300 | 2 | 6 | 10 | 1 |
| Will'm Hilles | 80 | 2 | 2 | 4 | -- |

| East Nottingham | Acres | Horses | Cattle | Sheep | Servants |
|---|---|---|---|---|---|
| Tho's Howard | 50 | 1 | 1 | -- | -- |
| Hugh Howard | 45 | 1 | -- | -- | -- |
| Margarett Hill | 6 | 1 | 1 | -- | -- |
| Jam's Hudders | 270 | 3 | 4 | 6 | 1 |
| Patrick Hambleton, weaver | 50 | 1 | 2 | -- | -- |
| John Hathorn, Sen'r | 200 | 2 | 3 | 8 | 1 |
| John Hathorn, Jun'r, weaver | 50 | 2 | 2 | -- | -- |
| Sam'l Hill | 80 | 2 | 2 | 11 | -- |
| Tho's Hill | 70 | -- | -- | -- | -- |
| David Hogg, weaver | 40 | -- | 2 | 6 | -- |
| Archabald Jobb, blacksmith | 80 | 2 | 2 | 6 | -- |
| David Junkin | 114 | 2 | 4 | 3 | -- |
| James Johnston | 100 | 2 | 2 | 6 | -- |
| Mordica James | 40 | -- | 2 | -- | -- |
| Tho's Jonston, cordwainer | 70 | 1 | 2 | 3 | -- |
| Timothy Kirk, g.m., s.m. | 260 | 5 | 10 | 10 | 2 |
| Mary Kirk, f.m. | 50 | 2 | 2 | 5 | -- |
| Sam'l England | 254 | 5 | 7 | 15 | 1 |
| John Lawson | 160 | 2 | 3 | 14 | -- |
| George Long | 100 | 2 | 2 | 3 | -- |
| Joseph Mahaffy | 120 | 2 | 2 | -- | -- |
| Matthew Henderson | 100 | 1 | 1 | 6 | 1 |
| Guyan Morrison | 150 | 3 | 3 | 6 | -- |
| James McCleane | 30 | -- | -- | -- | -- |
| Finley McGrew | 150 | 2 | 3 | 5 | -- |
| John Mears, joyner | 80 | 3 | 5 | 8 | -- |
| George Mitchel, miller, g.m. | 90 | 4 | 3 | 5 | -- |
| Wm. McLaughlin | 60 | 2 | 2 | 7 | -- |
| Jam's McCormick | 50 | 2 | 2 | 4 | -- |
| Jno. McClernon | 20 | 1 | 1 | -- | -- |
| Rob't Maxwell | 140 | 2 | 3 | 4 | -- |
| Jane McKee | 70 | 1 | 1 | 2 | -- |
| Wm. Mackey | 180 | -- | -- | -- | -- |
| Sampson Moor | 35 | 2 | 2 | 3 | -- |
| Jam's Mountgomery | 160 | 2 | 4 | -- | -- |
| James Maley, taylor | 18 | 1 | 1 | -- | -- |
| Wm. Mountgomery | 100 | 2 | 3 | 8 | -- |
| Jno. McConley | 40 | 1 | 1 | 2 | -- |
| Jno. Miller | 120 | 1 | -- | -- | -- |
| John Ogilby | 130 | 2 | 4 | 12 | 1 |
| John Oldham | 40 | -- | -- | -- | -- |
| John Pew | 150 | 3 | 6 | 10 | 1 |
| Joshua Pugh | 150 | 2 | 3 | 6 | -- |
| Josiah Porterfield | 100 | 2 | 3 | 4 | -- |
| Jam's Patterson | 40 | 2 | 2 | -- | -- |
| Jane Perry | 50 | 1 | 1 | -- | -- |
| David Price | 200 | 2 | 2 | 6 | 1 |
| Patrick Poor, weaver | 20 | 1 | -- | -- | -- |
| Geo'e Pasmoore | 150 | 2 | 1 | -- | -- |
| Patrick Poor, Sen'r | 160 | 3 | 3 | 8 | -- |
| Edw'd Parker, trader | 40 | 2 | 2 | -- | -- |
| Robert Currey | 26 | -- | -- | -- | -- |
| Thomas Rogers | 40 | -- | -- | -- | -- |
| Wm. Ramsey | 260 | 3 | 4 | 12 | -- |
| David Rankin | 60 | 2 | 4 | -- | -- |

| East Nottingham | Acres | Horses | Cattle | Sheep | Servants |
|---|---|---|---|---|---|
| Rowland Rogers | 350 | 6 | 7 | 20 | 1 |
| Will'm Rogers | 250 | 3 | 8 | 15 | -- |
| William Rogers, hatter | 70 | 1 | 2 | 6 | -- |
| John Rogers, smith | 50 | 1 | 2 | 6 | -- |
| Hezekiah Rowls, joyner | 75 | 2 | 2 | 8 | -- |
| Tho's Sharp | 50 | 2 | 2 | 5 | 2 |
| Jane Scott | 80 | 2 | 2 | -- | -- |
| Robert Shephard | 50 | 1 | 1 | -- | -- |
| Rich'd Sidwell | 150 | 2 | 3 | 7 | -- |
| Hugh Sidwell | 180 | 3 | 6 | 10 | -- |
| John Strawbridge | 100 | -- | -- | -- | -- |
| James Steel, weaver | 100 | 3 | 4 | 12 | 1 |
| Wm. Shephard | 80 | 1 | 2 | 3 | -- |
| Jno. Strithers | 100 | 2 | 1 | 5 | -- |
| Philip Scott, cooper | 90 | 2 | 2 | 6 | -- |
| Thomas Scott | 160 | 1 | 2 | 4 | -- |
| Patrick Scott, shoemaker | 60 | 2 | 1 | -- | -- |
| Jam's & Jno. Smith | 100 | 2 | 2 | 4 | -- |
| Joseph Trimble | 230 | 4 | 8 | 20 | -- |
| Phillip Tanner, f.m. | 280 | 4 | 5 | 20 | -- |
| Hugh Thompson | 250 | 2 | 4 | 10 | 1 |
| James Todd | 100 | 2 | 2 | -- | -- |
| James Wilson | 200 | 2 | 2 | -- | 1 |
| Flemming Wilson | 160 | 2 | 2 | -- | -- |
| Jno. White, on Tanner's Road | 160 | 2 | 3 | 6 | -- |
| Sam'l Wilson, joyner | 50 | 1 | 2 | 3 | -- |
| Jam's Wherrey | 260 | 3 | 6 | 10 | -- |
| John White, Jun'r, wheelwright | 80 | 1 | 1 | 6 | -- |
| Benjamin Wilson, joyner | 100 | 2 | 3 | -- | -- |
| David Wherrey | 226 | 3 | 7 | 12 | -- |
| Rob't Wilson | 200 | 3 | 4 | 8 | -- |
| John White, stiller | 100 | 3 | 3 | 6 | -- |
| Jonathan White | 90 | 2 | 1 | 4 | -- |
| Tho's Youle | 110 | 2 | -- | -- | -- |
| Hump'y Riddle, weaver | 110 | 1 | 2 | -- | -- |
| John Watt | 100 | 2 | 2 | -- | -- |
| Tho's Turner | -- | 2 | 3 | 8 | -- |
| Jno. Warnock, tavernkeeper | 200 | 2 | 3 | 6 | -- |
| David Worley, tavern & plantation | -- | -- | -- | -- | -- |
| Dan'l Turner | -- | 1 | -- | -- | -- |
| Jno. Vance, jockey | -- | 1 | 1 | -- | -- |
| Sam'l Colvin, smith | -- | 1 | 1 | -- | -- |
| Eliza Brisban | -- | -- | -- | -- | -- |
| Alex'r Frew | -- | 2 | 2 | 4 | -- |
| Joshua Cannon | -- | -- | -- | -- | -- |
| Wm. Brisland | -- | -- | -- | -- | -- |
| John Gilbreath, tavernkeeper | -- | 1 | -- | -- | -- |
| Nathan Boyde | -- | 1 | -- | -- | -- |
| Tho's Douglass & Sam'l Smith, millers | -- | 3 | 4 | 8 | -- |
| Henry McCormack | 140 | -- | -- | -- | -- |
| And'w Bryan | 150 | 2 | 2 | -- | -- |
| Jeremiah Brown | 8 | 1 | 1 | -- | -- |
| Jno. Hayes | 150 | 2 | 2 | -- | -- |

East Nottingham

| | Acres | Horses | Cattle | Sheep | Servants |
|---|---|---|---|---|---|
| Rob't Oldham | 60 | 2 | 2 | -- | -- |
| Alex'r Frew | -- | -- | -- | -- | -- |

### Freemen

| | |
|---|---|
| Wm. Carr | Joseph Stinson |
| Philip Donauly | Mich'l Randle |
| Moses McWhirler | Rob't Harvey |
| Jno. Cannon | Jam's Crawford |
| Jno. Morrison | James Steel |
| Jno. Ramsey | David White |
| Sampson Touchstone | Jno. Maxfield |
| James Smith | Rob't Salmon |

### Inmates

| | |
|---|---|
| Jonathan Hill | Jam's Wilson |
| Rob't Hill | Wm. Allaways |
| Jno. Rutherford | Joseph Harris |
| Tho's Harvey | Jeremiah Gatchell |
| Wm. Thompson | Jno. Day |
| Jno. Wilson | Jacob Anderson |
| Rob't McGrew | James Faules |
| Jno. Kincade | David Strawbridge |
| Wm. Mertle | Joseph Smith |
| Joseph Clark | James Flower |
| Henry Greames | James Dickey |
| Wm. Carson | Tho's Day |
| James Perry | |

### Astown Township Rate

| | Acres | Horses | Cattle | Sheep | Servants |
|---|---|---|---|---|---|
| Abram Ashton, tavernkeeper, tavern | -- | 1 | 2 | -- | -- |
| Hynn | 100 | 2 | 2 | 4 | -- |
| Hugh Kerns | 100 | 1 | 1 | -- | -- |
| Jno. Crowd | 150 | 2 | 2 | -- | -- |
| William Booth, wheelwright | 100 | 2 | 2 | 6 | -- |
| Jam's Craig | 100 | 4 | 7 | -- | -- |
| Marg't Richards | -- | 1 | 1 | -- | -- |
| Phillip Evans, s.m. | 166 | 2 | 5 | 2 | 1 |
| Sam'l Evans | -- | 1 | -- | -- | -- |
| Jam's Lindsey | 160 | 3 | 4 | 6 | -- |
| Isaac Ramond | 65 | 2 | -- | -- | -- |
| Phillip Romond, g.m. | 65 | 1 | 3 | -- | -- |
| Reese Peters, f.m., s.m., sawyer & fuller | 200 | 8 | 12 | -- | 3 |
| Wm. Peters | 172 | -- | -- | -- | -- |
| Jacob Pyke | 50 | 1 | 1 | -- | -- |
| Mordica Cloud | 100 | -- | -- | -- | -- |

| Astown Township | Acres | Horses | Cattle | Sheep | Servants |
|---|---|---|---|---|---|
| Jonathan Richards | 220 | 3 | 7 | -- | -- |
| John Chamberlin, sawyer & forgeman | 230 | 9 | 4 | -- | -- |
| Will'm Thompson | 80 | 2 | 2 | -- | 1 |
| Jam's McCloskey | 89 | 1 | 1 | -- | -- |
| Thomas Dutton | 120 | 3 | 4 | 6 | 1 |
| Richard Dutton | 80 | -- | -- | -- | -- |
| Morris Madson | 124 | 4 | 3 | 6 | -- |
| Nathan Yarnall, tanner, tanyard | 28 | 2 | 1 | -- | 1 |
| Wm. Griffits, s.m. | 200 | 4 | 6 | 6 | -- |
| Jacob Sharpless | 174 | 3 | 4 | -- | -- |
| Joseph Chamberlin | 135 | -- | -- | -- | -- |
| Isaac Chamberlin | 41 | 3 | 1 | 4 | -- |
| Joseph Sharpless | 170 | -- | -- | -- | -- |
| John Thompson, forgeman, forge | 40 | 6 | 2 | -- | 4 |
| John Ratew | 129 | 4 | 4 | 6 | -- |
| Abra'm Martin | 200 | 3 | 5 | 6 | -- |
| Jacob Richards | 150 | 5 | 6 | 10 | 3 |
| Jno. Linsay | 100 | 2 | 2 | 5 | -- |
| Rich'd Cheyney, miller, g.m. | -- | -- | -- | -- | -- |
| Dan'l Broomil | 97 | -- | -- | -- | -- |
| John McMin | 285 | 5 | 10 | 16 | -- |

Freemen

And'w McMin
Jam's Linsey
Rob't Murtlin
Jno. Derrah
Jno. Wilson
Jno. Matson

Tho's Marshall
Joseph Thompson
Jno. Ratew
Sam'l McMin
Jno. McMin, Jun'r

Inmates

Israel Taylor
Wm. Denin
Hezekiah Hall
Thomas Rummond
Martin Morton
Geo'e Johnston
Arthur O'Neal
Will'm Keepers
Barnibas McGinnis
Samuel Lindsey
Joseph Noblet
John Nesbitt
Tho's Walters
Godfrey Hivo
Geo. Mill
Abra'm Sharpless

Oliver Farah
John Farah, mason
Isaac Vanbought
Hugh Kirgin
Jno. Reed
Joshua Worrell
Will'm Withrow
Rob't Rankin
Sam'l Hughes
Dan'l Young
Jno. Walter
Jno. Knox
Will'm Elliot
David Wadle
Lewes Blackleg

## West Marlborough Rate

|  | Acres | Horses | Cattle | Sheep | Servants |
|---|---|---|---|---|---|
| Step'n Anderson | 180 | 2 | 2 | -- | 1 |
| Aron Baker, Sen'r | 50 | 2 | 2 | -- | -- |
| Jno. Baker | 200 | 4 | 5 | 7 | 1 |
| Aaron Baker, Jun'r | 153 | 3 | 6 | 9 | 1 |
| Joel Bailey | 160 | 4 | 4 | 10 | -- |
| Isaac Bailey, Jun'r | 160 | 1 | -- | -- | -- |
| Rob't Bell, weaver | 25 | 1 | 1 | -- | -- |
| Sam'l Baker | 150 | 3 | 3 | 6 | -- |
| Josiah Bailey | 140 | 2 | 2 | 6 | -- |
| Isaac Bailey | 140 | 2 | 2 | 6 | -- |
| Joel Bailey, Jun'r | 40 | -- | -- | -- | -- |
| Jeremiah Barnard, lime burner | 150 | 4 | 4 | 12 | 1 |
| Rich'd Barnard | 115 | -- | -- | -- | -- |
| John Bailey | 100 | 2 | 3 | 7 | -- |
| Will'm Bailey | 97 | 2 | 2 | 2 | -- |
| Tho's Barnett, s.m. | 200 | 2 | 5 | 10 | -- |
| Wm. Chalfant, wheelwright, s.m. | 100 | 3 | 3 | -- | -- |
| Henry Chalfant | 180 | 2 | 3 | 10 | -- |
| Joseph Davis, miller, g.m., s.m. | 258 | 4 | 4 | 6 | -- |
| Dan'l Avery | 100 | 3 | 2 | 5 | -- |
| Barnabas Fagan, shoemaker | 130 | 2 | 2 | -- | -- |
| Isaac Holton | 85 | 3 | 2 | 2 | -- |
| Fra's Fisher, cooper | 60 | 2 | 2 | -- | -- |
| Nathan Hayes | 170 | 3 | 4 | 8 | 1 |
| Hannah Hayes | 70 | 1 | 2 | -- | -- |
| And'w Jack | 200 | 2 | 3 | -- | -- |
| Mat'w McFetridge | 225 | 3 | 4 | -- | 1 |
| Jam's McClane | 45 | 1 | 2 | 2 | -- |
| Hector McNeal | 137 | 2 | 2 | -- | -- |
| Arch'd McNeal | 200 | 1 | 2 | -- | -- |
| Trustram Moor, cooper | 50 | 2 | 1 | -- | -- |
| Levis Pennock, malster | 600 | 4 | 7 | 3 | -- |
| Wm. Pusey | 100 | 2 | 3 | 10 | -- |
| John Pasmore, blacksmith | 190 | 2 | 4 | 15 | 1 |
| Thomas Plummer, shoemaker | 200 | 2 | 2 | -- | -- |
| Isaac Pyle | 220 | 3 | 4 | -- | -- |
| Joseph Pyle, joyner | 120 | 3 | 3 | 10 | -- |
| Nath'l Pennock, malthouse | 450 | 4 | 4 | -- | 1 |
| George Pasmore | 200 | 4 | 5 | 10 | -- |
| Eliz'th Ring, g.m., s.m. | 100 | 2 | 2 | 10 | 2 |
| Eliz'th Ring as Executor to Nath'l Ring | 180 | -- | -- | -- | -- |
| Moses Edwards | 250 | 5 | 4 | 12 | -- |
| Thomas Travilla | 170 | 2 | 2 | 6 | -- |
| John Kell | 70 | -- | -- | -- | -- |
| William Harlan | 350 | 4 | 3 | 10 | -- |
| Will'm Harlan, Jun'r | 200 | 4 | 3 | 6 | -- |
| Michael Harlan, s.m. | 109 | 2 | 1 | -- | -- |
| George Harlan | 109 | 3 | 4 | 8 | -- |
| Edward Swane | 124 | 2 | 2 | -- | -- |
| James Trimble, labourer | 45 | 1 | 1 | -- | -- |
| Joseph Pennock, Jun'r | 150 | -- | -- | -- | -- |
| Tho's Woodward | 100 | -- | -- | -- | -- |

| West Marlborough | Acres | Horses | Cattle | Sheep | Servants |
|---|---|---|---|---|---|
| And'w Mitchell | 127 | -- | -- | -- | -- |
| George Taylor | 165 | 2 | 3 | 6 | -- |

### Single Men

| | |
|---|---|
| John Sutor | John McHurd |
| Joshua Baker | James Reed |
| Amos McLaughlin | John Sharron |
| John Steel | Geo'e White |
| Samuel Hemphill | Jesse Swayne |
| Jonathan Chalfant | William Jones |
| Patrick McGee | Robert Wilson |
| William Fegan | Henry Hetherington |
| Tho's Fisher | |

### Inmates

| | |
|---|---|
| Tho's Reynolds | Jonathan Harlan |
| George Grist | James Harlan |
| Will'm Davis | Jam's Campbell |
| Barney Small | Jno. Buffington |
| Patrick Caveat | Jno. Kell |
| Nicolas Criberson | David Reynolds |
| Arthur Beaty | Jno. Maris |
| Zacarius Sugars | Joseph Taylor |
| Joseph Williams | Jam's Faron |
| Wm. Edwards | George Harlan |
| Robert McMin | Joshua Edwards |
| William Farlow | Jam's Pogue |

### Uwchland Rate

| | Acres | Horses | Cattle | Sheep | Servants |
|---|---|---|---|---|---|
| Rob't Allison | 260 | 3 | 4 | 4 | 1 |
| James Adams | 90 | 2 | 3 | 5 | -- |
| Daniel Brown | 160 | 3 | 3 | 6 | -- |
| Noble Butler, Sen'r | 90 | 2 | 2 | 5 | -- |
| Noble Butler, Jun'r | 90 | 2 | 1 | 3 | -- |
| Will'm Butler | 100 | 2 | 3 | -- | -- |
| John Butler | -- | 1 | 1 | -- | -- |
| David Beaty | 170 | 3 | 3 | -- | -- |
| Sam'l Bond | 162 | 1 | -- | -- | -- |
| Robert Beaty | 100 | 2 | 3 | 3 | -- |
| Enoch Butler | 150 | 2 | 3 | 5 | -- |
| William Benson | 47 | 2 | 5 | 4 | -- |
| Jam's Benson | 280 | 2 | 6 | 5 | -- |
| John Benson | 150 | 3 | 3 | 5 | -- |
| William Byers | 200 | 3 | 6 | 5 | -- |
| Rob't Carson | 100 | 2 | 3 | 6 | -- |
| Will'm Denney | 250 | 7 | 5 | 19 | 1 |
| Richard Downing | 150 | -- | -- | -- | -- |

| Uwchland | Acres | Horses | Cattle | Sheep | Servants |
|---|---|---|---|---|---|
| Miles Davis | 180 | 2 | 4 | 12 | -- |
| Daniel Davis | 100 | 2 | 4 | 4 | -- |
| Jermon Davis, g.m., s.m. | 50 | -- | 2 | 6 | -- |
| Daniel Evans | 150 | 2 | 3 | -- | -- |
| David Evans | 320 | 3 | 7 | 10 | -- |
| Thomas Evans | 180 | 3 | 5 | -- | -- |
| Rich'd Evans, s.m. | 40 | 2 | 2 | 5 | -- |
| Reece Gatles | 100 | 3 | 2 | 6 | -- |
| Tho's Guest | 120 | 3 | 3 | -- | -- |
| Will'm Griffith | 50 | -- | -- | -- | -- |
| Will'm Griffith, weaver | 100 | 2 | 2 | -- | -- |
| Sam'l Holliday, blacksmith | 90 | 3 | 4 | 6 | -- |
| Rudolph Harns, nursery | 90 | 1 | -- | -- | -- |
| John Jenkins | 100 | 2 | 3 | 6 | -- |
| Cadwalader Jones, storekeeper | 130 | 3 | 5 | -- | -- |
| Dan'l John | 100 | 2 | 2 | -- | 1 |
| Griffith John | 130 | 2 | 2 | 6 | -- |
| Evan Jones, saddler | 135 | 3 | 4 | -- | -- |
| Isaac Lewis | 200 | 2 | 5 | 10 | 1 |
| Robert Jones, mason | 93 | 2 | 3 | 6 | -- |
| Humphrey Loyde | 250 | 2 | 3 | 5 | -- |
| Tho's Martin | 120 | 2 | 3 | 6 | -- |
| John McClure | 250 | 4 | 5 | 14 | 1 |
| Rob't Millhouse | 100 | 2 | 4 | 8 | -- |
| Hance Nailor | 90 | 2 | 2 | -- | -- |
| David Owen | 188 | 2 | 9 | 10 | -- |
| Will'm Owen | 100 | 2 | 2 | -- | -- |
| David Peugh | 150 | 2 | 3 | -- | -- |
| Jam's Peugh | 69 | 1 | 1 | -- | -- |
| Joseph Phillips | 150 | 2 | 5 | 8 | -- |
| Stephen Phillips, taylor | 160 | 2 | 2 | 4 | -- |
| Geo'e Phipps | 300 | 3 | 3 | 6 | -- |
| Joseph Phipps | 450 | 1 | 3 | -- | -- |
| Aaron Phipps | 300 | 2 | 3 | 6 | -- |
| Nathan Phipps | 100 | 1 | 2 | 2 | -- |
| John Phipps | 250 | 2 | -- | -- | -- |
| Robert Smith | 200 | 3 | 3 | 10 | 2 |
| Abra'm Scott, g.m., s.m. | 23 | 1 | 2 | -- | 1 |
| Christian Treat | 130 | -- | -- | -- | -- |
| Joseph Willson | 100 | 2 | 5 | 2 | -- |
| Wm. Linsey, tinker | 50 | 3 | 3 | 9 | -- |
| Dennis Whealin, storekeeper | 200 | 5 | 5 | 10 | 1 |
| John Whealin | 200 | 3 | 5 | 10 | -- |
| David Williams, taylor | 260 | 3 | 2 | -- | -- |
| Abra'm Beatey | 50 | 2 | 1 | -- | -- |
| Joseph Bentley, t.k., tavern | -- | 2 | 3 | -- | -- |
| John Lewis | 200 | 2 | 4 | 5 | -- |
| Isaac Lewis, shoemaker | 100 | -- | -- | -- | -- |
| Jacob Graves | 200 | 2 | 2 | 6 | -- |
| John Taggart, weaver | 200 | 2 | 4 | 6 | -- |
| Clement Rigg | 150 | 2 | 4 | 10 | -- |
| David Philip, weaver | 40 | 2 | 4 | 4 | -- |
| John Hoskins | 100 | 3 | 2 | 2 | -- |
| Will'm John, cordwainer | 97 | 2 | 1 | -- | -- |
| Joshua Roberts | 60 | 2 | 1 | -- | -- |

| Uwchland | Acres | Horses | Cattle | Sheep | Servants |
|---|---|---|---|---|---|
| Joseph Roads, taylor | -- | 1 | 2 | -- | -- |
| Jacob Vogdes | -- | 1 | 1 | -- | -- |
| John Hatton, shoemaker | -- | 1 | -- | -- | -- |
| Charles Reed, mill, miller | -- | 2 | 2 | -- | -- |
| David Loyde, labourer | -- | -- | 1 | -- | -- |
| Humphrey Loyde, Junior | -- | -- | -- | -- | -- |
| Nath'n Cadwalader | -- | -- | -- | -- | -- |
| Jam's Spavin | -- | -- | -- | -- | -- |
| Tho's John | -- | 1 | 1 | -- | -- |
| Wm. Stanfield, sadler | -- | 1 | 1 | -- | -- |
| David McClure | -- | -- | -- | -- | -- |
| Tho's West | -- | -- | -- | -- | -- |
| Malica Jones | -- | 2 | 2 | -- | -- |

Inmates

Dan'l Arenton
Joshua Phipps
Robert Miller
Owen William
Bartley Lerl
Isaac Nutt
James John, Senior

James Edward
Ralph Helbsby
Jacob Nailor
Nath'l Jones
David Carson
Patrick Cullem

Freeman

Benj'n Davis
Reuben John
John Jones
Jno. McCord
Jno. McCarty
Jno. Davis
Jonathan McVaugh
Tho's Scott
Edward Jones
George Wilson
Joseph Collins
Tho's Jackson
John Phillips
Joseph Lancaster
Wm. Hanna
John Owen
Barnabas Hart
Robert Wilson

James Guest
Jno. Guest, Jun'r
Isaac Brown
Levy Jones
Francis Holmes
Wm. Beaty
Abra'm Beaty
Jam's McClure
Benjamin Butler
Rob't Benson
Patrick McGuire
Patrick McCealvy
Sam'l John
Rob't Richey
John Evans
John Mountgomery
Thomas John

Upper Providence Rate

| | Acres | Horses | Cattle | Sheep | Servants |
|---|---|---|---|---|---|
| George Miller | 400 | 6 | 7 | 20 | 1 |
| Joseph Worrel | 160 | 2 | 5 | 10 | -- |
| Cha's Linn, g.m. | 20 | 5 | 2 | -- | -- |

| Upper Providence | Acres | Horses | Cattle | Sheep | Servants |
|---|---|---|---|---|---|
| Nathan Taylor | 180 | 2 | 6 | 10 | -- |
| Thomas Bishop | 62 | 5 | 5 | -- | -- |
| James Moore | 228 | 4 | 5 | 6 | -- |
| Will'm Malin | 285 | 2 | 7 | 4 | -- |
| Gideon Malin | 110 | 2 | 4 | 4 | -- |
| Peter Taylor | 118 | 3 | 6 | 5 | -- |
| Tho's Prichat | 125 | -- | -- | -- | -- |
| Edw'd Worrel | 60 | 2 | 1 | 5 | -- |
| Samuel Worrel | 77 | 3 | 4 | 10 | -- |
| Daniel Thompson, t.k. | 150 | 2 | 3 | 6 | -- |
| John Johnston | 150 | 2 | 3 | -- | -- |
| Caleb James | 18 | -- | -- | -- | -- |
| Thomas Briggs | 100 | 1 | 4 | 6 | -- |
| Thos' Nuzun | 40 | -- | -- | -- | -- |
| Benjamin Worrel | 120 | 2 | 2 | 7 | -- |
| James Wilcox, s.m., p.m. | 53 | 1 | 4 | -- | -- |
| John Taylor | 70 | -- | 2 | -- | -- |
| Hugh Maxwell | 75 | 2 | 3 | -- | -- |
| John Calvert | 93 | 5 | 3 | -- | -- |
| James Black | 118 | -- | -- | -- | -- |
| Jacob Dunn | 75 | 2 | 3 | -- | -- |
| Mary Smedly | 88 | -- | 4 | -- | -- |
| Jam's Rhads | 6 | -- | -- | -- | -- |
| John Grant | 70 | 2 | 2 | 3 | -- |
| Joshua Kirk | 20 | 1 | 1 | -- | -- |
| Peter Worrel | 14 | 1 | 1 | -- | -- |
| Robert Stevenson | 50 | -- | -- | -- | -- |
| John Fox | 150 | 2 | 5 | 6 | -- |
| John Smith | 50 | -- | 2 | -- | -- |
| John Day | 42 | 1 | 1 | -- | -- |
| Rich'd Gorman | -- | -- | 9 | -- | -- |
| Joseph Swafar | 40 | -- | -- | -- | -- |
| Joseph Bell, labourer | -- | 1 | -- | -- | -- |

Freemen

Andrew Linn
Owen Worrel
Isaac Taylor
Rich'd Briggs
And'w Johnson
John Johnson
Adam Worrall

Samuel Swil
John Grant
George Hall
Joseph Jobson
Sam'l Moor
Nath'l Calvert
Isaiah Worrel

Inmates

James McColough

Wm. Dunn

## Lower Darby Rate

|  | Acres | Horses | Cattle | Sheep | Servants |
|---|---|---|---|---|---|
| Jesse Bonsall, taylor | 216 | 3 | 2 | 8 | -- |
| John Bartram | 19 | -- | -- | -- | -- |
| Josiah Bunting | 125 | 2 | 6 | 11 | 1 |
| Sam'l Bunting | 50 | -- | -- | -- | -- |
| Sarah Bunting | -- | -- | -- | -- | -- |
| Sarah Bonsall | 5 3/4 | -- | 1 | -- | -- |
| And'w Boon | 56 | -- | 3 | -- | -- |
| And'w Boon, taylor | 130 | 3 | 5 | -- | -- |
| And'w Boon, shoemaker | 10 | 1 | 1 | 6 | -- |
| Joseph Boon | 50 | 2 | 2 | 5 | -- |
| Hance Boon | 74 | 2 | 2 | -- | -- |
| Isaac Brook, mason | -- | -- | 1 | -- | -- |
| And'w Culin | 86 | 2 | 4 | 8 | -- |
| Paul Custulove, farmer | -- | -- | 1 | -- | -- |
| Eliz'th Buckram | -- | -- | -- | -- | -- |
| Benj'n Cherry, shoemaker | -- | 1 | 1 | -- | -- |
| John Croney | -- | -- | -- | -- | -- |
| James Dobbins | 125 | 4 | 6 | -- | -- |
| John Durnall | 97 | 5 | 4 | 5 | -- |
| John Elliot | 100 | 4 | 10 | -- | -- |
| Peter Elliot | 108 | 4 | 16 | 10 | 2 |
| Martha Elliot | -- | 1 | -- | 4 | 1 |
| Everard Ellis | 10 | 1 | 1 | -- | -- |
| Benjamin Jobb, Executor to ye Estate of Enoch Elliot | 30 | -- | -- | -- | -- |
| Joseph Fordom | 4 | 1 | 1 | -- | -- |
| Lawrence Fredirick | 36 | 3 | 3 | 6 | -- |
| Cha's Grantum | 120 | -- | -- | -- | -- |
| John Gruber, wheelwright | 37 | 2 | 2 | -- | -- |
| Daniel Humphreys, blacksmith | 21 | 2 | 3 | -- | -- |
| Rich'd Humphrey | 4 | -- | -- | -- | -- |
| John Hunt | 86 | 2 | 3 | 12 | 1 |
| Will'm Horn, tanyard | 166 | 2 | 5 | -- | -- |
| Will'm Helmes | 40 | 1 | 1 | 3 | -- |
| Wm. Herring, farmer | -- | -- | -- | -- | -- |
| Geo'e Hoffer, farmer | -- | -- | 1 | -- | -- |
| Jno. Kellvy, farmer | 4 | 1 | 2 | -- | -- |
| Jno. Knowl's, farmer | -- | -- | 1 | -- | -- |
| Jno. Lenderman, shoemaker | -- | -- | 1 | -- | -- |
| Isa'c Loyde, g.m. | 5 | 1 | 2 | 6 | -- |
| Isaac & Hugh Loyde | 18 | -- | -- | -- | -- |
| Will'm Linwill, shoemaker | 5 | 1 | 1 | -- | -- |
| Frederick Liking | -- | -- | -- | -- | -- |
| Geo'e Morton | 110 | 4 | 6 | 6 | 2 |
| Peter Madson | 9 | -- | -- | -- | -- |
| Tobiah Morton | -- | -- | -- | -- | -- |
| Alex'r Morrow | 19 | 2 | 6 | -- | -- |
| Jam's McCleoss | 100 | 4 | 4 | -- | -- |
| Rob't McCord, farmer | -- | -- | -- | -- | -- |
| Morton Morton | 9 | -- | -- | -- | -- |
| Arthur Nitfallus | 98 | 2 | 5 | 6 | 3 |
| Mathiak Nitfallus | 5 | 2 | 2 | 4 | -- |
| Aron Oakford, f.m., fuller | -- | 1 | -- | -- | -- |
| Wm. Parker, Esq'r | 167 | 4 | 10 | -- | -- |

| Lower Darby | Acres | Horses | Cattle | Sheep | Servants |
|---|---|---|---|---|---|
| Isaac Pearson, Esq'r | 90 | 4 | 4 | -- | -- |
| John Paschall, physician | 130 | 2 | 8 | -- | -- |
| Joseph Pearson, blacksmith | -- | 1 | 3 | -- | -- |
| Hannah Pearson | 39 | 1 | 2 | -- | -- |
| John Pearson, tanner | 18 | 1 | 2 | -- | -- |
| Jno. Palmer | 130 | 3 | 4 | 12 | -- |
| Daniel Rice | 68 | 2 | 3 | 3 | -- |
| John Rudolph | 96 | 2 | 10 | -- | -- |
| Joseph Rudolph, innkeeper, t.k. | -- | 1 | 1 | -- | -- |
| George Righter, wheelwright | -- | 1 | 1 | -- | -- |
| Jacob Rudolph, carpenter | -- | -- | 1 | -- | -- |
| Nicolas Randle | 100 | 3 | 4 | 8 | -- |
| Jacob Sullender, miller | -- | -- | 1 | -- | -- |
| John Trapnal, coroner's office | 85 | 2 | 10 | -- | 2 |
| And'w Urin | 38 | 3 | 2 | 6 | -- |
| Benj'n Urin | 50 | -- | 1 | 6 | -- |
| John Wilkinson, innkeeper, t.k. | 10 1/2 | 2 | 2 | -- | 1 |
| Hannah Wood, tavern, t.k. | -- | -- | 1 | -- | -- |
| Jacob Webber | 36 | 3 | 3 | -- | -- |
| Jonathan Wood, captain | -- | -- | -- | -- | -- |
| Jonathan Womsley, labourer | -- | -- | -- | -- | -- |
| John Kinde, butcher | -- | -- | -- | -- | -- |
| Silas Jones, grassier | 8 | 1 | -- | -- | -- |

Inmates

Tho's Anderson
George Bell
Joseph Bethel
Hance Conradtice
Morrice Lisk
Jno. McGilton

Joseph Polin
Jno. Hendrick Prisler
Jno. Reel
Mary Trayhorn
Peter Wood

Freemen

Wm. Ales
Manasah Connor
Jam's Griffith
Jno. Humphrey
Jno. Horn
Will'm Horn
Israel Morton

Jno. McCrackin
Rob't McCord, Jun'r
Jno. Paschall
Benj'n Paschall
Patrick Smith
Joshua Thomas

Coventry Rate

| | Acres | Horses | Cattle | Sheep | Servants |
|---|---|---|---|---|---|
| Jam's Arbeckle | 100 | 2 | 2 | -- | -- |
| Henry Brower | 260 | 2 | 5 | 5 | -- |
| Daniel Berry | 200 | 3 | 6 | 5 | -- |

| Coventry | Acres | Horses | Cattle | Sheep | Servants |
|---|---|---|---|---|---|
| Christian Brower | 200 | 2 | 4 | 4 | -- |
| Dan'l Brower | 100 | 2 | 4 | 4 | -- |
| Jno. Bough | 150 | 2 | 4 | 4 | -- |
| Henry Bear | 190 | 2 | 4 | 7 | -- |
| Henry Benner | 260 | 2 | 4 | 2 | -- |
| Jacob Bough | 240 | 2 | 4 | 4 | -- |
| John Brower | 45 | 1 | 2 | 5 | -- |
| Marg't Benner | 100 | 1 | 1 | -- | -- |
| Phillip Byer | 100 | 2 | 2 | -- | -- |
| Abra'm Crumbraker | 200 | 2 | 2 | -- | -- |
| Jno. Couchanour, g.m. | 300 | 3 | 5 | 12 | 1 |
| Peter Brumbaker | 180 | 2 | 4 | 6 | -- |
| Rich'd Custard | 120 | 1 | 2 | -- | -- |
| Rynord Contenhoser | 30 | -- | 1 | -- | -- |
| Godfry Duninghour | 70 | 1 | 2 | -- | -- |
| John Davis | 40 | -- | -- | -- | -- |
| Jacob Inglar, shoemaker | 100 | 1 | 3 | -- | -- |
| Abra. Grubb | 70 | 1 | 2 | -- | -- |
| John Grubb | 150 | 3 | 3 | 4 | -- |
| George Grouce | 100 | 2 | 2 | 2 | -- |
| George Garick | 30 | -- | -- | -- | -- |
| Conrod Grim | 25 | 2 | 1 | -- | -- |
| Henry Grubb | 300 | 2 | 3 | 5 | -- |
| Jacob Getinger | 100 | 2 | 2 | -- | -- |
| Jacob Garinger | 100 | 2 | 1 | -- | -- |
| Wm. Heterling | 200 | -- | -- | -- | -- |
| Andrew Heth | 180 | 2 | 3 | 6 | -- |
| Jam's Hackley | 150 | -- | -- | -- | -- |
| Mich'l Holderman | 120 | -- | -- | -- | -- |
| John High | 150 | 3 | 5 | -- | -- |
| Chris'r Holderman, g.m. | 325 | 2 | 6 | 6 | -- |
| Sam'l Himblerife | 100 | 2 | 2 | 5 | -- |
| Nicholas Hernick | 100 | 1 | 2 | -- | -- |
| Isaac John | -- | 1 | 1 | -- | -- |
| John Inhuff | 150 | 2 | 3 | -- | -- |
| Allen Jack | 200 | 3 | 3 | 4 | -- |
| Paul Cisor | 26 | 1 | 2 | -- | -- |
| Nich's Caller | 200 | 2 | 2 | 2 | -- |
| Jacob Longacre | 200 | 2 | 6 | 5 | 1 |
| John Light | 300 | 1 | 3 | 30 | -- |
| Jacob Light, s.m. | 200 | 2 | 3 | 3 | 1 |
| Justice Lenderman | 100 | 2 | 2 | 5 | -- |
| Phillip Loyde | 80 | 2 | 2 | 4 | -- |
| Peter Mook | 100 | 2 | 3 | 3 | -- |
| Tobias Miller | 100 | -- | 2 | -- | -- |
| Jacob Modary | 150 | -- | -- | -- | -- |
| Phillip Miller, labourer | -- | 2 | 3 | -- | -- |
| John Owen | 150 | 1 | 2 | -- | -- |
| Martin Orner | 236 | 3 | 6 | 6 | -- |
| John Potts | 150 | -- | -- | -- | -- |
| Will'm Blain | 100 | 1 | 2 | -- | -- |
| Christian Rife | 160 | 4 | 5 | 7 | 1 |
| Jonas Rudrough, weaver | 100 | -- | 2 | -- | -- |
| Fredirick Rinchard | -- | 2 | 4 | 4 | -- |
| John Rinchard, g.m., s.m. | 100 | 1 | 1 | -- | -- |

| Coventry | Acres | Horses | Cattle | Sheep | Servants |
|---|---|---|---|---|---|
| Uldrick Rinchard | 140 | 1 | 3 | 3 | -- |
| Will'm Ridge | -- | 2 | 1 | -- | -- |
| Fredirick Shull | 200 | 2 | 2 | 3 | -- |
| Henry Shankel | 140 | 2 | 3 | 5 | -- |
| Jacob Hoyer | 200 | 2 | 1 | -- | -- |
| John Sowder | 150 | 3 | 6 | 6 | -- |
| John Swarner, tavern | 150 | 2 | 3 | 7 | 1 |
| Uldrick Swisler | 165 | 3 | 5 | 9 | -- |
| John Switzar | 180 | 3 | 4 | 7 | -- |
| Michael Sink | 150 | 2 | 3 | 7 | -- |
| Jacob Thomas | 295 | 4 | 6 | 12 | -- |
| George Ditlaw | 140 | 2 | 4 | 4 | -- |
| Will'm Simplin | 100 | 2 | 2 | 6 | -- |
| And'w Woolf | 110 | 2 | 2 | -- | -- |
| Christian Wisler | 100 | 2 | 2 | 4 | -- |
| John Woolf, skinner | -- | 1 | 1 | -- | -- |
| Peter Wanger | 10 | -- | 2 | -- | -- |
| Rudolph Wise | 170 | 3 | 2 | -- | -- |
| Rich'd Willis | 45 | -- | -- | -- | -- |
| Susannah Wells | 300 | 3 | 4 | 6 | -- |
| Jacob Winger | 100 | 2 | 3 | 4 | -- |

Inmates

Geo'e Wideford
Phillip Rasmore
Dav'd Griffith
Richard Willis
John Bateman
Wm. Ridge
Geo'e West
John Saunders
Phi'p Sidestriker
John Smith
Christian Berry
Geo'e Westenberger

Dan'l Simmer
Tho's Butler
Pet'r Huttonstone
John Madary
Geo'e Sunligter
Anthony Barnherd
Fred'k Houk
Sebastian Wocchter
Henry Stuffle
Nicolas Munshour
Will'm Crow
Jacob Pefoutz

Single Men

Leonard Frisheom
Abra. Brower
Daniel Heath
Jacob Getinger
Peter Rincherd
Peter Susanner
And'w Woolf
Joseph Wolde
David Blain
Will'm Wolde

Martin Woolf
Leonard Snider
Dan'l Swityer
Jacob Creadler
Fred'k Evil
Mankin James
Jeremiah Talbot
Thomas Carter
Dan'l Switzer, Jun'r

## Pikeland Township Rate

| | Acres | Horses | Cattle | Sheep | Servants |
|---|---|---|---|---|---|
| Abra'm Turner | 100 | -- | -- | -- | -- |
| Adam Holman, s.m. | 150 | 3 | 4 | 10 | -- |
| Adam Mosses | 100 | 2 | 4 | 6 | -- |
| Adam Hartz | 65 | 3 | 3 | 6 | -- |
| Adam Axeline | 270 | 3 | 6 | 6 | -- |
| Alex'r McKinly | 50 | 1 | 1 | -- | -- |
| Benja'n Thomas, g.m., s.m. | 100 | 2 | 4 | -- | -- |
| Conrad Shimer, g.m., miller | 200 | -- | -- | -- | -- |
| Conrad Shearre | 99 | 2 | 2 | -- | -- |
| Conrad Miller | 60 | 2 | 3 | 6 | -- |
| Chris'r Ments | 160 | 2 | 2 | -- | -- |
| Gaspar Fitting | 120 | 2 | 2 | -- | -- |
| Fredirick Shimer | 150 | 3 | 2 | 7 | -- |
| Fra's Sole | 89 | 2 | 2 | -- | -- |
| George Lirish | 50 | 1 | 1 | -- | -- |
| Geo'e Maxton, tavern, s.m., t.k. | 140 | 3 | 3 | -- | -- |
| Geo'e Christman, s.m. | 150 | 3 | 3 | 6 | -- |
| Geo'e Emery | 250 | 2 | 4 | -- | -- |
| Henry Hipple | 100 | 2 | 3 | 6 | -- |
| John Hartman | 130 | 2 | 3 | 6 | -- |
| Jacob Ganter | 90 | 2 | 2 | -- | -- |
| John McKinly | 50 | 1 | 1 | -- | -- |
| John Boggs | 197 | 2 | 5 | 6 | -- |
| Joseph Jones | 200 | 2 | 5 | 8 | -- |
| John Buckwalter | 100 | -- | -- | -- | -- |
| Jacob Helvey | 100 | 2 | 3 | -- | 1 |
| Josiah Carles | 150 | 3 | 2 | 6 | -- |
| John Walter | 100 | 2 | 3 | -- | -- |
| John Urms | 150 | 2 | 4 | 6 | -- |
| James Starr | 200 | 2 | -- | -- | -- |
| John Wagoner | 200 | 2 | 4 | 6 | -- |
| Jacob Kirk | 50 | 2 | 1 | -- | -- |
| Jacob Slear | 85 | 2 | 2 | -- | -- |
| Jacob Hipple | 100 | 1 | 2 | -- | -- |
| John March | 70 | 2 | 2 | 6 | -- |
| John Snider | 100 | 2 | 3 | 6 | -- |
| Jam's Evans | 143 | 3 | 3 | 6 | -- |
| John Labach | 100 | 2 | 3 | -- | -- |
| John Davis | 143 | 2 | 4 | 6 | -- |
| John Henge | 150 | 4 | 5 | 6 | 1 |
| John Kluger, mill, miller | 20 | -- | 2 | -- | -- |
| John Francis | 184 | 4 | 6 | 8 | -- |
| Jam's McKleheny | 170 | 3 | 5 | -- | -- |
| John Milhouse, storekeeper | 100 | 3 | 6 | 8 | -- |
| Joshua John | 150 | 2 | 5 | 12 | -- |
| Jacob Danfettger | 150 | 2 | 4 | 6 | -- |
| Leonard Smith, blacksmith | 50 | 2 | 2 | -- | -- |
| Mich'l Teene | 150 | 3 | 4 | 6 | 1 |
| Mich'l King | 130 | 3 | 3 | 6 | -- |
| Philip Wagoner | 200 | 3 | 4 | 6 | -- |
| Philip Lodwig | 200 | 3 | 3 | 6 | -- |
| Peter Hankin | 25 | 1 | 2 | -- | -- |
| Peter Wagoner | 200 | 3 | 4 | 6 | -- |
| Philip Staffon | 194 | 3 | 3 | 7 | -- |

| Pikeland Township | Acres | Horses | Cattle | Sheep | Servants |
|---|---|---|---|---|---|
| Peter Shuman | 200 | 3 | 3 | 6 | -- |
| Peter Hartman | 200 | 4 | 5 | 8 | -- |
| Rowland Richards, labourer | 50 | 1 | 2 | -- | -- |
| Stephen Cayme | 55 | 4 | 2 | 4 | -- |
| Tho's Milhouse, Sr. | 200 | 5 | 8 | 12 | -- |
| Tho's Snider | 300 | 3 | 4 | 6 | -- |
| Timothy Kirk | 100 | 3 | 3 | 12 | -- |
| Tho's Lightfoot, Deputy Surveyor, s.m. | 250 | 6 | 7 | 12 | -- |
| Tho's Millhouse, Jun'r | 150 | 3 | 6 | -- | 1 |
| Vallentine Foos, wheelwright | 30 | 1 | 1 | -- | -- |
| Vallentine Smith | 180 | 2 | 3 | -- | -- |
| Vallentine Hinds | 250 | 4 | 6 | 10 | 1 |
| Vallentine Orner | 90 | 2 | 2 | -- | -- |
| Wm. Lewis | 150 | 2 | 4 | 12 | -- |
| Will'm Thomas | 250 | 3 | 4 | 6 | -- |
| Will'm Cowen, labourer | 100 | 2 | 2 | -- | -- |
| William Lightfoot, g.m., miller | 250 | 3 | 8 | -- | -- |
| Widow Andrew | 50 | -- | 2 | -- | -- |
| Widow Henry | 9 | -- | 1 | -- | -- |
| Zachariah Rice | 180 | 3 | 3 | 6 | -- |
| Casper Himes, carpenter | 4 | -- | 1 | -- | -- |
| Conrod Selenor | 14 | 1 | 2 | -- | -- |

Inmates

Philip Wayand
Leoanrd Daybel
John Teis
Olrick Brown
John Alder
Peter Huttonback
Peter Hailman
John Krank
Henry Shlir
Herman Burbower
Jacob Keer
Edw'd Herkins
Andrew Hick
Peter Seller
Peter Denmiller
Wm. Morgan
Martin Cuntman
Rob't Rigg
Henry Hanker
Jacob Moses

Simon Bouher
Tobias Bogens
Benedick Miller
Jno. Bosserd
John Cline
Jacob Riddleman
Jno. Rice
Jno. Kidd
Mathew Doyle
Mich'l Taylor
Wm. Christy
Nicolas Carter
Mich'l Road
John Fleeman
Amos Williams
Will'm Millhouse
George Fissiler
Mordica Williams
Tho's Dobbins

Freemen

John McKleheny
Balser Ladwigg
Will'm Walter
Peter Reym

Michael Clark
Philip Rice
John Kerr
Christopher Teene

## Freemen

Jno. Paton
Jam's Huston
Patrick McFall
John Edwards

John Brown
Neal Davis
Thomas Wilkinson

## Nether Providence Rate

|  | Acres | Horses | Cattle | Sheep | Servants |
|---|---|---|---|---|---|
| David Broomer, carpenter | 5 | 2 | 2 | --- | --- |
| Wm. Buntin | 50 | 2 | 2 | --- | --- |
| Sarah Dix | 150 | 3 | 5 | 6 | --- |
| Job Dix, s.m. | 15 | --- | --- | --- | --- |
| Joseph Dix | 150 | 6 | 8 | 20 | --- |
| Joseph Edwards, mason | 50 | 1 | 1 | --- | --- |
| Sarah Ely | 27 | 2 | 2 | --- | --- |
| Wm. Fell | 40 | --- | --- | --- | --- |
| John Hinkson | 240 | 4 | 6 | 12 | 1 |
| Joseph Heacock | 40 | --- | --- | --- | --- |
| Will'm Linsey | 165 | 2 | 4 | 6 | --- |
| Aaron Minshall | 2 3/4 | --- | --- | --- | --- |
| Wm. Mason | 100 | 3 | 4 | 2 | --- |
| Thomas Neezm, blacksmith | 28 | 3 | 2 | 8 | --- |
| Samuel Oliver | 100 | 4 | 5 | 6 | --- |
| John Powel | 68 | 3 | 2 | 6 | --- |
| John Sharpless | 170 | 4 | 2 | 2 | --- |
| Daniel Sharpless | 230 | 5 | 5 | 12 | --- |
| Jam's Sharpless | 162 | 3 | 3 | 3 | --- |
| Richard Smith | --- | 3 | 2 | 7 | --- |
| Wm. Slatton | --- | --- | --- | --- | --- |
| Wm. Starr | 48 | 2 | 2 | --- | --- |
| Hugh Traverse | 135 | 3 | 3 | 7 | --- |
| Jonathan Vernan | 60 | 3 | 2 | 3 | --- |
| Nath'l Vernun, s.m. | 386 | 4 | 5 | 10 | --- |
| Nathan Vernan | 120 | 3 | 1 | --- | --- |
| Moses Vernan | 60 | 2 | 1 | 5 | --- |
| Elias Vernan, taylor | 60 | 1 | --- | --- | --- |
| Edward Vernun | 61 | 1 | --- | --- | --- |
| Gedion Vernon | 71 | --- | --- | --- | --- |
| Mary Vernun | 11 | --- | --- | --- | --- |
| Abigal Vernun | --- | 1 | 1 | --- | --- |
| Isaac Weaver | 210 | 8 | 6 | --- | --- |
| And'w Wilson | 60 | 3 | 2 | 4 | --- |
| Tho's Worrall | 40 | 2 | 2 | 4 | --- |
| Nathan Vernun, Executor of M. Vernun | 50 | --- | --- | --- | --- |
| Elisha Jones | --- | --- | --- | --- | --- |
| Jam's Camel | --- | --- | --- | --- | --- |
| Sam'l Taylor, shoemaker | --- | --- | --- | --- | --- |
| Tho's Barns, labourer | --- | --- | --- | --- | --- |
| Roger & James Dicks | 12 | --- | --- | --- | --- |

Inmates

John Logmire  
Jonathan Vernun, Jun'r  
Reubin Roberts  

Wm. McClelland  
John O'Neal  
Jonathan Heacock  

Freemen

Thom's Linsey  
Job Vernum  
Nathan Milliner  
Jam's Dix  
Job Sharpless  
Dan'l Stephenson  

Jam's McCrackan  
Rob't Atkinson  
Rob't Linsey  
John Long  
William Armstrong  

Haverford Rate

|  | Acres | Horses | Cattle | Sheep | Servants |
|---|---|---|---|---|---|
| Cha's Crookshank | 80 | 3 | 4 | 8 | 3 |
| Sam'l Humphrey | 10 | 1 | -- | -- | -- |
| Edw'd Humphrey, f.m. | 50 | 1 | 2 | -- | -- |
| Lewes Davis, tanner | 150 | 3 | 6 | 10 | -- |
| Jeremiah Ellis | 100 | 2 | 3 | 6 | -- |
| Cha's Humphrey, g.m., s.m. | 100 | 5 | 2 | 6 | 2 |
| Will'm Lawrence | 160 | 2 | 2 | 6 | -- |
| John Greacy | 150 | 3 | 4 | 6 | -- |
| David Lewlyn | 100 | 2 | 2 | -- | -- |
| Closs Johnson | 200 | 3 | 4 | 8 | -- |
| Tho's Cornock | 80 | 2 | 3 | 4 | 1 |
| Matthew Brooks | 100 | 2 | 6 | 5 | 1 |
| John Lewis | 200 | 4 | 4 | 8 | 1 |
| Obediah Wictden | 50 | 2 | 2 | 5 | -- |
| Moses Packer | 100 | 2 | 2 | 6 | -- |
| Aaron Coates | 150 | 2 | 3 | -- | -- |
| Joseph Miller | 93 | 2 | 2 | 4 | -- |
| John Davis, shoemaker | 60 | 2 | 2 | 6 | -- |
| Joseph Callwell | 150 | 2 | 6 | 8 | -- |
| Sam'l Johnson | 75 | 2 | 2 | 6 | -- |
| John Johnson | 100 | 1 | -- | -- | -- |
| Simon Litzenberg, cooper | 80 | 2 | 3 | -- | -- |
| George Bosler | 30 | 1 | 1 | -- | -- |
| Isaac Davis, g.m. | 100 | -- | -- | -- | -- |
| Geo. Smith, g.m. | -- | -- | -- | -- | -- |
| Abra. Lewis, g.m. | -- | -- | -- | -- | -- |
| Abraham Lewis | 90 | -- | -- | -- | -- |
| Jesse Davis, shoemaker | 10 | 1 | 1 | -- | -- |
| Peter Pecheen, innkeeper | 140 | 2 | 4 | 6 | -- |
| Abraham Cornock | 120 | 2 | 2 | -- | -- |
| Jacob Berry | 100 | 2 | 2 | -- | -- |
| John Thomas | 150 | 2 | 4 | 6 | -- |
| Thomas Ellis | 66 | 1 | 3 | 4 | -- |
| Isaac Vaughen | 90 | 2 | 2 | -- | -- |
| Joshua Hardy, shoemaker | 10 | -- | -- | -- | -- |
| Rich'd Barry | 70 | 1 | 1 | -- | -- |
| Evan Watkin, taylor | 10 | 1 | 1 | -- | -- |

| Haverford | Acres | Horses | Cattle | Sheep | Servants |
|---|---|---|---|---|---|
| Chris'r Kitselman | 50 | 1 | 1 | -- | -- |
| Samuel Lander | 120 | 2 | 3 | -- | -- |
| Morris Fowler | 200 | 3 | 4 | 5 | -- |
| Tho's Vaughan | 130 | 2 | 3 | 3 | -- |
| Jacob Charles | 280 | 2 | 3 | 6 | -- |
| Jam's Doherty | 80 | 1 | 2 | -- | -- |
| Vellentine Nanholt | 150 | 2 | 4 | -- | -- |
| John Waiting | 9 | 1 | 2 | -- | -- |
| Gyles Pearman | 80 | 1 | 2 | -- | -- |
| Philip Super | -- | 1 | 1 | -- | -- |
| Will'm Townsend | -- | -- | 1 | -- | -- |
| Alexander Solely, blacksmith | -- | -- | 1 | -- | -- |
| James Thompson, mason | 20 | 1 | 1 | -- | -- |
| David Richards, blacksmith | -- | 1 | -- | -- | -- |
| Jacob Tuston | 100 | 1 | 2 | -- | -- |
| John Kearn, shoemaker | -- | 1 | 1 | -- | -- |
| David Rees, shoemaker | -- | 1 | 1 | -- | -- |
| Eliz'th Foreman | 2 | -- | 1 | -- | -- |
| John Earl | -- | -- | -- | -- | -- |

Inmates

James Calwell          Elisha Taylor
Tho's Lawrence         Samuel McBride
Jacob Johnston

Freemen

Jesse Ellis            Wm. Rees
David Ellis            Griffith David
Jonathan Ellis         Obediah Wieldy
Will'm Griffith        Jacob Femble
Tho's Simon

Upper Chichester Rate

| | Acres | Horses | Cattle | Sheep | Servants |
|---|---|---|---|---|---|
| Mordica Cloud | 196 | 6 | 8 | 3 | 1 |
| Nicolas Newlin | 100 | 4 | 5 | 6 | -- |
| Robert Eyere, tanner | 100 | 2 | 5 | 9 | -- |
| Sam'l Walker | 150 | 3 | 6 | 6 | 1 |
| Will'm Haston, s.m. | 220 | 4 | 5 | 4 | 1 |
| James Shelley | 75 | 3 | 4 | -- | -- |
| Will'm Lamplugh | 80 | 3 | 2 | 8 | -- |
| Benj'n Reynolds | 18 | 3 | 4 | 4 | -- |
| Jacob Dingee | 90 | 4 | 5 | 8 | -- |
| Robert Jack | 130 | 2 | 1 | -- | -- |
| Wm. Linsey | 70 | 3 | 5 | -- | -- |
| Christ'r Dingee | 42 | 2 | 2 | -- | -- |
| Edward Linvill | 100 | 3 | 3 | -- | -- |
| Joseph Brown | 96 | 3 | 2 | 4 | -- |

| Upper Chichester | Acres | Horses | Cattle | Sheep | Servants |
|---|---|---|---|---|---|
| Joseph Askew | 120 | 2 | 4 | 4 | -- |
| John Cook | 45 | 2 | 1 | -- | -- |
| Jeremy Booth | 80 | 2 | 1 | -- | -- |
| E'd Whitaker | 85 | 2 | 6 | -- | -- |
| John Dutton, Jun'r | 74 | -- | -- | -- | -- |
| Martin Carter | 127 | 2 | 2 | -- | -- |
| Tho's Edwards | 200 | 2 | 2 | 2 | -- |
| Rich'd Dutton | 150 | 3 | 4 | 10 | 1 |
| James Smith | 100 | 1 | 3 | 4 | -- |
| Levy Gregory, labourer | -- | -- | 1 | -- | -- |
| Peter Leonard, labourer | -- | -- | 1 | -- | -- |
| Daniel Brown | 70 | 2 | 1 | -- | -- |
| Jacob Howell | 148 | -- | -- | -- | -- |
| Arch'd McMitchell | 2 | 2 | 2 | 7 | -- |
| John Ford | 100 | -- | -- | -- | -- |
| Jacob Richards | 70 | -- | -- | -- | -- |
| Dennis Whealin, labourer | 20 | 1 | -- | -- | -- |
| Sam'l Walker | 130 | -- | -- | -- | -- |
| Mathias Kirlin | 115 | -- | -- | -- | -- |
| Alex'dr Tussy, weaver | 5 | 1 | 1 | -- | -- |
| Isabella Bernard, widow | 8 | -- | 1 | -- | -- |
| Jeremy Booth | 50 | -- | -- | -- | -- |
| Lewis Eyere | 5 | -- | -- | -- | -- |
| Tho's Robinsoin Estate, deceased | 50 | -- | -- | -- | -- |
| Hannah Flower | -- | -- | -- | -- | -- |
| John Alley, labourer | 5 | 1 | 1 | -- | -- |
| Mary Scott | -- | -- | 1 | -- | -- |
| Ann Dutton | -- | -- | -- | -- | -- |
| Sarah Reynolds | -- | 1 | 1 | -- | -- |
| John Talbot | 190 | 3 | 8 | 2 | -- |
| Nath'l Brown | 75 | 4 | -- | 10 | -- |
| Sam'l Reynolds | 40 | -- | -- | -- | -- |
| Jno. Derrough | -- | -- | 1 | -- | -- |
| Jacob Richard | 50 | -- | -- | -- | -- |
| Joseph Talbert | 35 | -- | -- | -- | -- |

Inmates

Sam'l Dutton         John Kirkpatrick
Joseph Sivill        Arch'd Steward

Freemen

Arch'd Sheerer       Jacob Lamplugh
John Askew           James Huston
Isaac Pennall        John McGuire
Tho's Edwards        Jacob Dingee

## Bethel Township Rate

|                          | Acres | Horses | Cattle | Sheep | Servants |
|--------------------------|-------|--------|--------|-------|----------|
| John Larkan              | 170   | 3      | 7      | --    | 1        |
| Will'm Eyers             | 180   | 2      | 1      | 20    | --       |
| Robert Booth             | 100   | 3      | 5      | 16    | --       |
| Joseph Booth             | 100   | 4      | 6      | 6     | --       |
| John Ford                | 215   | 6      | 7      | 10    | --       |
| John Nory                | 4     | --     | --     | --    | --       |
| Richard Hew, blacksmith  | 10    | --     | 1      | --    | --       |
| Will'm Nory, taylor      | --    | --     | --     | --    | --       |
| James Bratton            | 150   | 3      | 4      | 6     | 1        |
| Will'm Baldwin           | 150   | 3      | 6      | 3     | --       |
| Will'm Peter             | 90    | --     | --     | --    | --       |
| Jarrat Allison           | 10    | --     | --     | --    | --       |
| Abra. Swangor            | 100   | 2      | 3      | 2     | --       |
| Joseph Larkan            | 120   | 3      | 2      | 4     | --       |
| Isaac Larkan             | --    | 2      | 2      | 6     | --       |
| John Foulk               | 100   | 3      | 3      | 10    | --       |
| Eneas Foulk              | 60    | 1      | 3      | --    | --       |
| David McGorman           | 83    | 2      | 3      | 2     | --       |
| Isaac Pyle               | 160   | 4      | 4      | 3     | 1        |
| Will'm Guest, carpenter  | 100   | 2      | 4      | 6     | --       |
| Tho's Hampton            | 7     | --     | --     | --    | --       |
| Rob't Pyle               | 20    | 3      | 4      | 4     | --       |
| Wm. Crose, comber        | 38    | 1      | 1      | --    | --       |
| Giles Sankey             | 140   | 2      | 2      | --    | --       |
| James Hunter             | 70    | 2      | 4      | 4     | --       |
| And'w Hunter             | 122   | 2      | 2      | 3     | --       |
| John Kenny, labourer     | --    | --     | 1      | --    | --       |
| Joseph Lloyde            | --    | 2      | 2      | --    | --       |
| John Walter              | --    | --     | --     | --    | --       |

### Freemen

Sam'l Withrow  
Robert Mortlin  
John Phillips  
Jam's Anderson  
John Booth  

Rob't Steel  
Jam's Brattn  
Lewis Eyres  
Cornelius McGlaughlin  

## Springfield Township Rate

|                              | Acres | Horses | Cattle | Sheep | Servants |
|------------------------------|-------|--------|--------|-------|----------|
| Jam's Crozier, shopkeeper    | 110   | 3      | 4      | 6     | --       |
| Jno. Camerron                | 55    | 2      | 2      | 3     | --       |
| Dugall Cameron, farmer       | 100   | 2      | 2      | 5     | --       |
| Lewis Davis                  | 150   | --     | --     | --    | --       |
| Will'm Fell, s.m.            | 255   | 6      | 6      | 15    | --       |
| William Forrest              | 200   | 3      | 8      | 6     | --       |
| Joseph Gibbins, tavern,      |       |        |        |       |          |
|   tavernkeeper     | 150   | 3      | 2      | 14    | 1        |
| John Hall, shoemaker         | 118   | 3      | 3      | --    | --       |

| Springfield Township | Acres | Horses | Cattle | Sheep | Servants |
|---|---|---|---|---|---|
| Joseph Haycock, s.m. | -- | -- | -- | -- | -- |
| Abraham Holmes | 48 | 1 | 2 | -- | -- |
| Elisha Jones, mill, miller | 29 | 6 | 4 | -- | -- |
| John Levis | 300 | 5 | 14 | 8 | 2 |
| Samuel Levis, miller, g.m. | 280 | 6 | 8 | 6 | 3 |
| George Lownes, blacksmith | 92 | 4 | 5 | 10 | -- |
| Alice Lownes | 150 | 3 | 2 | -- | 1 |
| Thomas Levis | 165 | 3 | 7 | 6 | 1 |
| James Maddock, millwright | 75 | 2 | 1 | -- | -- |
| Ann Maris, shopkeeper | 60 | 2 | 3 | -- | 1 |
| Jesse Maris, tavernkeeper, county treasurer | 88 | 3 | 3 | -- | -- |
| John Maris, taylor | 45 | 2 | 4 | -- | -- |
| John Morris | 50 | -- | -- | -- | -- |
| Will'm Maddock | 85 | 2 | 2 | -- | -- |
| Hannah Ogden | 171 | 4 | 7 | 4 | -- |
| Seth Pancast | 138 | -- | -- | -- | -- |
| Dan'l Reese, blacksmith | 50 | 1 | 1 | -- | -- |
| Walter Roberts | 100 | 5 | 4 | 4 | -- |
| Tho's Shoemaker | 40 | -- | -- | -- | -- |
| Tho's Taylor | 50 | 2 | 3 | -- | -- |
| John Thompson | 217 | 5 | 12 | 8 | -- |
| Nathan Thompson | 190 | 2 | 2 | 6 | -- |
| John Tennant | 110 | 1 | 2 | -- | -- |
| Joel Willis | 250 | 3 | 3 | 6 | 1 |
| Joseph Wilkinson | 200 | 4 | 7 | 12 | -- |
| Dan'l Yarnill | 160 | 3 | 5 | 4 | -- |
| Sam'l Parke | 42 | -- | -- | -- | -- |
| Nath'l Pennock | 133 | -- | -- | -- | -- |

Freemen

Jno. Maris
Dan'l Brown
Jam's Lowns
Tho's Broom
Abra'm Pyatt
Hugh Kennedy

Edward Fell
Tho's Pheenix
John Dobbins
Wm. Jones
Hezekiah Camp

Inmates

Benjamin Morgan
Joseph Tanyers
Wm. Paste
John Caldwell
Mich'l Lights

Finley Cameron
Henry McClenan
Isaac Davis
Charles Carey
John Dicks, taylor

## Edgement Rate

|  | Acres | Horses | Cattle | Sheep | Servants |
|---|---|---|---|---|---|
| Cadwalader Evans, tanner | 300 | 5 | 7 | 15 | 1 |
| Nath'n Yarnall, weaver | 173 | 3 | 6 | 10 | -- |
| Mary Yarnall | 130 | 2 | 4 | 6 | -- |
| Moses Meridith | 200 | 4 | 10 | 12 | -- |
| James Sill | 120 | 3 | 5 | 8 | -- |
| William Russell | 200 | 3 | 7 | 4 | 1 |
| Edward Farr | 100 | 2 | 4 | 6 | -- |
| Susannah Griffith | 100 | 1 | 2 | -- | -- |
| Abel Green | 193 | 3 | 5 | 8 | -- |
| Abra. Hoops | 170 | 4 | 4 | 6 | -- |
| Nehemiah Baker | 96 | 3 | 3 | 6 | -- |
| John Worrell | 300 | 4 | 5 | 10 | -- |
| Joseph Pratt | 235 | 6 | 7 | 10 | -- |
| Josiah Lewis | 200 | 4 | 5 | -- | -- |
| Jacob Yarnall | 100 | 3 | 3 | -- | -- |
| Daniel Calvert | 36 | 3 | 1 | -- | -- |
| Joseph Black | 120 | 2 | 3 | 6 | -- |
| Aron Baker, blacksmith | 120 | 3 | 4 | -- | -- |
| George Bishop | 100 | 4 | 3 | 6 | -- |
| Will'm Prichett | 100 | 2 | 3 | 6 | -- |
| Jam's Howard | 100 | 3 | 3 | 7 | -- |
| John Howard | 60 | -- | -- | -- | -- |
| Wm. McAfee | 150 | 3 | 5 | 5 | 1 |
| Will'm Russell, sadler | 100 | 2 | 2 | 3 | -- |
| John Regester | 100 | 2 | 3 | 4 | -- |
| Daniel Thompson, labourer | 97 | 1 | 1 | -- | -- |
| John Holston | 151 | 3 | 4 | 10 | 1 |
| Will'm Yarnall | 90 | 2 | 3 | 3 | -- |
| Jonathan Hunter | 250 | 3 | 4 | 10 | 1 |
| George Hunter | 250 | 3 | 4 | -- | 1 |
| John Hoops, tavernkeeper | 200 | 3 | 8 | 6 | -- |
| David Yarnall | 70 | 2 | 2 | 4 | -- |
| Dan'l Bromall | 165 | 3 | 5 | 4 | -- |
| Rob't Thompson | 60 | 2 | 1 | -- | -- |
| Tho's Bishop | 72 | -- | -- | -- | -- |
| Caleb Yarnall | 100 | 1 | -- | -- | -- |
| Elias Pearson, white smith | 80 | 2 | 2 | -- | -- |
| Nath'l Mercer, labourer | -- | -- | 1 | -- | -- |
| Will'm Regester, mason | -- | 2 | 1 | -- | -- |
| Tho's Cookson | -- | -- | -- | -- | -- |
| Tho's Grisell, labourer | -- | -- | 1 | -- | -- |

Inmates

James Russell            Will'm Tharlow
Edw'd Churchman          John Otley
John Grimes

Freemen

Rob't Evans              Job Yarnall
Rich'd Beats             Joseph Robins

## Freemen

Thomas Prichard
Wm. Prichard
Jonathan Esery
Wm. Wiseley
Thomas Evans
Joseph Beaker
Aaron Madson

John Sill
Isaac Hoops
Will'm Black
Daniel McAfee
Abra'm Pratt
Dan'l Williamson
John Black

## Concord Rate

|  | Acres | Horses | Cattle | Sheep | Servants |
|---|---|---|---|---|---|
| John Arment | 50 | 3 | 3 | -- | -- |
| John Baldwin | 250 | 3 | 4 | 6 | -- |
| John Brinton, miller | 4 | 1 | 1 | -- | -- |
| Isaac Bullock, blacksmith | 150 | 3 | 4 | 6 | -- |
| Abra'm Barnett | 50 | 2 | 1 | -- | -- |
| Rich'd Beates | 50 | -- | -- | -- | -- |
| John Bale, wool comer | 160 | 1 | 2 | 2 | -- |
| John Burnett | 60 | 1 | 4 | -- | -- |
| Joseph Chamberlin | 113 | 6 | 7 | 9 | -- |
| Joseph Cloud, S'r | 100 | 4 | 4 | 6 | -- |
| Joseph Cloud, carp'r | 150 | 2 | 2 | -- | -- |
| John Cambel | 50 | 1 | 1 | -- | -- |
| Tho's Evans | 85 | 1 | 2 | -- | -- |
| Rob't Green, S'r | 39 | -- | -- | -- | -- |
| Rob't Green, Jun'r | 180 | 2 | 4 | 16 | -- |
| Pat'k Gambel | 100 | 2 | 4 | 5 | -- |
| Phebe Guest | 145 | 1 | 1 | -- | -- |
| John Hannum, Esq'r | 257 | 5 | 8 | 18 | 1 |
| Peter Hatton, wheelwright | 100 | 4 | 6 | 5 | -- |
| Rob't Hall, tavernkeeper, tavern | 50 | 2 | 3 | 5 | -- |
| Stephen Hall | 100 | 4 | 5 | 8 | -- |
| John Hall | 250 | 6 | 7 | 17 | -- |
| George Harlin, mason | 5 | 1 | 1 | -- | -- |
| John Jordan | 80 | 1 | 2 | -- | -- |
| Joseph Kerlin, blacksmith | 73 | 2 | 2 | -- | -- |
| Alex'r Lockard | 130 | 2 | 4 | 8 | 1 |
| Sam'l Mendenhall | 287 | 6 | 8 | 10 | 1 |
| Rob't Mendenhall, s.m. | 298 | 6 | 8 | 10 | 2 |
| Benjamin Marshal, labourer | 148 | 1 | 2 | 8 | -- |
| Will'm McCay | 159 | 1 | 3 | 7 | -- |
| Henry Myre, labourer | 120 | 2 | 2 | -- | -- |
| And'w Mitchell, leed maker | 50 | 1 | 3 | -- | -- |
| Tho's McCall | 100 | 3 | 3 | 7 | -- |
| Mary Morison | 50 | 1 | 2 | 2 | -- |
| Nic's Nulin, g.m. | 190 | 6 | 4 | 22 | 1 |
| Nath'l Nulin | 340 | 2 | 5 | 6 | -- |
| Joseph Niclin | 65 | 2 | 3 | 3 | -- |
| John Nicklin, labourer | 117 | 2 | 2 | 6 | -- |
| Moses Palmer | 240 | 5 | 7 | 8 | 1 |
| John Peirce | 111 | 3 | 10 | -- | -- |
| Caleb Peirce, Sen'r | 60 | 1 | -- | -- | -- |

| Concord | Acres | Horses | Cattle | Sheep | Servants |
|---|---|---|---|---|---|
| John Palmer, blacksmith | 70 | 2 | 2 | 4 | -- |
| John Palmer, S'r | 100 | -- | 1 | -- | -- |
| Henry Peirce | 80 | 2 | 3 | 2 | -- |
| Will'm Peirce | 140 | -- | -- | -- | -- |
| Jno. Piper | 150 | 3 | 2 | 5 | 1 |
| Wm. Peters, Guard'n for Jno. Guest | 200 | -- | -- | -- | -- |
| Jno. Russell, labourer | 120 | 2 | 2 | 3 | -- |
| Rich'd Sanderson | 150 | 3 | 4 | 4 | 2 |
| Will'm Smith | 100 | 2 | 4 | 12 | -- |
| John Trimble, shopkeeper, s.m. | 55 | 5 | 4 | 8 | 1 |
| Sam'l Trimble, hatter | 8 | 1 | 1 | -- | -- |
| Edith Thatcher | 50 | -- | 2 | -- | -- |
| Jacob Taylor | 8 | 1 | 1 | -- | -- |
| Will'm Walter | 105 | 2 | 4 | 6 | -- |
| Tho's Wilcox, p.m. | 140 | 6 | 6 | 12 | 2 |
| John Steen | 200 | 3 | 4 | -- | 1 |
| John Steward | 100 | 2 | 4 | 2 | -- |
| Micajah Spickman, blacksmith and servant | 72 | 2 | 3 | 8 | -- |
| Predick Kimber | 100 | 3 | 1 | 5 | -- |
| Sam'l Talkinton | 92 | 4 | 4 | 8 | -- |
| John Reynolds, cooper | 3 | -- | 1 | -- | -- |
| William Hawley, carpenter | 50 | 2 | 1 | 8 | -- |
| Jam's Hatten | 70 | 1 | 2 | -- | -- |

Inmates

Mich'l Monagan
Phi'p Mendenhall
Will Rowle
Caleb Pyle
Robert Earl
Jam's Curry

Daniel Webb
Valentine Weaver
John Sullen
Jno. Chamberlin
Jam's Johnston
Nicholas Fling

Freemen

Nath'l Morrison
Moses Mendenhall
Will'm Vernon
And'w Carson
Tho's Ball
Lawrence McConally
Joshua Morrison
John Allin
Thomas Arment
David Morrison
John Bohanan
Daniel Harris
Syles Pryor
Caleb Perkins
Levy Mersey
Benj'n Mendenhall

Jam's Clark
Richard Webb
Charles Linn
Will'm Armet
Mark Wilcox
James Hall
William Boyde
Peter Plankenton
James Eliot
John Palmer
John Bullock
Geo. Ball
William Frith
Abraham Randle
George Ganger

## Marple Township Rate

| | Acres | Horses | Cattle | Sheep | Servants |
|---|---|---|---|---|---|
| Bern'd Vanlier, physician | 200 | 3 | 5 | 12 | 2 |
| Jam's Roads, tanner | 236 | 7 | 5 | 12 | 1 |
| Jam's Bartram | 240 | 5 | 10 | 6 | -- |
| Hen'y Lawrence | 240 | 4 | 5 | 12 | -- |
| Jos'h Haycock | 100 | 3 | 4 | 5 | -- |
| David Hall | 200 | 3 | 6 | 3 | 1 |
| Joseph Shelden | 100 | 2 | 3 | -- | -- |
| John Morris | 195 | 6 | 5 | 5 | 2 |
| Law'e Howard | 160 | 4 | 8 | -- | 1 |
| Eliz'th Moore | 200 | 3 | 4 | -- | -- |
| Joseph Powel | 100 | 3 | 4 | 6 | -- |
| Jam's Powel | 90 | 1 | 1 | 3 | -- |
| Isaac Roads | 100 | 3 | 6 | 8 | -- |
| Joseph Roads | 100 | 2 | 3 | 6 | -- |
| Nath'l Holland | 100 | 2 | 5 | -- | -- |
| Seth Pancost, s.m. | 180 | 3 | 9 | 7 | 1 |
| Wm. Burns | 24 | 4 | 10 | 5 | 1 |
| Jonathan Maris | 190 | 2 | 5 | -- | -- |
| Mordica Morris | 177 | 3 | 2 | -- | -- |
| Tho's Select, shoemaker | 10 | 1 | 1 | 1 | -- |
| Jam's Logan, labourer | 10 | -- | 1 | -- | -- |
| Rich'd Maris | 60 | 1 | 2 | -- | -- |
| Mary Morris | -- | -- | -- | -- | -- |
| Moses Thompson | 140 | 2 | 6 | 4 | 1 |
| Cha's Lynn | 34 | -- | -- | -- | -- |
| Hen'y Effinger | 100 | 1 | 3 | -- | -- |
| Hayes Pennall | 200 | 2 | 1 | -- | -- |
| Joshua Pennall, Jun'r | 60 | 2 | 3 | -- | -- |
| Jonathan Worrall | 100 | 3 | 3 | 4 | -- |
| Jam's Worrall | 50 | 2 | 2 | 6 | -- |
| Phebe Worrall | 100 | 2 | 3 | 4 | -- |
| Peter Worrall | 70 | 2 | 3 | -- | -- |
| Isaac Maris | 200 | 3 | 5 | -- | -- |
| Edw'd Hughes | 100 | 1 | 1 | -- | -- |
| Nathan Davis | 140 | 3 | 5 | -- | -- |
| Aron Vernum, weaver | 8 | -- | 2 | -- | -- |
| David Melan | 200 | 3 | 8 | -- | 1 |
| Will'm Quin | 100 | 2 | 3 | 6 | -- |
| Ann Taylor, widow | 50 | 1 | 1 | -- | -- |
| John Coppock, shoemaker | 16 | 1 | 1 | -- | -- |
| Will'm Maxwell | 70 | 2 | 4 | 3 | -- |
| Conrod Sinclair | 59 | 2 | 2 | 3 | -- |
| John Nicolson | -- | -- | 1 | -- | -- |
| Dan'l Cameron | 30 | 2 | 2 | -- | -- |
| John Mason | 75 | 2 | 1 | -- | -- |
| Alex'r Oliver | 90 | 3 | 5 | 5 | -- |
| Nathan Yarnall | 100 | 2 | 4 | 6 | -- |
| Elisha Worrall, shopkeeper | 10 | 2 | 1 | -- | -- |
| Jam's Cohran | 40 | 2 | 2 | -- | -- |
| Wm. Field | 50 | 2 | 2 | 5 | -- |
| Sarah Caldwell | 60 | 2 | 4 | 5 | -- |
| Tho's Leech | -- | -- | 2 | 1 | -- |
| Jam's Worrall, Jun'r, labourer | -- | -- | 1 | -- | -- |
| Edw'd Hughes, carpenter | 60 | 1 | 2 | -- | -- |

Marple                          Acres   Horses  Cattle  Sheep   Servants

David Fisher                    --      --      --      --      --
Joseph Thomas, taylor           --      --      --      --      --

                                Inmates

Joseph Baldwin                          Josh. Pennall
Sam'l Grasy                             Benj'n Taylor

                                Freemen

Peter Higgins                           Elisha Worrall
John Sarah Check                        Joseph Worrall
Michael Cope                            Sam'l Vanleer
John Wolly                              Andrew Dimond
Isaac Hughes                            David Moor
John Ferree                             Tho's Wooley
Tho's Powell                            Will'm Shilden
Joseph Powell, Jun'r

                        Ridley Township Rate

|  | Acres | Horses | Cattle | Sheep | Servants |
|---|---|---|---|---|---|
| Wm. Archer | 135 | 5 | 6 | 6 | 1 |
| John Archer | 55 | 2 | 4 | 6 | -- |
| Wm. Boon | 160 | 4 | 4 | 6 | 1 |
| James Barton | 4 | -- | -- | -- | -- |
| John Crozby, s.q. | 158 | 5 | 4 | 10 | -- |
| Rich'd Crozby, Jun'r, s.q. | 66 | 2 | 3 | -- | -- |
| Rich'd Crozby, Sen'r | 105 | 4 | 3 | -- | -- |
| Swan Culing | 125 | 3 | 6 | 8 | 1 |
| Daniel Culin | 230 | 3 | 8 | 20 | 1 |
| John Culin, carpenter | 40 | 2 | 1 | -- | -- |
| Wm. Cowan | 7 | 2 | 1 | 4 | -- |
| Tho's Cobourn | 117 | 1 | 6 | 6 | -- |
| Phillip Climes, shoemaker | -- | 1 | -- | -- | -- |
| James Cherry, taylor | -- | -- | -- | -- | -- |
| John Craig | 12 | -- | -- | -- | -- |
| Joseph Dicks | 8 | -- | -- | -- | -- |
| Lewis Davis | 100 | 5 | 6 | -- | 1 |
| Christopher Elliot | 245 | 3 | 5 | -- | 1 |
| William Edwards | 150 | 5 | 6 | -- | 1 |
| Roger & John Dicks | 12 | -- | -- | -- | -- |
| Peter Elliot | 20 | -- | -- | -- | -- |
| Rob't Edwards, carpenter | -- | -- | -- | -- | -- |
| Margaret Ford | 112 | 1 | 2 | -- | 1 |
| Cha's Grantham | 180 | 5 | 11 | 30 | 3 |
| Margaret Grantham | 97 | 1 | 2 | -- | -- |
| Jacob Gally | 80 | 2 | 4 | -- | 1 |
| Isaac Hendrickson | 161 | 3 | 18 | -- | -- |
| Susan'h Hendrickson | 30 | 1 | 1 | -- | -- |
| John Knowls | 147 | 4 | 3 | -- | 2 |

| Ridley Township | Acres | Horses | Cattle | Sheep | Servants |
|---|---|---|---|---|---|
| Jacob Kitz, weaver | 200 | 2 | 2 | -- | -- |
| Jno. Lewes, s.m. | 300 | 6 | 4 | 10 | 1 |
| Isaac Levis | 100 | 3 | 6 | 6 | 1 |
| Sam'l Levis | -- | -- | -- | -- | -- |
| Hugh Lloyd, g.m., miller | -- | 2 | 2 | -- | -- |
| Israel Longacre, chairmaker | 33 | 2 | 5 | 8 | -- |
| John Morton, Esq'r, High Sheriff for the County of Chester | 240 | 4 | 8 | 20 | 2 |
| Morton Morton | 139 | 4 | 6 | 10 | 2 |
| James Mather | 46 | -- | -- | -- | -- |
| Dan'l Morton, taylor | 40 | 1 | 2 | -- | -- |
| Jno. McIlvain, s.q. | 118 | 3 | 3 | 10 | -- |
| Hugh McIlvain, s.q. | 6 | 1 | -- | 6 | -- |
| John McMickoll | -- | -- | -- | -- | -- |
| Lucas Nether Mark | 240 | 7 | 20 | -- | 1 |
| Caleb Phipps, g.m., miller | 13 | 3 | 3 | -- | -- |
| Ed. Pennington | 40 | -- | -- | -- | -- |
| Daniel Price | 42 | 3 | 3 | -- | -- |
| Patrick Ryan | 105 | 2 | 4 | 3 | -- |
| Wm. Rushton, shoemaker | 6 | 1 | 1 | -- | -- |
| John Ralston, labourer | -- | -- | -- | -- | -- |
| Jam's Ross | 170 | 2 | 25 | -- | -- |
| Tho's Smith | 250 | 5 | 10 | 30 | 2 |
| Tho's Swayne | 225 | 4 | 10 | 6 | -- |
| Will'm Smith, ferry | 8 | 1 | 3 | -- | -- |
| Edward Shaw, carpenter | -- | 1 | -- | -- | -- |
| Mary Sketchly | 25 | 1 | 2 | 4 | -- |
| John & Daniel Sharpless | 15 | -- | -- | -- | -- |
| Tho's Sharpless | 8 | -- | -- | -- | -- |
| Jacob Stork | 105 | 4 | 6 | 6 | -- |
| Henry Trimble | 310 | 3 | 12 | 12 | 3 |
| John Taylor | 55 | 4 | 4 | -- | -- |
| Joseph Taylor | 152 | 4 | 6 | -- | -- |
| John Bryan, tavern | 112 | 2 | 6 | 20 | 3 |
| Benj'n Thomas | 200 | 3 | 2 | -- | -- |
| Lewes Trimble | 300 | 4 | 10 | -- | 1 |
| John Vandorin | 13 | -- | -- | -- | -- |
| Will'm Worrall | 102 | 3 | 3 | 6 | -- |
| Jacob Worrall | 65 | 2 | 2 | 4 | -- |
| Chris'r Wilson | 250 | 7 | 20 | -- | 1 |
| Jno. Worrall | 100 | 3 | 4 | -- | -- |
| Tho's West | 100 | 3 | 4 | -- | 1 |
| Joseph Worrall | -- | -- | -- | -- | -- |
| Mich'l Walker | -- | -- | -- | -- | -- |
| Fredrick Wilks | -- | -- | -- | -- | -- |
| John Lardner, shoemaker | -- | -- | -- | -- | -- |
| Benj'n Maddock, shoemaker | -- | -- | -- | -- | -- |
| Tho's Manly | -- | -- | -- | -- | -- |
| Nicolas Deal | 105 | -- | 20 | -- | -- |
| Tho's Haddon, labourer | -- | -- | 1 | -- | -- |
| Philip Corodon | 20 | -- | -- | -- | -- |
| And'w Longacre, labourer | -- | -- | 1 | -- | -- |

                              Inmates

Joseph Menion                   Rich'd Wright

                              Freemen

William Bratton                 Lawrence Cox
Daniel Culin, Jun'r             Caleb Davis
Tho's Care                      Patrick Doran
Rob't Colvin                    Will'm Emblen
Samuel Colvin                   David George
Patrick Gaff                    John Barnhill
John Hendrickson                Elijah Worrall
Samuel Henderson                Wm. Prim
George Hartshorn                Tho's Prim
John Johnson                    William Porter
John Hogan                      Robert Nixon
Andrew Justison                 John Reynold
John Justison                   Robert Steward
Harvey Lewis                    James Smith
Samuel Lewis                    John Taggart
Andrew McIlvaine                Andrew Tartan
John McCormack                  Lewis Thomas
John Morton                     Elisha Worrall
John Miller                     Ezekiel Wickwere
Francis Moore                   Tho's Willis
Duncan McSparrow                Benj'n Flemming
Thomas Johnson


                        Lower Chichester Rate

|  | Acres | Horses | Cattle | Sheep | Servants |
| --- | --- | --- | --- | --- | --- |
| Samuel Armor, cordwainer | 8 1/2 | 1 | 1 | 5 | -- |
| Joseph Buffington | -- | -- | -- | -- | -- |
| Benj'n Black, ferryman | 12 | 2 | 1 | -- | -- |
| Thomas Barnett, tanner | -- | 1 | -- | -- | 1 |
| Wm. Burns, cordwainer | -- | 1 | 1 | -- | -- |
| Jno. Brown | 20 | 2 | 2 | -- | -- |
| Mary Barclay | 16 | -- | -- | -- | -- |
| Peter Brown | -- | -- | -- | -- | -- |
| Adam Clayton, tavern, t.k. | 30 | 1 | 1 | 5 | -- |
| Rich'd Clayton, cordwainer | 22 | 2 | 1 | 5 | -- |
| Joseph Clayton | 7 | 1 | -- | -- | -- |
| John Crawford, shopkeeper & ship carpenter | 14 | -- | -- | -- | -- |
| Wm. Crabb | 10 | 1 | 2 | -- | -- |
| Tho's Cobourn | 32 | 2 | 3 | -- | -- |
| Will'm Cobourn | 15 | 2 | -- | -- | -- |
| John Cobourn | 30 | 2 | 4 | -- | -- |
| Jacob Cobourn | 33 | 2 | 2 | -- | -- |
| Joseph Cobourn | 13 | -- | -- | -- | -- |
| Hugh Conn | 30 | 2 | 1 | -- | -- |
| John Cloud | 100 | 1 | 2 | 6 | -- |
| William Connell, joyner | -- | -- | 1 | -- | -- |
| Zachariah Derrick, wheelwright | 20 | 1 | 2 | 5 | -- |

Lower Chichester

| | Acres | Horses | Cattle | Sheep | Servants |
|---|---|---|---|---|---|
| Thomas Derrick, house carpenter | -- | -- | -- | -- | -- |
| John Druitt | 40 | 1 | 4 | 9 | -- |
| Archibald Dick | 38 | 2 | 1 | -- | 1 |
| David Duncan, shopkeeper | 15 | 1 | 1 | -- | -- |
| John Flower, shallop man and hatter | 4 | -- | 1 | -- | -- |
| Hannah Flower, tavern, inkeeper | 8 1/2 | 1 | 1 | -- | -- |
| Daniel Frich, innkeeper | 12 | 1 | 1 | -- | 2 |
| Jam's Forgy, labourer | 4 | -- | 1 | -- | -- |
| George Grist | -- | 2 | 5 | 10 | -- |
| Joseph Gribble, whitesmith | -- | 1 | 1 | -- | -- |
| Samuel Grist, labourer | -- | -- | -- | -- | -- |
| Joseph Grangee, waterman | -- | -- | -- | -- | -- |
| Will'm Henderson | 130 | 2 | 2 | -- | 2 |
| Jacob Howell, cordwainer | 30 | 2 | 2 | -- | -- |
| Mary Howell | 20 | -- | -- | -- | -- |
| William Henry | 56 | 2 | 3 | -- | -- |
| Elis'h Hartley | -- | -- | -- | -- | -- |
| Tho's Hutcheson | -- | -- | -- | -- | -- |
| David Johnson | 114 | 5 | 4 | 10 | -- |
| Catherine Jackson | -- | -- | -- | -- | -- |
| Sam'l Lamply | 15 | 1 | 4 | -- | -- |
| Catherine Lawrence | 2 | -- | 2 | -- | -- |
| Rich'd Leonard, labourer | -- | -- | 1 | -- | -- |
| Allin Muris | -- | -- | -- | -- | -- |
| John McCoy, t.k. | 40 | 2 | 1 | 10 | -- |
| Robert Moulder, tavern, innkeeper | 79 | 1 | 5 | 20 | 1 |
| Benj'n Moulder, ship carpenter | -- | -- | -- | -- | -- |
| John Marshall, sadler | 31 | 2 | 2 | 11 | -- |
| Mary Moore | 14 | -- | 1 | -- | -- |
| Matthew McLaughlin, labourer | 15 | 2 | 2 | -- | -- |
| Richard Moseley, shopkeeper | -- | 1 | -- | -- | -- |
| John Moreton, taylor | -- | -- | -- | -- | -- |
| John Meal | -- | 1 | 1 | -- | -- |
| John Price, Esq'r, g.m., s.m., miller | 178 | 4 | 8 | 16 | 2 |
| John Power, scrivener | 3 | 2 | 1 | -- | -- |
| Edward Pilkenton, whitesmith | -- | 1 | -- | -- | -- |
| Thomas Phillips, blacksmith | -- | 1 | -- | -- | -- |
| Martha Rowan | -- | -- | -- | -- | -- |
| Richard Riley, Esq'r | 15 1/3 | 1 | 1 | 5 | -- |
| John Reynolds, malt house | -- | -- | -- | -- | -- |
| Samuel Reynolds, g.m., s.m. | 13 | 1 | 2 | -- | -- |
| James Rowan, shopkeeper | 4 | 1 | 1 | -- | 1 |
| Allen Robenett, joyner | 2 | 1 | 2 | -- | -- |
| Mary Raine | -- | -- | -- | -- | -- |
| Moses Rawson, wool comber | -- | -- | -- | -- | -- |
| James Rigby, schoolmaster | -- | -- | 1 | -- | -- |
| Paul Stern, cooper | -- | -- | -- | -- | -- |
| Susannah Brockden | -- | -- | -- | -- | -- |
| Anthony Sumption, smith | 5 | 1 | 1 | 3 | -- |
| Joseph Stow | 17 3/4 | -- | -- | -- | -- |
| Isaac Wood, waterman | 2 | -- | -- | -- | 1 |
| Jacob Worril | -- | -- | 1 | -- | -- |

| Lower Chichester | Acres | Horses | Cattle | Sheep | Servants |
|---|---|---|---|---|---|
| Samuel Williams, physician | -- | 1 | 1 | -- | -- |
| John Wade | 2 | 3 | 2 | -- | -- |
| James Weer | -- | -- | -- | -- | -- |
| Elizabeth Willis | -- | -- | -- | -- | -- |
| James Young, shoemaker | -- | -- | -- | -- | -- |
| Elisha Price | 58 | -- | -- | -- | -- |
| John Hall | 105 | -- | -- | -- | -- |

## Non-Residents

| | Acres | Horses | Cattle | Sheep | Servants |
|---|---|---|---|---|---|
| Charles Norris's Estate | -- | -- | -- | -- | -- |
| Robert Cobourn | 154 | -- | -- | -- | -- |
| Mordecai Cloud | 30 | -- | -- | -- | -- |
| Thomas Perkins | 3 | -- | -- | -- | -- |
| Benja. Ford | -- | -- | -- | -- | -- |
| Richard Moore | -- | -- | -- | -- | -- |
| Tho's Robinson's administrators | 20 | -- | -- | -- | -- |
| Dan'l Brown | 2 | -- | -- | -- | -- |
| Jno. Williamson | 8 | -- | -- | -- | -- |
| Grubbs Family | 4 | -- | -- | -- | -- |
| Francis Ruth, Junior | -- | -- | -- | -- | -- |
| Adam Price | -- | -- | -- | -- | -- |
| Sam'l Raine | 3 | -- | -- | -- | -- |
| Geo. Gilpin | -- | -- | -- | -- | -- |
| Robert O'Neal | -- | -- | -- | -- | -- |
| Howels Family | -- | -- | -- | -- | -- |
| John Downing, malt house | 5 | -- | -- | -- | -- |
| John Buffington | 2 | -- | -- | -- | -- |
| Peter Valoe | -- | -- | -- | -- | -- |
| William Stow | -- | -- | -- | -- | -- |

## Single Men

Solomon Brown
John Brown
Joseph Cloud
John Wall
John Conrad

Robert Moulder
Hugh O'Neal
Andrew McIntire
William Flower
Joseph Few

## Charles Town Rate

| | Acres | Horses | Cattle | Sheep | Servants |
|---|---|---|---|---|---|
| Patrick Anderson, s.m. | 300 | 4 | 4 | 4 | 1 |
| John Buckwalter | 400 | 4 | 5 | 12 | -- |
| Benj'n Byers | 160 | 2 | 2 | -- | -- |
| John Beaton | 200 | 2 | 4 | 3 | -- |
| Alexander Balah | 200 | 4 | 4 | 4 | -- |
| Frederick Bussard | 100 | 2 | 2 | 5 | 1 |

| Charles Town | Acres | Horses | Cattle | Sheep | Servants |
|---|---|---|---|---|---|
| Elias Brown | 134 | 1 | -- | -- | -- |
| Jonathan Coates | 50 | 3 | 3 | 8 | 1 |
| Moses Coates | 280 | 3 | 5 | 7 | 1 |
| Benja. Coates | 100 | 3 | 4 | 5 | 1 |
| John Campbell | -- | 2 | -- | -- | -- |
| Alexander Campbell | 100 | 2 | 1 | -- | -- |
| David Davis, M.P. | 334 | 4 | 4 | -- | -- |
| Lewellyn Davis | 300 | 4 | 6 | 10 | -- |
| John David, taylor | 115 | 1 | -- | -- | -- |
| David Davis, Gland | 143 | 3 | 5 | 6 | -- |
| John David | 100 | 2 | 4 | 3 | -- |
| Godfrey Deel | 190 | 2 | 1 | 2 | -- |
| Jeremiah David | 100 | -- | 1 | -- | -- |
| Jenkin David | -- | 3 | 6 | 8 | -- |
| John Francis | 144 | 2 | 4 | 6 | -- |
| William Fussell, chairmaker | 4 | 1 | 1 | -- | -- |
| John Griffith | 290 | 3 | 3 | 5 | -- |
| William Graham | 200 | -- | -- | -- | -- |
| Frederick Geerhart, blacksmith | 3 | 1 | 1 | -- | -- |
| David Humphreys | 100 | 2 | 2 | 5 | -- |
| Samuel Harvey, f.m., fuller | 200 | 2 | 3 | -- | -- |
| James Hancock | 40 | 1 | 3 | 2 | -- |
| William Hancock | 100 | -- | -- | -- | -- |
| Nicholas Holderman | 235 | 3 | 4 | 8 | -- |
| Nicholas Holderman, Jun'r | -- | 3 | 3 | -- | -- |
| Nicholas Foos | 100 | 2 | 3 | 5 | -- |
| Griffith Jones | 150 | 4 | 6 | 10 | 1 |
| David John | 100 | 1 | 3 | 5 | -- |
| Thomas Ives, tavern, t.k. | 150 | 2 | 3 | 6 | 1 |
| John Longstreath, g.m., miller | 63 | 4 | 3 | 4 | -- |
| Benj'n Longstreath | 63 | -- | -- | -- | -- |
| George Luther | 100 | 2 | 2 | 3 | -- |
| James Lewis | 45 | -- | -- | -- | -- |
| George Leip | 150 | 4 | 4 | 10 | -- |
| Jacob Lobb | 100 | 1 | 1 | 3 | -- |
| Henry Low | 200 | 2 | 1 | -- | -- |
| Samuel Lewis | -- | 1 | 1 | -- | -- |
| David Linsey | 200 | 4 | 2 | -- | 2 |
| James Martin | 140 | 3 | 3 | 6 | -- |
| William Moore, Esq'r, g.m., s.m. | 510 | 10 | 10 | 20 | 1 |
| David Matthias | 190 | 4 | 4 | 7 | -- |
| Henry Miller | 150 | 2 | 3 | 6 | -- |
| Lewis Morgan | 227 | 3 | 4 | 4 | -- |
| William Martin | 120 | -- | -- | -- | -- |
| Mathias Martin | 200 | 4 | 3 | 3 | -- |
| Joel Martin | 150 | 4 | 3 | 3 | -- |
| Roger Martin | 50 | 2 | 2 | 4 | -- |
| David Mathias, Sen'r | 14 | 2 | 2 | 2 | -- |
| George McHaney | 200 | 3 | 4 | 2 | -- |
| Francis O'Neal | 70 | 2 | 2 | -- | -- |
| Anthony Pritchard | 174 | 4 | 8 | 10 | 2 |
| Stephen Paschall | 150 | -- | -- | -- | -- |
| Samuel Potts | 190 | -- | -- | -- | -- |
| Joseph Randle | 235 | 4 | 4 | 10 | -- |

## Charles Town

| | Acres | Horses | Cattle | Sheep | Servants |
|---|---|---|---|---|---|
| Nicholas Riffitt | 100 | 2 | 4 | 8 | 1 |
| Thomas Robinson | 250 | 2 | 2 | 5 | 1 |
| Thomas Roberts, Sen'r | 120 | -- | -- | -- | -- |
| Tho's Roberts, Jun'r | 150 | 4 | 4 | 3 | -- |
| Joseph Starr, Sen'r | 100 | 4 | 9 | 7 | -- |
| Joseph Starr, Jun'r | 100 | 2 | 3 | 6 | -- |
| Jacob Stickle | 400 | 5 | 4 | -- | -- |
| Martin Shinholt | 100 | 2 | 3 | 3 | -- |
| Jost Smith, blacksmith | 100 | 2 | 2 | -- | -- |
| George Scoffield, taylor | -- | 1 | 1 | -- | -- |
| Christopher Stickle | 250 | 1 | 2 | -- | 1 |
| Henry Sheiffer | 50 | 1 | 2 | -- | -- |
| Andrew Turk | 235 | 3 | 4 | 3 | -- |
| John Thomas, W. | 150 | 2 | 2 | 4 | -- |
| John Thomas, R.M. | 190 | 2 | 3 | 8 | -- |
| Mary Thomas | 100 | 2 | 2 | 5 | 2 |
| Ann Tomkin | -- | 1 | 1 | -- | 1 |
| John Varley | 180 | 2 | 3 | 3 | -- |
| James Thomas | 245 | 3 | 3 | 9 | -- |
| Bernard Vanhorn | 187 | 4 | 3 | -- | -- |
| Abraham Welts | 200 | 1 | 3 | 6 | -- |
| Isaac Wayne | 198 | -- | -- | -- | -- |
| Bastian Waggoner | 300 | 4 | 5 | 10 | 1 |
| Joseph William | 105 | 3 | 3 | 2 | -- |
| John White | 200 | -- | -- | -- | 1 |
| Jonathan Wells | 147 | 2 | 4 | 2 | -- |
| James William | 100 | 2 | 1 | 6 | 1 |
| John William | 200 | 1 | 1 | 2 | -- |
| Dan'l Wilson | 85 | 2 | 1 | -- | -- |
| John Youngblood, shoemaker | 27 | 1 | 1 | -- | -- |
| Thomas William | 106 | 2 | 2 | 3 | -- |
| John Humphreys, tanyard | -- | 1 | -- | -- | -- |

Freemen

John Arskine
Jacob Bookter
Thomas Beard
James Craven
Joseph Conrad
Zepheniah David
Alexander Dempsey
Adam Huffman
John John
Reese John
Hugh Loyd
Alexander McCallah
James Marshall
Francis McKay
John O'Neal
John Rogers
George Pean

Elisha Edwards
Roger Gelespy
Nicholas Grant
Christ'r Hulderman
Job Harvey
Jonat'n Humphreys
Joshua Humphreys
John Shintz
Robert Shepard
Tho's Thomas
James Waters
John William
Hugh William
James White
William White
John Harvey

## Inmates

Richard Darby
John Dwire
Amos Edwards
James Gardner
Andrew Hall
David John, Glandy
David Englis
William Johnson
Edward Jones
William Llewellin
Alexander Lindsey
Jacob Miller
Darby Murphy
Peter Mathers

William Palmer
Lewis Peirce
William Potts
Nicholas Peregrine
Thomas Riley
John Stuart
James Smith
Wyant Spiker
James Spotswood
William Turk
James William
David William
Thomas William
Richard White

## Birmingham Rate

| | Acres | Horses | Cattle | Sheep | Servants |
|---|---|---|---|---|---|
| Edward Brinton, Esq'r, g.m., s.m. | 525 | 5 | 10 | 18 | 1 |
| George Brinton | 180 | 5 | 6 | -- | 1 |
| Caleb Brinton | 260 | 5 | 13 | 20 | 1 |
| John Bennett | 200 | 4 | 4 | 6 | -- |
| Obadiah Bonsall | 100 | 3 | 4 | 6 | -- |
| Robert Chamberlain | 200 | 4 | 6 | 6 | -- |
| Emmor Chandler, blacksmith | 50 | 2 | 2 | -- | 1 |
| Thomas Chandler | 60 | 3 | 5 | 11 | -- |
| James Chandler, labourer | 100 | 3 | 1 | 5 | -- |
| John Cry, labourer | 200 | 2 | 2 | -- | -- |
| Thomas Chalfant, cordwainer | 40 | 1 | 1 | -- | -- |
| Martha Chalfant | 60 | -- | -- | -- | -- |
| James Dilworth | 500 | 5 | 8 | 12 | 2 |
| Abraham Darlington | 200 | 1 | 5 | -- | 1 |
| Abrah'm Darlington, Jun'r | 100 | 5 | 3 | 12 | -- |
| Nathan Frame, shoemaker | 40 | 2 | 2 | 4 | -- |
| George Gilpin, s.m. | 280 | 4 | 4 | 5 | -- |
| William Gibbons | 25 | -- | -- | -- | -- |
| Harry Gordon, Esq'r, s.m. | 200 | 6 | 2 | 6 | 2 |
| Gideon Gilpin | 178 | 4 | 6 | 8 | 1 |
| Robert Green | 80 | 2 | 2 | 4 | -- |
| Amos House, chairmaker | 100 | 4 | 5 | 15 | 1 |
| Thomas Hall, farmer | 120 | 2 | 4 | 6 | -- |
| Thomas Hannum | 200 | 1 | 3 | 10 | -- |
| William Harvey | 150 | 2 | 3 | -- | -- |
| John Henderson, weaver | 100 | 2 | 2 | -- | -- |
| William Jones, tavern, t.k. | 260 | 5 | 7 | 12 | -- |
| William Kerlin, tavern, t.k. | 300 | 4 | 10 | 10 | -- |
| John Kimbler | 150 | 3 | 6 | 4 | -- |
| Rob't Mc'leHoe | 67 | 2 | 2 | 3 | -- |
| Robert Mercer | 50 | 1 | 1 | 3 | -- |
| Elias Neal, joyner | 25 | 1 | 1 | -- | -- |
| Joseph Peirce, tanner | 117 | 2 | 4 | -- | -- |
| John Pyle, tanner | 140 | 2 | 2 | -- | -- |

| Birmingham | Acres | Horses | Cattle | Sheep | Servants |
|---|---|---|---|---|---|
| Sarah Painter | 12 | -- | 2 | -- | -- |
| James Russell | 100 | 3 | 2 | 6 | -- |
| Benj'n Ring, f.m., s.m., fuller | 140 | 3 | 6 | 12 | 1 |
| Nathaniel Ring | 130 | 3 | 2 | 6 | -- |
| James Smith | 100 | 2 | 3 | -- | -- |
| Christian & Frederick Starker, farmer | 150 | 3 | 2 | 6 | -- |
| Will'm Smith | 100 | -- | -- | -- | -- |
| Will'm Simonson | 50 | 2 | -- | -- | 1 |
| Edward Simonson | 100 | 1 | -- | -- | -- |
| William Seal | 175 | 4 | 5 | 10 | -- |
| John Thatcher, shoemaker | 50 | 2 | 2 | -- | -- |
| Jno. Underwood, taylor | 70 | 1 | 2 | -- | -- |
| John Woodward | 100 | -- | -- | -- | -- |
| Matthew Warson | 150 | 3 | 2 | 8 | -- |

Inmates

Cha's Dilworth
Rich'd Stroud
David Brinton
Wm. Dilworth
Benj'n Hawley
Sam'l Way
Paul Selcus
George Martin
Joseph James
John Rowles
John Harper

John Barefield
Wm. Chapman
Simon Christie
John Hook
Peter Glansey
David Waddle
Isaac Barry
James Porter
John Gordon
Isaac Strode

Freemen

David May
George Solsus
Jonathan Thatcher
Aron Duncin
Will Jones, Jun'r

John Frame
Tho's Strode
John Mote
Joseph Port

London Britain Rate

| | Acres | Horses | Cattle | Sheep | Servants |
|---|---|---|---|---|---|
| Will'm Alexander | 60 | 2 | 3 | 5 | -- |
| Charles Black | 250 | 4 | 4 | 12 | 2 |
| John Bruton | 50 | 2 | 3 | 3 | -- |
| James Crawford | 100 | 2 | 3 | 6 | -- |
| Catherine Crawford | 100 | 2 | 2 | 4 | -- |
| Moses Crow | 100 | 2 | 3 | 6 | -- |
| John Chambers | 100 | -- | -- | -- | -- |
| Sam'l Eakins | 70 | 2 | 1 | -- | -- |
| Evan Evans, s.m., f.m. | 250 | 5 | 8 | 15 | 2 |
| Charles Hughes | 200 | 3 | 4 | 8 | 1 |

London Britain

| | Acres | Horses | Cattle | Sheep | Servants |
|---|---|---|---|---|---|
| Will'm Hutcheson, labourer | 50 | -- | 1 | -- | -- |
| James Kennedy | 250 | 4 | 6 | 20 | 1 |
| Tho's Lunn | 156 | 2 | 2 | -- | -- |
| Murtough Menough | 30 | 2 | 2 | 3 | -- |
| And'w McClelland | 60 | 2 | 2 | 3 | -- |
| Joshua McDowel | 150 | 2 | 4 | 8 | 1 |
| Tho's Morgan | 100 | 2 | 2 | -- | -- |
| John Miller | -- | 4 | 2 | 5 | 1 |
| Tho's Oram | 100 | 2 | 3 | 6 | -- |
| Rees Price | 100 | 3 | 5 | 6 | -- |
| John Ross | 60 | 2 | 2 | 4 | -- |
| Stephen Parr | 100 | 3 | 2 | 4 | 1 |
| Jam's Reed | 100 | 2 | 4 | 7 | -- |
| Morris Thomas | 100 | 2 | 2 | 10 | -- |
| James Taylor | 80 | 2 | 2 | 6 | -- |
| James Willson | 160 | 2 | 1 | 6 | -- |
| John Whitton | 200 | 3 | 2 | 10 | 1 |
| John Williams | 100 | 3 | 3 | 8 | -- |
| Benja. Whitton | 100 | 2 | 4 | 6 | 1 |
| Isaac Johnston | 100 | 2 | 4 | 8 | -- |
| John Alexander | 43 | -- | -- | -- | -- |
| John Jordan, shoemaker | -- | 1 | 1 | -- | -- |
| John Porter | 100 | 2 | 4 | 5 | -- |

N. B. the Several Names following is Below ye Line & therefore makes no return but Taken from ye Old Book ye transcript

Sterret Gray
Tho's Singleton
John Whan
John Rankin
Joseph Ralston
William Scott
Wm. Fryer

Rob't Sergeant
George Crow
Tho's Jordan
John Reed
Hugh McGregor
Moses Scott

Freemen

Hugh Smith
Joseph Scott
Wm. Kennedy
Wm. Scott
Jam's Taylor
David Rogers
John Connelly
Sam'l Porter

Adam Dinsmore
Tho's Scott
Alex'r Rankin
Moses Scott
Wm. Reed
Sam'l McGregor
Tho's Johnson
Jam's Johnson

Inmates

Dan'l Cuney
Tho's Jordan
James Alexander
Edward Styatt

William Giffen
William Spear
Patrick Kalahan

## London Grove Rate

| | Acres | Horses | Cattle | Sheep | Servants |
|---|---|---|---|---|---|
| Elizabeth Anderson | 60 | -- | -- | -- | -- |
| John Allen, as Guardian for Children, g.m. | 200 | 2 | 2 | 6 | -- |
| Joseph Allen, blacksmith | 120 | 2 | 2 | 6 | -- |
| Wm. Arthur | 100 | 2 | 2 | -- | -- |
| Sam'l Alexander, tavern, t.k. | 200 | 3 | 4 | 5 | -- |
| Rob't Baldwin | 100 | 2 | 2 | -- | -- |
| Joseph Baldwin | 120 | 1 | 1 | -- | -- |
| Cha's Booth | 88 | 2 | 3 | 5 | -- |
| Stephen Cook, f.m. | 150 | 1 | 3 | 6 | -- |
| Wm. Chandler | 150 | 2 | 4 | 8 | -- |
| John Culbertson | 220 | 4 | 4 | 6 | 1 |
| Mathew Shields, g.m., miller | 30 | 1 | 2 | -- | -- |
| Edw'd Crooks | 100 | 2 | 2 | -- | 1 |
| Rebecca Cook | 100 | -- | -- | -- | -- |
| Rob't Cain | 150 | 3 | 2 | 6 | -- |
| Will'm Clinton | 87 | 2 | 1 | -- | -- |
| And'w Caldwell | 100 | -- | -- | -- | -- |
| David England, joyner | 100 | 2 | 2 | 5 | -- |
| Rich'd Flower | 250 | 3 | 4 | 10 | -- |
| Moses Frazier | 150 | 2 | 2 | 6 | -- |
| Fra's Fosster | 157 | 1 | -- | -- | -- |
| Jam's Greenfield | 256 | 3 | 3 | 9 | -- |
| David Harlan, s.m. | 200 | 4 | 4 | 6 | 1 |
| Soloman Harlan | 200 | 2 | 2 | 7 | -- |
| Caleb Harlan | 200 | 3 | 3 | 3 | -- |
| Edward Henderson | 230 | 2 | 2 | 4 | -- |
| Cha's Holdman | 100 | 1 | 1 | 4 | -- |
| John Hindman | 100 | 2 | 4 | 10 | -- |
| Joseph Hobson | 33 | 1 | 1 | -- | -- |
| Will'm Jackson | 400 | 4 | 5 | 9 | -- |
| Joshua Jackson | 150 | 3 | 2 | 8 | -- |
| John Jackson, s.m., g.m. | 150 | 4 | 4 | 6 | 1 |
| Josiah Jackson | 100 | 1 | -- | -- | -- |
| Wm. Jones, spinning wheel maker | -- | 1 | 1 | -- | -- |
| Rich'd Jacobs, tavern, t.k. | 130 | 2 | 2 | -- | -- |
| Jam's Kelton | 190 | 2 | 2 | 2 | -- |
| Ed. Kirkpatrick, weaver | -- | -- | 1 | -- | -- |
| Jonathan Linley | 200 | 3 | 4 | -- | -- |
| Hugh Larman | 100 | 2 | 3 | -- | -- |
| Margret Linsfield | 60 | 1 | 2 | -- | -- |
| Fra's Lambourn, sadler | 95 | 2 | 2 | 6 | -- |
| Josiah Lambourn | 70 | 2 | 3 | 6 | -- |
| Tho's Lambourn, tanyard, tanner | 22 | 2 | 1 | -- | -- |
| Lodowick Lemart | 100 | 2 | 3 | 4 | -- |
| Sam'l Morton, millwright | 90 | -- | -- | -- | -- |
| Wm. Morton | 100 | 1 | 2 | 3 | -- |
| Tho's Morton | 100 | 2 | 2 | 5 | -- |
| Joseph Mull | 100 | 1 | 1 | 4 | -- |
| Joseph Moor, g.m., miller | 55 | 1 | 2 | 6 | -- |
| David Matthews | 200 | 2 | -- | -- | -- |
| Sam'l Moor | 200 | 3 | 3 | 5 | -- |
| John Norris, tinker | 120 | 1 | 1 | -- | -- |
| Nath'l Penock | 380 | -- | -- | -- | -- |

| London Grove | Acres | Horses | Cattle | Sheep | Servants |
|---|---|---|---|---|---|
| Joshua Pusey, g.m., miller | 165 | 3 | 8 | 10 | -- |
| John Pusey | 200 | 2 | 3 | 8 | -- |
| John Reed | 200 | -- | -- | -- | -- |
| John Ross | 120 | 3 | 3 | 6 | -- |
| Joseph Shields | 90 | 2 | 2 | 6 | -- |
| John Swan | 80 | 2 | 3 | 3 | -- |
| Hugh Speakman | 170 | 2 | 2 | 6 | -- |
| Jonathan Swayne | 150 | 1 | 1 | 2 | -- |
| Alex'r Starr | 200 | 1 | 3 | 6 | -- |
| Sam'l Sharp | 250 | 3 | 4 | 9 | -- |
| Jno. Williamson | 163 | 2 | 2 | 5 | -- |
| Sam'l Wilson | 100 | -- | 1 | -- | -- |
| Tho's Woodward | 50 | -- | -- | -- | -- |
| Nath'l Wollis | 90 | 1 | -- | -- | -- |
| John Waugh | 130 | 1 | 1 | -- | 1 |
| Wm. Wood, f.m. | 300 | 2 | 4 | 6 | -- |
| David Wiley | 160 | 3 | 4 | 10 | -- |

Inmates

Benjamin Allen         Jam's Ray
Robert Allen           Jno. Matthews
Nehemiah Hatton        Tho's Underwood
John Marshall          John Baldwin
Stephen Harlan         John Russell
Patrick Burns

Freemen

John Bartley           Michael Harlan
John Shields           Wm. Johnson
James Moor             George Whipo
Moses Chandler         Sam'l Withers
Peter Wilson           Jeremy Underwood
Henry Chalton          John Dickey
Patrick Louge          Dennis McConnel
John England           John Ward
Samuel Crumpton        John Wilson
Samuel Warton          Francis Carson
Henry Harlan           Alex'r Walker

East Marlborough Rate

| | Acres | Horses | Cattle | Sheep | Servants |
|---|---|---|---|---|---|
| Jam's Allen | 350 | 4 | 12 | 12 | -- |
| Edw'd Bennet | 200 | 4 | 4 | 6 | -- |
| Joel Bailey | 195 | 4 | 5 | 10 | -- |
| Isaac Bailey | 160 | 2 | 5 | 10 | -- |
| William Bailey | 260 | 4 | 4 | 8 | -- |
| John Bratton | 80 | 2 | 3 | 4 | -- |
| Caleb Baily | 200 | 3 | 3 | 6 | -- |

| East Marlborough | Acres | Horses | Cattle | Sheep | Servants |
|---|---|---|---|---|---|
| Sam'l Beverly | 10 | 1 | 1 | -- | -- |
| Moses McGomery, storekeeper | 20 | 1 | 1 | -- | -- |
| Wm. Cloud | 200 | 4 | 6 | 8 | -- |
| Abner Cloud, g.m., miller | 170 | 4 | 8 | 3 | -- |
| Mordica Cloud, g.m., s.m., miller | 350 | 5 | -- | 15 | -- |
| Tho's Carrington | 100 | 3 | 4 | 10 | -- |
| John Calvert | 50 | 1 | -- | -- | -- |
| John Chandler | 23 | 1 | 1 | -- | -- |
| Jeremy Cloud | 35 | -- | -- | -- | -- |
| John Taylor | 195 | 2 | 1 | -- | -- |
| Timothy Cavenaugh | 12 | 1 | -- | -- | -- |
| John Doudall | 25 | 2 | 1 | -- | -- |
| Will'm Harry | 150 | 3 | 2 | -- | -- |
| Mordica Hayes | 96 | 1 | 5 | 5 | -- |
| Samuel Hayes | 177 | 3 | 7 | -- | -- |
| James Marsh | 177 | 4 | 3 | 10 | -- |
| Caleb Johnson, g.m., s.m., miller | 200 | 3 | 4 | 12 | -- |
| John Jackson | 330 | 4 | 4 | 6 | -- |
| Joseph Pearson, weaver | 10 | 1 | 2 | -- | -- |
| Rob't Gaff, labourer | 30 | -- | 1 | -- | -- |
| Jonathan Jackson | 177 | 3 | 4 | 8 | -- |
| Sam'l Jefferis | 80 | 3 | 3 | -- | -- |
| Geo'e Jackson | 15 | 2 | 2 | 4 | -- |
| John Martin | 290 | 4 | 4 | 8 | -- |
| Caleb Jackson | -- | -- | -- | -- | -- |
| Benj'n Leonard, shoemaker | 15 | -- | 1 | -- | -- |
| Jonathan Morris, physician | 75 | 3 | 2 | -- | 1 |
| Daniel Mercer | 300 | 3 | 4 | 5 | -- |
| John Bartly, labourer | 30 | -- | 1 | -- | -- |
| James McMaster | 30 | 2 | 2 | 4 | -- |
| Henry Neal | 140 | 3 | 3 | 6 | -- |
| Moses Penock | 360 | 4 | 4 | 22 | 1 |
| Joseph Penock, malt house, malster | 280 | 4 | 4 | 10 | 1 |
| Thomas Pusey | 230 | 2 | 5 | 10 | -- |
| Joshua Peirce, s.m. | 170 | 3 | 4 | 10 | -- |
| Caleb Peirce | 250 | 4 | 5 | 14 | -- |
| Isaac Peirce, s.m. | 250 | 2 | 3 | 5 | -- |
| David Pusey, wheelwright | 140 | 2 | 2 | 4 | -- |
| Mich'l Pepper | 30 | 2 | 2 | -- | -- |
| Joseph Pyle | 220 | 3 | 4 | 6 | 1 |
| Will'm Swayne, tanyard | 185 | 3 | 5 | 6 | -- |
| Sam'l Swayne | 91 | 2 | 3 | 4 | -- |
| Isaa. Swayne | 200 | 3 | 3 | 5 | -- |
| And'w Shiverly | 150 | 2 | 2 | 4 | -- |
| Tho's Sugar, spinning wheeler | 40 | 2 | 2 | -- | -- |
| Jacob Taggart | 200 | 3 | 3 | 6 | -- |
| Mordica Vernon | 100 | 3 | 3 | 5 | -- |
| Jesse Jackson | 180 | 2 | 3 | 3 | -- |
| Fra's Windle | 160 | 4 | 4 | 6 | -- |
| John Webster, sadler | 186 | 3 | 5 | -- | -- |
| Tho's Newman | -- | 2 | -- | -- | -- |
| Jam's Wickersham | 100 | 2 | 4 | 8 | -- |

East Marlborough

| | Acres | Horses | Cattle | Sheep | Servants |
|---|---|---|---|---|---|
| Jacob Wright | 170 | 4 | 5 | 5 | 1 |
| Tho's Woodward, suveyor | 41 | 3 | 3 | -- | 1 |
| Tho's Welsh | 75 | -- | -- | -- | -- |
| Will'm Windle | 50 | 3 | 3 | 5 | -- |
| Enoch Wickersham, joyner | 100 | 1 | -- | -- | -- |
| Wm. Williams | 150 | 2 | 4 | 4 | -- |
| John Wilson, blacksmith | 100 | 2 | 4 | 6 | -- |
| Nayle Woodward | 177 | 4 | 3 | 6 | -- |
| Tho's Preston | -- | 1 | -- | -- | -- |
| Alex'r Skelton, shoemaker | -- | 1 | 1 | -- | -- |
| Isaac Chalfant, cooper | -- | -- | 1 | -- | -- |
| Will'm Brown, hatter | 60 | 1 | 1 | -- | -- |
| Tho's McFaddin | -- | -- | 1 | -- | -- |
| Abel Wickersham, blacksmith | -- | -- | 1 | -- | -- |
| John Jones, stiller | -- | -- | 1 | -- | -- |
| Rob't Story, weaver | -- | -- | 1 | -- | -- |
| Solomon Mercer | 50 | 3 | 1 | -- | -- |
| Sam'l White | 25 | -- | 1 | -- | -- |
| Nath'l Keetch | -- | -- | -- | -- | -- |
| Sam'l Keetch | -- | -- | -- | -- | -- |
| John McNeil, weaver | 25 | -- | 1 | -- | -- |

Inmates

David Echuff
Nicolas Moor
Silas Harry
James Thomson

John McCormack
Wm. Neal
Joseph Anderson
Christopher Rix

Freemen

Jam's Wickersham
Jesse Wickersham
Joel Cloud
Jno. Williamson
Jesse Cloud
Wm. Allen
Nathan Baily
Jno. McDade
Cha's Diblin
John Windle

John Witcraft
Wm. Swayne
Jonathan Brown
Cornelius McConaway
Jam's Hardy
Jesse Swayne
Rich'd Trouton
Rob't Fletcher
Joseph Norman
Dan'l Colbert

West Bradford Rate

| | Acres | Horses | Cattle | Sheep | Servants |
|---|---|---|---|---|---|
| Sarah Arnol | 30 | 1 | 1 | -- | -- |
| Rich'd Baker | 212 | 4 | 5 | 2 | 1 |
| John Batton | 130 | 5 | 3 | -- | -- |
| John Buffington | 200 | 4 | 4 | 7 | -- |
| Jam's Brown | 160 | 2 | 3 | 6 | -- |
| Joel Bailey | 130 | 4 | 3 | 8 | -- |

| West Bradford | Acres | Horses | Cattle | Sheep | Servants |
|---|---|---|---|---|---|
| Rob't Buffington | 136 | 3 | 2 | 3 | -- |
| Will'm Buffington | 300 | 4 | 4 | 10 | -- |
| Jam's Bane, weaver | 90 | 2 | 1 | 4 | -- |
| Jno. Bane | 90 | -- | -- | -- | -- |
| Rich'd Buffington | 139 | 4 | 3 | 6 | -- |
| James Bruce, weavery | 200 | 3 | 4 | 10 | -- |
| John Chalfant | 200 | 3 | 2 | -- | -- |
| Joshua Clayton, cooper | 160 | 3 | 3 | 8 | -- |
| Will'm Clayton, smith | 97 | 2 | 2 | 2 | -- |
| Will'm Clark | 120 | 3 | 4 | 10 | -- |
| Wm. Cooper, f.m., fuller | 100 | 2 | 2 | -- | -- |
| Jam's Chalfant | 170 | 3 | 2 | 4 | -- |
| John Clayton, weaver | 50 | 2 | 2 | 1 | -- |
| Jno. Carpenter | 200 | 2 | 6 | 10 | -- |
| Rich'd Downing | 70 | -- | -- | -- | -- |
| Abraham Ford | 110 | 3 | 3 | 4 | -- |
| John Ford | 65 | 1 | 1 | -- | -- |
| Abel Griffith | 218 | 1 | -- | -- | -- |
| Tho's Gheen | 200 | -- | -- | -- | -- |
| Wm. Woodward | 282 | 2 | 2 | 4 | -- |
| Stephen Harlan | 307 | 5 | 8 | -- | -- |
| Joseph Hawley, taylor | 50 | 1 | 1 | -- | -- |
| Jno. Hannums, in Trust for Taylors | 85 | -- | -- | -- | -- |
| Tho's Rossiter | 100 | -- | -- | -- | -- |
| Benj'n Jefferis | 113 | 2 | 2 | -- | -- |
| John Jackson | 130 | 1 | 1 | 6 | -- |
| Eliz'th Ligott | 260 | 3 | 4 | 6 | -- |
| Hump'y Marshall, g.m., s.m., dealer in meal | 333 | 4 | 15 | 18 | 1 |
| Jam's Marshall, shopkeeper, surveyor | 125 | 4 | 4 | 4 | -- |
| John Marshall | 200 | 3 | 3 | 6 | -- |
| Joseph Martin, tavern, t.k. | -- | 1 | 2 | 6 | -- |
| James Milleson | 150 | 2 | 3 | 3 | -- |
| Isaac Marshall | 160 | 5 | 3 | -- | -- |
| John McCormack | 200 | 2 | 2 | -- | -- |
| Cornelius McGuire | 260 | 2 | 2 | -- | -- |
| Will'm Ball | 65 | -- | -- | -- | -- |
| George Martin, Jun'r | 160 | 3 | 3 | 6 | -- |
| Caleb Martin | 194 | 3 | 3 | 6 | -- |
| George Martin | 70 | 1 | 1 | 6 | -- |
| Sam'l Marshall | 180 | 2 | -- | 16 | -- |
| Cha's Norris' heirs | 75 | -- | -- | -- | -- |
| John Powell | 200 | 2 | 2 | -- | -- |
| Wm. Pyle | 150 | 2 | 2 | -- | -- |
| Jam's Ramsey | 80 | 2 | 2 | -- | -- |
| Sam'l Sellers, weaver | 200 | 2 | 3 | 6 | -- |
| Tho's Sheward | 298 | 4 | 5 | 10 | -- |
| Geo'e Stalker | 100 | 3 | 4 | 6 | -- |
| James Trimble, g.m., s.m., miller | 90 | 3 | 5 | -- | -- |
| John Thompson, blacksmith | 30 | -- | 1 | -- | -- |
| Rich'd Townsend | 234 | 2 | 1 | -- | -- |
| Rob't Thornton | 83 | -- | -- | -- | -- |

| West Bradford | Acres | Horses | Cattle | Sheep | Servants |
|---|---|---|---|---|---|
| Sam'l Thornton | 40 | 1 | 1 | -- | -- |
| Sam'l Worth | 503 | 5 | 5 | 8 | -- |
| Wm. Woodward | 160 | 3 | 6 | 15 | -- |
| Joseph Woodward | 95 | 2 | 2 | -- | -- |
| John Woodward | 200 | 4 | 5 | 15 | -- |
| Wm. Woodward, carp'r | 75 | 2 | 2 | -- | -- |
| Robert Wilson | 150 | 2 | 2 | 6 | -- |
| Jam's Woodward | 112 | -- | -- | -- | -- |
| Rob't Woodward | 50 | 1 | 1 | -- | -- |
| James Woodward | 70 | 1 | -- | -- | -- |
| John Young | 260 | 3 | 5 | 3 | -- |
| Arch'd Young | 240 | 1 | 1 | -- | -- |
| Ed. Bartholomew | 166 | -- | -- | -- | -- |
| John Powell | -- | 2 | 1 | 3 | -- |
| David Powell, labourer | -- | 1 | 1 | -- | -- |
| Will'm Boys, labourer | -- | 2 | 1 | -- | -- |
| Geo'e Fisher | -- | -- | -- | -- | -- |

### Freemen

| | |
|---|---|
| Tho's Baldwin | James Trimble |
| Curtis Buffington | Tho's Brown |
| Jno. Whippo | Jno. Headdin |
| James Pyle | Arc'd Young |
| John Pyle | Rob't Gilfellin |
| David Erwin | Absolam Wall |
| Rob't Chalfant | Joseph Gheen |
| Henry McIntire | Rob't Hindman |
| Benj'n McGloughlen | John Worth |
| Rich'd Buffington | John Weston |
| Wm. Lassley | Isaac Speckman |

### Inmates

| | |
|---|---|
| Wm. Clark, Jun'r | Joseph Thornborough |
| Hugh Crawford | Richard Wilson |
| John Clark | William Wilson |
| John Cremer | Francis Wallace |
| Geo'e Fosset | William White |
| Joshua Woodrow | John Underhill |
| James Furey | William Thornborough |
| Henry Hollis | Joseph Clark |
| Wm. Keetch | Wm. Hoops |
| Patrick McCurty | Samuel Hunt |
| Rob't McIntire | Peter Hunt |
| Geo'e Martin, tanner | R'd Downing |
| Peter O'Daniel | John Downing |
| James Reiley | Rob't Taylor |
| Will'm Stephens | John McCullack |
| Sam'l Sellers, Jun'r | James McMasters |

## West Nantmill Rate

| | Acres | Horses | Cattle | Sheep | Servants |
|---|---|---|---|---|---|
| James McCroskey, tavern, innkeeper | 250 | 4 | 5 | 15 | -- |
| Rob't Starrat | 200 | 1 | 1 | -- | -- |
| Will'm Rolston | 100 | -- | -- | -- | -- |
| John Gardner | 250 | 4 | 6 | 20 | -- |
| Joseph Karr | 150 | 3 | 4 | 6 | 1 |
| James Karr | 100 | 2 | 3 | -- | -- |
| William Sheerer | 150 | 3 | 6 | 2 | -- |
| John Thompson, carpenter | 100 | 3 | 1 | 5 | -- |
| Arthur Graham | 100 | 1 | 1 | -- | -- |
| Jane Graham | 150 | 1 | -- | -- | -- |
| Adam Gattrey, shoemaker | 100 | -- | -- | -- | -- |
| Robert Matthews | 120 | -- | -- | -- | -- |
| Andrew Cristie | 120 | 3 | 3 | 8 | -- |
| Joseph Martin | 89 | 2 | 2 | 6 | -- |
| Robert Lask | 150 | 3 | 3 | 12 | -- |
| Michael Graham | 200 | 4 | 6 | 6 | -- |
| James Hannah | 200 | 3 | 4 | 10 | -- |
| Samuel Cunningham, carpenter | 100 | 2 | 1 | 6 | -- |
| Jason Cloud, Jun'r | 200 | 3 | 3 | -- | 1 |
| James Hare | 100 | 2 | 4 | 6 | -- |
| George Irwin | 150 | 2 | 4 | 6 | -- |
| Jerrard Irwin | 80 | 1 | 4 | 10 | -- |
| John Irwin, s.m. | 25 | 1 | 3 | 4 | -- |
| Rob't Gilmore | 250 | 4 | 4 | 5 | -- |
| Jacob Miller, t.k. | 500 | 5 | 4 | 10 | -- |
| James Waddle | -- | 3 | 3 | -- | -- |
| Nathan Porter | 150 | 2 | 1 | 12 | -- |
| Will Porter | 150 | 4 | 4 | 12 | 1 |
| Joshua Cope | 100 | 2 | 2 | -- | -- |
| Tho's Elliott | 100 | -- | -- | -- | -- |
| Mary Brown | 100 | -- | 1 | -- | -- |
| John Lashey, g.m., miller | 80 | -- | -- | -- | -- |
| Evan Jenkins | 100 | 2 | 1 | -- | -- |
| Terence Conly | 150 | 2 | 2 | 6 | -- |
| Jacob Cambell | -- | -- | -- | -- | -- |
| James Skeen | 100 | 1 | 1 | 7 | -- |
| Jacob Pearsall | -- | 2 | 1 | -- | -- |
| Custin Fisher | 150 | -- | -- | -- | -- |
| James Graham | 310 | 4 | 4 | 10 | 1 |
| John Graham, tavern, t.k. | 100 | 1 | 1 | -- | -- |
| Samuel Buhannan | 120 | 2 | 2 | -- | -- |
| Mathew Buhannan | 120 | 4 | 2 | 10 | -- |
| And'w Buhannah | 120 | 3 | 3 | 6 | -- |
| Mathew Brown | 140 | 2 | 2 | -- | -- |
| Mathew Curry | 86 | 2 | 4 | 6 | -- |
| John Campbell | 150 | 3 | 4 | 5 | -- |
| Wm. Tregoe | 150 | 4 | 4 | 10 | -- |
| Sam'l Logan | 150 | 5 | 4 | 10 | -- |
| Dinah Pearsall | 100 | 1 | 1 | -- | -- |
| Jeremiah Pearsall, g.m., s.m., miller | 100 | 4 | 3 | -- | -- |
| Abel Griffith | 100 | 2 | 5 | 5 | -- |
| Wm. Ashton | 200 | 4 | 6 | 12 | -- |

| West Nantmill | Acres | Horses | Cattle | Sheep | Servants |
|---|---|---|---|---|---|
| Sam'l Allen | 150 | 2 | 3 | 6 | -- |
| John Henderson, blacksmith | 80 | 2 | 1 | 3 | -- |
| Fra's Alexander | 130 | 3 | 2 | 10 | -- |
| John Hambleton | 200 | 4 | 4 | 6 | -- |
| William Kennedy | 170 | 2 | 2 | 4 | -- |
| James Moor, g.m., s.m., miller | 125 | 4 | 4 | 12 | 1 |
| James Beaty | 170 | 3 | 4 | 12 | -- |
| John Starr | 40 | 2 | 3 | -- | -- |
| Henry Iddings | 80 | 2 | 2 | 5 | -- |
| Will'm Millekin | 50 | 2 | 1 | -- | -- |
| David McConaway | -- | -- | -- | -- | -- |
| Will'm Barr | -- | -- | -- | -- | -- |
| Sam'l Charlton | 50 | 1 | 1 | -- | -- |
| Will'm Bruce | 30 | 1 | 1 | -- | -- |
| John Brown | 210 | 2 | 2 | 6 | -- |
| Jam's McCochran | 200 | 2 | 2 | 6 | -- |
| Will'm Rogers | 100 | 4 | 4 | 6 | -- |
| Will'm Ferguson | 300 | 3 | 2 | 5 | -- |
| John Thompson, wheelwright | -- | 4 | 4 | 6 | -- |
| Rob't Wallace | 100 | 4 | 4 | 6 | -- |
| Guyan Wallace | 150 | 4 | 2 | 6 | -- |
| Isaac Wynn | 100 | 2 | 2 | 6 | -- |
| Paul McNight, tavern, t.k. | 150 | 4 | 2 | -- | -- |
| Alex'r Craig | 180 | 3 | 3 | -- | -- |
| Dan'l Henderson | 300 | 4 | 3 | 8 | 1 |
| Sam'l Henderson | 200 | 2 | 2 | 6 | -- |
| Jam's Scott | 300 | 3 | 3 | 6 | -- |
| Tho's Alford | 100 | 2 | 2 | 4 | -- |
| Tho's Kennedy | 100 | 3 | 3 | 8 | -- |
| James Hambleton | 200 | 4 | 4 | 10 | -- |
| Jam's Stanley | 200 | 4 | 2 | 5 | -- |
| Rob't McConaughy, s.m. | 1,000 | 6 | 4 | 12 | -- |
| John Jack | -- | 4 | 2 | 6 | --- |
| Wm. Kennedy | 90 | 2 | 2 | 4 | -- |
| Jacob Alexander | -- | 3 | 2 | 4 | -- |
| Sam'l Caruthers | 100 | 2 | 2 | -- | -- |
| John Mackey | 100 | 3 | 3 | 18 | -- |
| And'w Willson, Sen'r | 160 | 3 | 2 | 6 | -- |
| Joseph Long | 150 | 4 | 3 | 12 | 1 |
| James Willson | 150 | 4 | 3 | 10 | -- |
| And'w Wilson, Jun'r | 150 | 1 | -- | -- | 1 |
| And'w Spence, weaver | 130 | 2 | 3 | 5 | -- |
| Abra'm Pearsall | 200 | 4 | 3 | -- | -- |
| John Smith | 150 | 3 | 4 | 6 | -- |
| Ephraim Robinson, distiller | 150 | 2 | 2 | -- | -- |
| Thomas Boyle | 40 | 2 | 2 | 4 | -- |
| Mathew Robinson | 300 | 4 | 6 | 12 | -- |
| John Robinson, tan yard, tanner | 50 | 4 | 2 | -- | 1 |
| Will'm Dunwoddy | 270 | 4 | 6 | 10 | -- |
| Jam's Anderson | 100 | 2 | 5 | 8 | -- |
| John Starratt | 100 | 2 | 3 | 6 | -- |
| Will Logan | 500 | -- | -- | -- | -- |
| John Sook | -- | 3 | 4 | 2 | -- |
| Christian Winder | -- | 1 | 2 | -- | -- |
| John Phillips | 150 | 2 | 4 | -- | -- |

| West Nantmill | Acres | Horses | Cattle | Sheep | Servants |
|---|---|---|---|---|---|
| James Carswell | 100 | 4 | 5 | -- | -- |
| John Iddings | 97 | 2 | 4 | 6 | -- |
| John Moor, shoemaker | 120 | 3 | 3 | 5 | -- |
| Jacob Cosman | 93 | 1 | 2 | 2 | -- |
| Wm. Irwin | 150 | 3 | 4 | 10 | -- |
| Jacob Borgy | 100 | 2 | 2 | -- | -- |
| Jacob Cochran | 200 | 4 | 6 | 10 | 1 |
| Jam's Cochran | 100 | 2 | 1 | -- | -- |
| Rob't Brown | 150 | 2 | 3 | 10 | -- |
| Tho's Green | -- | -- | -- | -- | -- |
| Rob't Darlington, sadler | 100 | 2 | 3 | -- | -- |
| Sam'l McDuff, g.m., s.m. | 900 | 5 | 6 | 30 | 1 |
| John Strong, miller | 200 | 1 | 2 | 6 | -- |
| Jos'h Darlington, tanner, tanyard | 150 | 3 | 4 | 10 | 1 |
| John Dunwoddle | 250 | 4 | 5 | 10 | 1 |
| Arch'd Thompson | 30 | 1 | 1 | -- | -- |
| Peter Hunter | 370 | 3 | 3 | 13 | 1 |
| Dan'l Moore | 100 | 1 | 2 | 4 | -- |
| John Moore, Jun'r | 100 | 3 | 4 | 4 | -- |
| Will'm Gilkie | 150 | -- | -- | -- | -- |
| Ann Thomas | 100 | -- | -- | -- | -- |
| Joseph Tregoe | 150 | 4 | 5 | 4 | -- |
| Rich'd Pearsall | 350 | 3 | 4 | 8 | 1 |
| Isaac Gibson | 240 | 4 | 3 | 4 | -- |
| Francis Gardner | 300 | 5 | 5 | 20 | -- |
| Geo'e Hunter | 200 | -- | -- | -- | -- |
| James Starrett | 250 | 5 | 3 | 6 | 2 |

Freemen

John Millison
Mathew Bohanan
William Smith
Wm. Neally
Henry Graham
Fra's Wilson
Alex'r McClean
Jam's Currey
John Black
John Ward
Will'm Caldwell
Will'm Steal
Rob't Scott
Will'm Averett
Adam Hopman
William Gould
Alex'r Gould
Nathan Darling
Alex'r Wiley
Colin Spence
William Lowry
Joseph Carr
Hugh Wallace

Joseph Russel
William Dixson
Jam's Kerr
William Hill
Jam's Hillhouse
Alexander Martin
William Cunningham
John Early
Mark Cant
William Frame
Joseph Stretch
John Sommerfield
Robert Grey
Robert Robinson
Alexander Henderson
James Moore
James Kennedy
Jam's Garman
James Smith
James Hambleton
Rob't Dunwooddy
Rob't Barr

Inmates

Archabald Carson
Andrew Barr
John Wallace
James Lockard
John McGowen
Hambleton Gamble
William Waddle
John Hambleton
Samuel Christie
Gilbert Gray
John Gardner
David McConaughey
John Guttry
James Bighart
Cha's McKinley
William Bolling
John Bishop
Jacob Alexander
William Logan

Samuel Mountgomery
John McKetrick
Daniel McCurdy
William Robinson
William Donaldson
William Rogers
Thomas Forster
Thomas Hunter
James Porter
John Hannah
David Long
Will'm Wilson
Patrick McDermont
Isaac Nanny
Sam'l McCaskey
James Purvain
John Fulton
James Beverland

Oxford Rate

|  | Acres | Horses | Cattle | Sheep | Servants |
| --- | --- | --- | --- | --- | --- |
| Job Ruston, g.m. | 700 | 4 | 8 | 15 | 4 |
| John Hinkead | 100 | 2 | 2 | 5 | -- |
| Hugh Luckey | 245 | 2 | 2 | 5 | -- |
| Tho's Armstrong | 150 | 2 | 4 | 5 | -- |
| Wm. Pinkerton | 60 | 2 | 3 | -- | -- |
| Fra's Modrell, tavernkeeper | 20 | 2 | 2 | -- | -- |
| Rob't Poston | 90 | 2 | 2 | 5 | -- |
| Step'n Cornelius | 100 | 2 | 2 | 5 | -- |
| Wm. Ross | 60 | 2 | 2 | 5 | -- |
| Wm. Donoughy | 50 | 1 | 1 | -- | -- |
| Wm. Breeden | 32 | 1 | 1 | -- | -- |
| Will'm Edmunston | 60 | 1 | 2 | -- | -- |
| Andrew Walker | 100 | 2 | 2 | 8 | -- |
| Arch'd Fowles | 15 | 1 | 1 | -- | -- |
| Rob't Hogg | 50 | 1 | 1 | -- | -- |
| Will'm Huett | 50 | 2 | 2 | 5 | -- |
| Wm. Hopkins | 50 | 1 | 1 | -- | -- |
| James Criswell | 80 | 1 | 2 |  |  |
| Isabel Gui | 80 | 1 | 1 | -- | -- |
| Robert Cammel | 60 | 1 | 1 | -- | -- |
| Will'm Robb | 70 | 2 | 2 | 5 | -- |
| Sam'l Robb | 20 | 1 | 1 | -- | -- |
| Andrew Richie | 100 | 2 | 2 | 5 | -- |
| Thomas Cloyd | 60 | 2 | 2 | -- | -- |
| Robert Criswell | 200 | 3 | 3 | 8 | -- |
| Jam's Boyde | 180 | 2 | 2 | 5 | -- |
| James Fleming | 100 | 2 | 2 | -- | -- |
| William Glen | 30 | 1 | 1 | -- | -- |
| Hugh Miller | 100 | 2 | 2 | -- | -- |
| Hugh Russell | 120 | 2 | 2 | -- | -- |

| Oxford | Acres | Horses | Cattle | Sheep | Servants |
|---|---|---|---|---|---|
| Thomas White | 50 | 1 | 1 | -- | -- |
| John Wallace | 75 | 1 | 1 | -- | -- |
| John White | 120 | 2 | 2 | 5 | -- |
| Jno. McClenichen, tavernkeeper, tavern | 100 | 2 | 3 | 5 | -- |
| John Culbreath | 100 | -- | -- | -- | -- |
| George Churchman | 200 | -- | -- | -- | -- |
| Catherine Torbert | 100 | 2 | 2 | 5 | -- |
| Arch'd Tagart, labourer | 70 | 1 | 1 | -- | -- |
| David Fleming | 200 | 2 | 2 | 5 | -- |
| Rachel Jorden, g.m. | 100 | 3 | 4 | 8 | -- |
| James Kennedy | 40 | 1 | 2 | -- | -- |
| Will'm Bunting, g.m. | 300 | 3 | 3 | 10 | -- |
| David Drew | 50 | 1 | -- | -- | -- |
| Samuel McNeal | 200 | 2 | 2 | 6 | -- |
| Adam Cooper | 100 | 2 | 2 | 5 | -- |
| Thomas Cooper | 100 | 1 | 1 | -- | -- |
| John Grey | 60 | 2 | 2 | 5 | -- |
| John Black | 100 | 3 | 3 | 6 | -- |
| John Ross | 200 | 2 | 2 | 8 | -- |
| Will'm Woods | 40 | 1 | 1 | -- | -- |
| George McColough | 80 | 2 | 2 | 8 | -- |
| George Cruswell | 60 | 1 | 2 | -- | -- |
| Wm. Ligett | 40 | 1 | 1 | 5 | -- |
| Tho's Barrett | 10 | 1 | 1 | -- | -- |
| Robert Smith | 200 | 2 | 2 | 7 | -- |
| Jam's Dysart | 100 | 2 | 3 | -- | -- |
| Arthur McKiscock | 40 | 2 | 2 | -- | -- |
| Wm. Disart | 40 | 2 | 1 | -- | -- |
| John Smith | 100 | 1 | 2 | -- | -- |
| James Simpson | 100 | 2 | 1 | -- | -- |
| Hugh Tarbet | 100 | 1 | 2 | 5 | -- |
| Will'm Porter | 100 | 2 | 2 | -- | -- |
| David Hayes | 100 | 2 | 2 | 5 | -- |
| Allen Simson | 100 | 2 | 2 | -- | -- |
| Rob't Law | 40 | 2 | 2 | 8 | -- |
| John Wallace | 30 | 1 | 1 | -- | -- |
| Thomas Wallace | 100 | 2 | 2 | -- | -- |
| John Gibson | 200 | 2 | 2 | 8 | -- |
| James Cooper | 100 | 2 | 3 | -- | -- |
| Thomas Cooper | 100 | | -- | -- | -- |
| Will Maxwell | 100 | 2 | 2 | 5 | -- |
| James Stockman | 100 | 2 | 2 | 6 | -- |
| Will'm Wilson | 100 | 2 | 3 | 5 | -- |
| Henry Ewing | 100 | 2 | 2 | 4 | -- |
| James Ewing | 50 | 2 | 1 | 2 | -- |
| David Watt | 200 | 2 | 3 | 5 | -- |
| John Steward | 100 | 2 | 3 | 5 | -- |
| John Gottry | 50 | 2 | 4 | 8 | -- |
| Samuel Jackson | 200 | 2 | 2 | -- | -- |
| Alex'r Ewing | 100 | 2 | 2 | 7 | -- |
| Sam'l Dicky | 100 | -- | -- | -- | -- |
| Will'm Carlisle | 100 | 2 | 2 | -- | -- |
| Tho's Mease | 100 | 2 | 2 | 5 | -- |
| James McDowel | 100 | 2 | 2 | 5 | -- |

| Oxford | Acres | Horses | Cattle | Sheep | Servants |
|---|---|---|---|---|---|
| John McKisock | 100 | 2 | 2 | 5 | -- |
| David Simson | 146 | 2 | 3 | 8 | -- |
| John Turner | 140 | 2 | 3 | -- | -- |
| James Turner | 100 | 2 | 2 | -- | -- |
| Walter Hood | 200 | 2 | 3 | 5 | 1 |
| John Smith, Sen'r | 200 | 2 | 3 | 9 | -- |
| Tho's Greer, labourer | 200 | 2 | 2 | -- | -- |
| Will'm Sterrett, labourer | 210 | 1 | 1 | -- | -- |
| Will'm Dickey | 100 | 2 | 2 | 5 | -- |
| William Lowry | 100 | 2 | 2 | 4 | -- |
| John Huston | 60 | 1 | 2 | -- | -- |

Inmates

John Fleming
Elijah Creswell
Robert Smith
John Porter
Sam'l Warnock
Rob't Walker
Rob't Munton
Robert Henderson
Will'm Moor
Jno. Parks
Henry Simpson
John Cooper

Isaac Rogers
James Harris
James Reed
Jno. McAlister
Samuel Criswell
Rob't Ralston
John Richey
Wm. Richey
Will'm Bailey
John McKusick
John Kithcart

Freemen

John Smith
James Morrison
Hance Fleming
William Geety
William Smith
William McCalister
John Pinkerton
Samuel Smith
Henry Ewing
James Guttry
Samuel Fulton
David Brown

James Liget
Hugh Bond
Alex'r Gibson
Jam's Lowry
Joseph Creswell
John Fleming
Alexander McNeal
James Bayley
George Munrow
Will'm Luckey
Arch'd Fleming

London Derry Rate

| | Acres | Horses | Cattle | Sheep | Servants |
|---|---|---|---|---|---|
| David Allen | 100 | 2 | 3 | 6 | -- |
| Josiah Allen, carpenter | 90 | 2 | 2 | 9 | -- |
| David Bohannan, blacksmith | 100 | 2 | 3 | 6 | -- |
| Francis Blair | 150 | 2 | 4 | 6 | -- |
| David Breicenridge | 80 | 2 | 2 | 2 | -- |
| Joseph Calvel | 150 | 2 | 3 | 8 | -- |

| London Derry | Acres | Horses | Cattle | Sheep | Servants |
|---|---|---|---|---|---|
| Thomas Charlton | 100 | 2 | 4 | 10 | 1 |
| John Carswell | 100 | 2 | 4 | 10 | -- |
| Alexander Cammel | 100 | 2 | 4 | 10 | -- |
| Wm. Crosby | 50 | 2 | 2 | 6 | -- |
| Samuel Crosby & Hugh Michel | 100 | 1 | -- | -- | -- |
| Samuel Carswell | 100 | 2 | 3 | 6 | -- |
| Sam'l Clelland | 100 | -- | -- | -- | -- |
| Sam'l Croos | 150 | 2 | 2 | 6 | -- |
| James Carswell | 130 | 2 | 3 | 7 | -- |
| Moses Correy | 90 | 2 | 1 | -- | -- |
| Will'm Cummens | 100 | 2 | 2 | 4 | -- |
| Jno. Flatcher | 50 | 2 | 1 | 4 | -- |
| Alex'r Fulton | 170 | 3 | 3 | 6 | 1 |
| John Donlay | 100 | 2 | 2 | 6 | -- |
| Will'm Grimes, s.m. | 250 | 3 | 3 | 10 | -- |
| Jam's Gilleland | 100 | 2 | 3 | 8 | -- |
| Joseph Hall | 140 | -- | -- | -- | -- |
| Will'm Hall, weaver | 100 | 1 | -- | -- | -- |
| Walter Hall | 100 | 2 | 2 | 6 | -- |
| Rob't Hucheson | 70 | 2 | 1 | -- | -- |
| Will'm Kerr | 200 | 2 | 4 | 10 | -- |
| David Kennedy | 200 | 4 | 6 | 9 | -- |
| Mondgory Kennedy | 150 | 3 | 3 | 4 | -- |
| David Kinkad | 160 | 2 | 3 | 8 | -- |
| James Law | 150 | 2 | 2 | 5 | 1 |
| Will'm Love | 150 | 2 | 2 | 3 | 1 |
| Will'm Mountgomery | 300 | 4 | 4 | 6 | 1 |
| Dan'l McClain | 100 | 2 | 2 | 5 | 1 |
| Jam's Mackey | 100 | 2 | 2 | -- | -- |
| Henry McAdams | 100 | 2 | 2 | 6 | -- |
| Tho's McGuire | 250 | 2 | 4 | 10 | -- |
| Fra's Modril | 90 | -- | -- | -- | -- |
| Elisha McClanahan | 100 | 2 | 3 | 6 | -- |
| John McClantick | 60 | 2 | 2 | 5 | -- |
| Will'm Mitchel | 100 | 2 | 2 | 5 | 1 |
| And'w Michel | 80 | 2 | -- | -- | -- |
| Joshua McCraken | 60 | 2 | 3 | 4 | -- |
| Tho's Mehaffey | 100 | 2 | 3 | 6 | -- |
| Mary Miller | 40 | 2 | 2 | -- | -- |
| Jno. Moss | 100 | -- | -- | -- | -- |
| Jno. McClair | 70 | 2 | 2 | 6 | 1 |
| Wm. Nail | 30 | 2 | 1 | 3 | -- |
| John Nuby | 150 | 1 | -- | -- | -- |
| David Ramsey | 100 | 2 | 9 | 6 | 2 |
| Sam'l Ramsey | 60 | 1 | 1 | 5 | -- |
| John Ramsey | 60 | 1 | 1 | 5 | -- |
| Mich'l Rowan | 100 | 2 | 2 | 4 | -- |
| John Richey | 120 | 2 | 3 | 6 | 1 |
| James Steel | 200 | 2 | 4 | 6 | -- |
| Martha Shields | 100 | 2 | 3 | 6 | -- |
| Rob't Slone, tavernkeeper | 140 | 2 | 3 | 6 | -- |
| Joseph Strawbridge | 130 | 2 | 2 | 6 | 1 |
| Tho's Strawbridge, tanner | 70 | 2 | 2 | 6 | 1 |
| Will'm Thompson, stiller | 20 | 2 | 1 | -- | -- |
| Ann Thompson | 60 | 2 | 2 | 2 | -- |

| London Derry | Acres | Horses | Cattle | Sheep | Servants |
|---|---|---|---|---|---|
| John Thompson | 100 | 1 | 2 | 3 | -- |
| Job Ward | 150 | 2 | 2 | 4 | -- |
| Will'm Wallace | 60 | 2 | 2 | 4 | -- |
| Jacob Woolson, taylor | 20 | 2 | 2 | 5 | -- |
| George Wallis | 50 | 2 | 2 | 4 | -- |
| Nath'l Walker | 100 | 2 | 2 | 6 | -- |
| John Wikersham, stiller | 100 | 3 | 4 | 4 | -- |
| Mathew Young | 60 | 2 | 2 | 6 | -- |
| Robert Paterson | 10 | 2 | 2 | -- | 1 |

### Freemen

| | |
|---|---|
| Walter Davis | Benj'n Croswell |
| Joseph Porter | John Widdas |
| James Strawbridge | Peter Blew |
| Thomas Thompson | Patrick Graham |
| George Brown | John Camble |
| David Richly | Ringen Steel |

### Inmates

| | |
|---|---|
| George Coughran | Jane Garbison |
| James McCrackin | Robert Arteer |
| Arch'd Hamble | Will'm Nugin |
| Alex'r McClery | Will'm Cummins |
| Alex'r Harrison | Rob't Graham |
| David Moor | John Mitchel |
| Thomas Hamors | George Matthews |
| Jam's Oghaltree | Patrick Obrian |

### West Fallowfield Rate

| | Acres | Horses | Cattle | Sheep | Servants |
|---|---|---|---|---|---|
| Arthur Park | 100 | 2 | 2 | 6 | -- |
| And'w Gibson, s.m., f.m. | 150 | 3 | 3 | 10 | -- |
| Arch'd Guy | 100 | -- | -- | -- | -- |
| And'w Noble | 100 | 1 | 1 | -- | -- |
| Alex'r Dunlap | 100 | 1 | 2 | -- | -- |
| And'w Reed | 50 | 2 | 2 | 4 | -- |
| And'w Kirkpatrick | 50 | 2 | 2 | 5 | -- |
| David Hastings | 120 | 2 | 2 | 2 | -- |
| David Cochran | 150 | 3 | 2 | 6 | -- |
| Dorington Boyle, tanner, tan house | 250 | 4 | 6 | 10 | 2 |
| David Brooks | 100 | 3 | 2 | 2 | 1 |
| David Ligott | 50 | 2 | 2 | -- | -- |
| Ellis Pusey, miller, g.m. | 180 | 3 | 4 | 15 | 2 |
| George Cowpland | 50 | 2 | 2 | 4 | -- |
| George Lackey | 200 | 2 | 2 | 3 | -- |
| John Caruthers | 388 | 2 | 3 | 6 | -- |
| James Caruthers | 150 | 2 | 2 | 4 | -- |

West Fallowfield

| | Acres | Horses | Cattle | Sheep | Servants |
|---|---|---|---|---|---|
| James Cochran, tavernkeeper, tavern | 180 | 3 | 3 | 8 | 2 |
| Jam's Gibson | 100 | 3 | 2 | 6 | -- |
| Joseph Adams | 100 | -- | 3 | 9 | 1 |
| Jam's Gillalen, sadler | 50 | 2 | 2 | 3 | -- |
| John Wilson | -- | 1 | 2 | 3 | -- |
| Isaac Pennington | 100 | 2 | 2 | 2 | -- |
| John Erwin, tavernkeeper, tavern | 100 | 2 | 10 | 2 | 1 |
| John Dunn | 250 | 4 | 4 | 6 | -- |
| Jam's Laughlin, g.m., s.m. | 150 | 2 | 2 | 6 | -- |
| Jno. Love | 150 | 2 | 4 | 10 | -- |
| John Watson | 50 | 2 | 2 | 6 | -- |
| John Park | 150 | 2 | 3 | 6 | -- |
| James Gray | 120 | 1 | 1 | 2 | -- |
| John Poe | 300 | 2 | 2 | 2 | -- |
| Jos'h Wilson | 100 | 2 | 2 | 4 | -- |
| John Young, weaver | 50 | 1 | 2 | -- | -- |
| Jno. Kirkpatrick | 30 | 1 | 1 | 2 | -- |
| James Wilson | 100 | 2 | 2 | 3 | -- |
| Joseph Thyle | 60 | 2 | 2 | -- | -- |
| Jam's Allison | 100 | 2 | 2 | 4 | -- |
| Isaac Allison | 40 | 2 | 2 | -- | -- |
| James Smith | 250 | 5 | 6 | 10 | -- |
| Jam's Glendenning | 307 | 3 | 4 | 20 | -- |
| John Bell | 300 | 4 | 4 | 10 | 3 |
| James Adams | 100 | 2 | 2 | 6 | -- |
| Patrick McLaughlin | 230 | 2 | 1 | 6 | -- |
| Robert Burns | 100 | 2 | 2 | 2 | -- |
| Rob't Wilson | 100 | 2 | 2 | 7 | -- |
| Robert McCormick | 100 | 2 | 2 | 6 | 1 |
| Rob't Mercer, cooper | 60 | 2 | 2 | 5 | -- |
| Philip Roddan | 80 | 1 | -- | -- | -- |
| Robert Cowdan | 50 | 2 | 2 | -- | -- |
| Robert Hamel | 60 | 2 | 2 | 4 | -- |
| Richard Lee | 125 | 2 | 1 | -- | -- |
| Stephen Cochran | 150 | 2 | 2 | 6 | -- |
| Stephen Cochran, Junior, shopkeeper | 100 | 2 | 4 | 8 | 1 |
| Sam'l Tate, storekeeper | 300 | 2 | 1 | 2 | -- |
| Sam'l Futhey, tavernkeeper, tavern | 105 | 2 | 3 | 6 | -- |
| Sam'l Wilson | 250 | 2 | 3 | -- | 1 |
| Thomas Elder | 200 | 1 | 1 | 4 | -- |
| Tho's Officer | 100 | 2 | 3 | 6 | -- |
| Thomas Thompson | 160 | 2 | 1 | -- | -- |
| Will'm Adams | 100 | 3 | 3 | 4 | -- |
| Will'm Reed, cooper | 70 | 2 | 3 | 4 | -- |
| Will'm Hazlett | 200 | 2 | 2 | 4 | 1 |
| Will'm Stringer | 150 | 2 | 3 | 6 | -- |
| Wm. Mcl'eHaney | 100 | 2 | 2 | 3 | -- |
| Will'm Buntin | 100 | 2 | 3 | 6 | 1 |
| Will'm Bogs | 60 | 2 | 2 | 2 | -- |
| Tho's Irwin | 100 | 2 | 2 | 2 | -- |
| Thomas Kerr | 100 | 2 | 4 | 4 | 1 |

## Freemen

| | |
|---|---|
| Joseph Gardner | Archabald Flemmin |
| Edward Latmer | Alexander Dunlap |
| Rob't Taylor | Alexander Caruthers |
| Bryan Muloy | George Gibson |
| Hugh Dougherty | William Bogs |
| John McleHaney | James Sharkpatrick |
| John Netherington | Robert Rogers |
| William Holmes | Will Parte |
| Barney Broadley | Patrick Davlin |

## Inmates

| | |
|---|---|
| John Mathews | Joseph Beaty |
| James Allen | Jno. Kyles |
| Rob't Futhey | John Crow |
| Robert Adams | John Donally |
| John Gibson | Charles McGlaughlan |
| James Dunn | James Evers |
| David Dunlap | Wm. Rob |

## East Caln Rate

| | Acres | Horses | Cattle | Sheep | Servants |
|---|---|---|---|---|---|
| Rich'd Buffington, nursery | 150 | 2 | 2 | -- | -- |
| Wm. Bennett | 70 | 2 | 2 | 5 | -- |
| John Baldwin, tin manufacturer | 300 | 5 | 5 | 12 | -- |
| Joshua Baldwin | 300 | 6 | 7 | 8 | -- |
| Sam'l Byers, miller, g.m. | 290 | 5 | 6 | 6 | -- |
| John Barr | 30 | 1 | 2 | -- | -- |
| Tho's Coates | 240 | 4 | 7 | 8 | -- |
| Moses Coates | 80 | 2 | -- | -- | -- |
| Mordica Cloud | 350 | 3 | 4 | 10 | -- |
| John Cretam | 50 | 2 | 2 | 6 | -- |
| John Clark | 150 | 2 | 3 | 6 | -- |
| John Culbertson, f.m. | 150 | 2 | 4 | 4 | 1 |
| Abigal Culbertson | 150 | -- | -- | -- | -- |
| Lawrence Cox | 150 | 2 | 2 | 3 | -- |
| Andrew Cox | 20 | 4 | 1 | -- | -- |
| John Downing, tavernkeeper, tavern | 300 | 4 | 8 | 12 | 1 |
| Joseph Downing | 600 | 6 | 15 | 5 | -- |
| Rich'd Downing, g.m., s.m. | 300 | 5 | 9 | 12 | -- |
| Will'm Baldwin, sadler | 12 | 1 | 2 | -- | -- |
| David Jenkins | 9 | 1 | -- | -- | -- |
| Isaac Jacobs, tanner, tanyard | 10 | 1 | 2 | -- | 1 |
| Will Roberts, fuller, f.m. | 8 | 1 | 1 | -- | -- |
| Joshua Way, malster, malt house | -- | 1 | 2 | -- | -- |
| Rob't Darlington | 200 | 4 | 3 | 6 | -- |
| John Edge, g.m. | 50 | 1 | 1 | -- | -- |
| John Eaton, fuller, f.m. | 100 | 2 | 2 | -- | -- |
| Theophelus Erwin | 100 | 2 | 2 | -- | -- |

| East Caln | Acres | Horses | Cattle | Sheep | Servants |
|---|---|---|---|---|---|
| Arch'd Erwin | 100 | 2 | 3 | 8 | -- |
| Robert Erwin | 200 | 2 | 2 | 5 | -- |
| James Erwin | 50 | 4 | -- | -- | -- |
| John Erwin | 100 | 3 | 1 | 9 | 1 |
| Tho's Fisher, coooper | 100 | 3 | 3 | -- | -- |
| Sam'l Fisher | 150 | 3 | 3 | -- | -- |
| Alexander Fleming | 100 | 2 | 2 | 4 | -- |
| Joseph Fleming | 100 | 2 | 4 | 3 | -- |
| Ann Fleming | 100 | 1 | 2 | 4 | -- |
| Peter Fleming | 150 | 3 | 4 | 5 | -- |
| Hugh Glen | 50 | 4 | 2 | 4 | -- |
| Tho's Green, Jun'r | 100 | -- | -- | -- | -- |
| Peter Grimes | 60 | 3 | 3 | -- | -- |
| John Gilleland | 420 | 4 | 4 | 9 | 4 |
| Isaac Green | 60 | 2 | 2 | 5 | -- |
| Joseph Green | 125 | 1 | -- | -- | -- |
| Peter Hunt | 100 | 3 | 2 | 3 | -- |
| Sam'l Hunt | 120 | 1 | -- | -- | -- |
| John Hastand | 13 | 1 | -- | -- | -- |
| Jam's Hickey | 100 | 2 | 3 | 3 | -- |
| James Jack | 200 | -- | -- | -- | -- |
| Cha's Jack | 250 | 2 | 4 | -- | -- |
| Robert Kincade | 300 | 1 | 2 | -- | -- |
| Caleb Kirk, joyner | 160 | 4 | 4 | 4 | -- |
| Rob't Lockard | 250 | 3 | 4 | 4 | 1 |
| Lodowick Liggit | 200 | 2 | 6 | 6 | 1 |
| Will Littler | 200 | 2 | 2 | 20 | -- |
| Phineas Lewes | 200 | 3 | 5 | 10 | -- |
| Curtis Lewes, smith | 118 | 5 | 5 | 10 | -- |
| Henry Lewes | 200 | 3 | 4 | 9 | -- |
| Tho's McAnteer | 120 | 2 | 2 | 2 | -- |
| Wm. McFarlan | 50 | 2 | 1 | 3 | -- |
| Benj'n McCarty | 50 | 2 | 2 | 6 | -- |
| Jam's McFarlan | 100 | 2 | 3 | 6 | -- |
| Jam's McKelvy | 280 | 2 | 3 | 4 | -- |
| Jno. McFarren | 200 | -- | -- | -- | -- |
| Grif'th Mendenhall, sadler | 69 | 2 | 3 | -- | -- |
| Joshua Mendenhall | 200 | 5 | 3 | 4 | -- |
| Mich'l Miller | 200 | 3 | 3 | 6 | -- |
| Will'm McKinly | 200 | 2 | 4 | 6 | -- |
| Wm. McClean | 50 | 2 | 2 | 6 | -- |
| Mich'l McClean | 200 | 1 | 4 | -- | -- |
| Warrick Miller, tavern, t.k. | 333 | 6 | 5 | 14 | 3 |
| Jam's Niesbit | 200 | 2 | 3 | -- | -- |
| Tho's Pimm | 383 | 5 | 8 | 13 | 2 |
| Hannah Pimm | 200 | 4 | 5 | 6 | -- |
| James Packer | 250 | 7 | 12 | 8 | 1 |
| Sam'l Picking | 150 | 2 | 3 | 6 | -- |
| Rob't Park | 394 | 5 | 8 | -- | 2 |
| Obiah Park | 100 | 2 | 5 | 6 | 1 |
| Joseph Phipps, Junior, g.m., miller | 100 | 1 | 2 | -- | -- |
| Fra's Pearson, weaver | 28 | 1 | 1 | -- | -- |
| Wm. Quaintance | 310 | 3 | 6 | 9 | -- |
| Tho's Rossiter | 245 | 4 | 6 | 8 | 2 |

East Caln

| | Acres | Horses | Cattle | Sheep | Servants |
|---|---|---|---|---|---|
| Rach'l Rommans | 85 | 2 | 2 | 6 | -- |
| Mosses Scott, phycitian | 40 | 1 | 2 | -- | -- |
| Tho's Stalker, tanyard, tanner | 399 | 5 | 5 | 6 | 1 |
| James Steel | 85 | 2 | 1 | 4 | -- |
| Tho's Shirley | 50 | 2 | 3 | 6 | -- |
| John Smith | 280 | 4 | 5 | 6 | -- |
| Tho's Temple | 150 | 2 | 3 | -- | -- |
| Jam's Thompson | 100 | 3 | 3 | 6 | -- |
| Robert Valintine, shopkeeper | 130 | 4 | 4 | 6 | -- |
| Jonathan Valentine | 250 | 2 | 4 | 6 | -- |
| Sam'l Underwood | 66 | 2 | 1 | -- | -- |
| Isaac Webb, tavern, t.k. | 200 | 3 | 4 | 8 | -- |
| Jam's Webb | 150 | -- | -- | -- | -- |
| David Walker | 300 | 2 | 1 | -- | -- |
| John Walker | 400 | 4 | 4 | 6 | -- |
| Moses Wait | 100 | 2 | 3 | 6 | -- |
| George Wilson | 50 | 1 | 2 | 4 | -- |
| Leonard Wilkin | 100 | 2 | 3 | -- | -- |
| Tho's Windle, s.m. | 180 | 3 | 1 | -- | 1 |
| Oliver Wallace | 250 | 2 | 3 | 4 | -- |
| Tho's White | 100 | 2 | 4 | 4 | 1 |
| Sam'l White | 150 | 3 | 4 | -- | -- |
| Will'm Wilson | 50 | 3 | 3 | 6 | -- |
| Will'm Byers | 108 | -- | -- | -- | -- |
| John Carmickle | 228 | 3 | 4 | 4 | 1 |
| Wm. Meredith, tavern | 200 | 3 | 4 | 6 | -- |
| Israel & James Pemberton | 300 | -- | -- | -- | -- |
| Wm. Ralston | 100 | -- | -- | -- | -- |
| Tho's Hart | 500 | 7 | 6 | 10 | 2 |
| Andrew Elliott, shopkeeper | 100 | 1 | 2 | -- | -- |

Freemen

Edw'd Barran
Henry Barker
Rob't Bearns
Mathew Brown
Peter Burgindine
Jno. Danalson
Owen Danaly
Robert Elliot
James McGee
Cain Mahony
Will'm McCoy
Samuel McMahon
Wm. McConnell
Wm. Meridith
David Owen
Robert Porter
Gideon Pearson
Geo'e Quaintance
John Rommons
Adam Richards

James Eaton
Ginnings Field
James Goudy
John Hall
Will'm Hoops
Thomas Jackson
James Jack
Bryan McCune
Peter Shields
Mathew Taylor
Abra'm Temple
David Walker
Fra's Wilkinson
Tho's Wilkinson
Barney McFailey
John Denney
Dennis Beagly
Sam'l Culbertson
Barney Hanley
James McClane

Freemen

Daniel Rossiter            Joseph Miller
And'w Ross                 John Miles
John Scott

Inmates

Wm. McCarakan              John Parker
Wm. Berry                  Wm. Purdy
Robert Carson              James Reed
Edward Early               Ralph Robinson
James Erwin                Joseph Skeen
Andrew Forbus              James Sheward
Wm. Hunt                   Magnus Snowder
James Johnson              Jonathan Stalker
Sam'l Johnson              Jacob Tate
Andrew Knox                Will'm Temple
John Lewes                 Morris Thomas
Lewes Lewes                John Temple
John Mountgomery           Henry Thompson
John Man                   Joshua Webb
Wm. Mills                  John White
George Niece               Will'm Reed
James Porter               Joseph Adams

West Caln Rate

|  | Acres | Horses | Cattle | Sheep | Servants |
|---|---|---|---|---|---|
| Rob't Anderson | 243 | 3 | 3 | 6 | -- |
| Fra's Alexander | 120 | 2 | 4 | -- | -- |
| Hance Attleman, s.m. | 85 | 2 | 3 | 6 | -- |
| Peter Babb | 337 | 3 | 4 | 10 | -- |
| Joseph Bishop, Jun'r | 260 | 5 | 4 | -- | 2 |
| Tho's Babb | 198 | 5 | 3 | 5 | 1 |
| Joseph Bishop | 50 | 2 | 2 | 3 | -- |
| Thomas Boyd | 100 | 2 | 2 | 2 | -- |
| And'w Burnside | 7 | -- | 1 | -- | -- |
| Rob't Brakenrig | 220 | 2 | 6 | -- | -- |
| Tho's Clark | 40 | 1 | 1 | 7 | -- |
| Joseph Clark, sadler | 100 | 2 | 3 | 5 | 1 |
| Will'm Clingan, shopkeeper | 120 | 3 | 4 | 6 | 1 |
| Richard Cox | 30 | -- | 1 | -- | -- |
| Josiah Cambell | 100 | 2 | 2 | -- | -- |
| Will'm Crawford, tavern, t.k. | 100 | 3 | 1 | 6 | 1 |
| And'w Culberson, s.m. | 60 | 1 | 2 | 6 | -- |
| John Cambell | 150 | 3 | 5 | 10 | -- |
| Will'm Crawford | 100 | 2 | 4 | 8 | -- |
| Robert Cooper | 150 | -- | -- | -- | -- |
| John Darlington, tanner | -- | 1 | 1 | -- | -- |
| Alexander Davidson | 200 | 1 | 2 | 10 | -- |
| Will'm Davidson | 100 | 2 | 3 | 6 | -- |
| Tho's Dawson | 150 | -- | -- | -- | -- |
| Thomas Dawson, Jun'r | 400 | 4 | 6 | 10 | 1 |
| Samuel Dencey | 119 | -- | -- | -- | -- |

| West Caln | Acres | Horses | Cattle | Sheep | Servants |
|---|---|---|---|---|---|
| Samuel Entrikin | 145 | 2 | 3 | 2 | -- |
| John Fleming, g.m., miller | 117 | 2 | 2 | -- | -- |
| Will'm Fleming | 100 | 2 | 3 | 4 | -- |
| Mat'w Ferguson | 100 | 2 | 2 | 1 | -- |
| James Gibb | 100 | 2 | 4 | 6 | -- |
| Hugh Gibb | -- | 1 | 1 | 4 | -- |
| James Gabey | 40 | -- | 1 | -- | -- |
| Rob't Gilkey | 150 | -- | -- | -- | -- |
| Geo'e Harison, weaver | 80 | 1 | 1 | 7 | -- |
| John Hart, brewery | 25 | 2 | 3 | -- | -- |
| Jam's Henderson, mill, miller | 50 | 1 | 1 | -- | -- |
| Will'm Henry | 100 | 3 | 3 | 6 | -- |
| Wm. Hambleton | 180 | -- | -- | -- | -- |
| Rich'd Hope | 200 | 2 | 4 | 6 | -- |
| John Jack | 150 | 3 | 4 | 14 | 1 |
| John Johnson | 100 | 2 | 3 | 7 | -- |
| Jam's Kelly | 150 | 2 | 3 | 8 | -- |
| Sam'l Kincade | 150 | -- | -- | -- | -- |
| Tho's Kennedy | 30 | 1 | 2 | 6 | -- |
| Rob't Kincade | 70 | 1 | 1 | 1 | -- |
| Jam's Keys | 100 | 1 | 2 | 2 | -- |
| Alex'r Lewes, s.m. | 213 | 2 | 3 | 1 | 1 |
| Will'm Long | 100 | 2 | 4 | 2 | -- |
| Wm. Lyon, joyner | 50 | 2 | 3 | 3 | 1 |
| Thomas Law, cordwainer | 40 | 1 | 2 | 3 | -- |
| John Miller, g.m., miller | 50 | 4 | 6 | 12 | 3 |
| John Murphy | 50 | 1 | 1 | 1 | -- |
| John McVicker | 150 | 2 | 3 | 6 | -- |
| Alex'r McMullen | 100 | 1 | 2 | -- | -- |
| Tho's McGraw | 40 | -- | 1 | -- | -- |
| Ann McIlvain | 100 | 1 | -- | -- | -- |
| Alex'r McFerson | 100 | -- | -- | -- | -- |
| John Martin | 50 | 2 | 1 | 4 | 1 |
| Wm. Moore | 339 | 2 | 3 | 10 | -- |
| Benjamin Parvin | 50 | -- | -- | -- | -- |
| Tho's Lightfoot | 100 | -- | -- | -- | -- |
| Joseph Park, tan yard, tanner | 110 | 5 | 4 | 8 | -- |
| Jam's Peirce, wheelwright | 106 | 1 | 2 | 3 | -- |
| Patrick Porter | 50 | 2 | 2 | 6 | -- |
| John Porter | 200 | 2 | 1 | -- | -- |
| Dan'l Richardson, cordwainer | 30 | 1 | 1 | -- | -- |
| Rob't Rodgers | 200 | 1 | 1 | -- | -- |
| Jam's Reed | 50 | 1 | 1 | -- | -- |
| Alex'r Rodgers | 200 | 3 | 3 | 10 | 1 |
| John Rhea | 60 | 1 | 2 | 2 | -- |
| Tho's Ratcliffe | 92 | 2 | 1 | -- | -- |
| Tho's Sherron, s.s. | -- | 2 | 1 | -- | -- |
| John McKnee, g.m. | -- | -- | -- | -- | -- |
| John Sinkler | 100 | 2 | 2 | 4 | -- |
| Will'm Sinkler, s.m. | 98 | 2 | 3 | 2 | -- |
| Abraham Smith | 100 | 2 | 2 | 3 | -- |
| Edward Vernon, millwright | 140 | 2 | 4 | 6 | -- |
| Will'm Brown | 80 | 2 | 1 | -- | -- |
| Caleb Way, Jun'r, tavern, t.k. | 113 | 2 | 2 | 2 | 1 |
| Mary Way | 80 | 1 | 1 | 3 | -- |

West Caln

| | Acres | Horses | Cattle | Sheep | Servants |
|---|---|---|---|---|---|
| John Whitaker, malt house, brewery, malster | 4 | 1 | 1 | -- | -- |
| Nath'l White | 225 | 3 | 3 | 6 | -- |
| John Waggoner, miller | -- | 1 | 3 | -- | 1 |
| Josiah Wallace | 100 | 3 | 3 | 6 | -- |
| John Wallace | 50 | 2 | 3 | 6 | -- |
| Rob't Withrow | 200 | 4 | 6 | 15 | -- |
| Sam'l Withrow | 150 | 1 | 6 | 6 | -- |
| Tho's Wilson | 120 | 2 | 4 | -- | -- |
| Jam's Wilson | 150 | 2 | 5 | 6 | -- |
| Rob't Wilson | 50 | 1 | -- | -- | -- |

Freemen

Joseph Ash
Will'm Brown
Cha's Cambell
Geo'e Cummins
Gilbert Gibbs
John Hill
James Hood
Will'm Hunter

John Long
And'w McNab
Will'm Withrow
Thos's Warner
Nath'l Maxwell
Peter Pursel
Jam's Keys
John Angel

Inmates

Sam'l Bishop
Joseph Cummins
Rob't Cole
Geo'e Cambell
Jam's Cochran
William Downey
Jacob Dawson
Felix Deving
Jam's Gutrey
Adam Hope
Dennis Herkin
Tho's Isburn

Robert Kerns
Jam's Longmore
Jesse Lewes
David Lewes
Enoch Lewes
John Marshall
Duncin McAlister
James Ray
John Vernon
George Warner
Sam'l Hart

East Nantmill Rate

| | Acres | Horses | Cattle | Sheep | Servants |
|---|---|---|---|---|---|
| Linford Lardner | 5,591 | 14 | 8 | 30 | 4 |
| John Potts, iron master | 1,200 | 12 | 10 | 20 | 10 |
| Jam's Hockley, g.m., s.m., miller | 200 | 6 | 8 | 20 | 1 |
| Chris'r Knower, g.m., miller | 200 | 3 | 5 | 6 | -- |
| Evan Griffith | 200 | 1 | 2 | 6 | -- |
| David Rodgers | 150 | 3 | 7 | 6 | -- |
| Abner Evans | 150 | 3 | 5 | 6 | -- |
| Will'm James | 200 | 2 | 5 | 6 | -- |
| Evan William | 150 | 3 | 5 | 8 | -- |

| East Nantmill | Acres | Horses | Cattle | Sheep | Servants |
|---|---|---|---|---|---|
| John Loyde | 130 | 3 | 4 | 7 | -- |
| Jonathan Pugh, s.m. | 150 | 3 | 4 | 4 | -- |
| Simon Meridith | 160 | 3 | 5 | -- | -- |
| Will'm Kirk | 100 | 3 | 3 | 4 | -- |
| John Griffith | 100 | 4 | 5 | -- | -- |
| Jona'n Winn | 150 | 2 | 5 | 7 | -- |
| Jam's Abraham | 200 | 2 | 3 | 6 | -- |
| Wm. Sterrett | 200 | 4 | 6 | 8 | -- |
| John Sterrett | 155 | 2 | 1 | -- | -- |
| Joseph McKinley | 200 | 4 | 4 | -- | -- |
| Thomas Loyd | 300 | 2 | 10 | -- | -- |
| David Stephens | 100 | 2 | 4 | 5 | -- |
| John Stephens | 50 | 1 | 2 | -- | -- |
| Joshua Stephens | 50 | -- | -- | -- | -- |
| Jam's Guest | 130 | 2 | 3 | 3 | -- |
| David Yarnall | 150 | 1 | 3 | 6 | -- |
| Jacob Williams, carpenter | 40 | 1 | 2 | 4 | -- |
| John Pugh, shoemaker | 100 | 3 | 3 | 7 | -- |
| Sam'l Robinson | 130 | 2 | 2 | -- | -- |
| Reuben Thomas | 100 | 2 | 3 | -- | -- |
| Wm. Griffith | -- | 3 | 3 | 7 | -- |
| Wm. Griffith, smith | 50 | 1 | 2 | -- | -- |
| Jno. Johnston | 80 | 2 | 3 | -- | -- |
| Peter Moses, | 100 | 1 | 1 | -- | -- |
| Geo'e & Elihu Evans | 200 | -- | -- | -- | -- |
| Sam'l John | -- | 4 | 6 | 8 | -- |
| John Boyer | 100 | -- | -- | -- | -- |
| Will'm Brown | 100 | 2 | 4 | 8 | -- |
| Patrick Dymon | 100 | 2 | 2 | -- | -- |
| Robert McConoughy | 300 | -- | -- | -- | -- |
| John McKnight, labourer | 100 | 1 | 2 | -- | -- |
| Sebastian Frank | 200 | 3 | 3 | 4 | -- |
| Tho's Morgan, carpenter | 100 | 2 | 2 | -- | -- |
| John John | 120 | -- | -- | -- | -- |
| Borick Peholt | 140 | 2 | 4 | 8 | -- |
| Jacob Myre | 80 | 2 | 2 | -- | -- |
| Adam Miller | 150 | 2 | 3 | 4 | -- |
| Dan Griffith | 185 | 4 | 3 | 4 | -- |
| Rob't Steward | 150 | 2 | 5 | 5 | -- |
| Will'm Richards | 200 | 3 | 3 | -- | -- |
| Will'm Thomas | 100 | 2 | 5 | 6 | -- |
| Rich'd Tmplin | 60 | -- | -- | -- | -- |
| David Steel, weaver | 100 | 1 | 2 | -- | -- |
| Jacob Murrey | 80 | 1 | 3 | -- | -- |
| John Horn | 100 | 2 | 3 | 3 | -- |
| Jacob Ketcher | 20 | 1 | 1 | -- | -- |
| George Gerick | 50 | 2 | 3 | 3 | -- |
| Jacob Shooster | 110 | 2 | 2 | 3 | -- |
| Dan'l Hie | 200 | 2 | 4 | 4 | -- |
| Martin Roads | 100 | 2 | 2 | -- | -- |
| Wintle Dunfelton | 100 | 2 | 2 | 2 | -- |
| Mich'l Haws | 100 | 2 | 3 | -- | -- |
| Chri's Fuller, s.m. | 160 | 1 | 2 | 2 | -- |
| Tho's Jenkins | 150 | 2 | 4 | -- | -- |
| John Jenkins | 100 | 1 | 1 | -- | -- |

East Nantmill

| | Acres | Horses | Cattle | Sheep | Servants |
|---|---|---|---|---|---|
| Mich'l Boyer | 100 | 2 | 4 | 4 | -- |
| Jacob High | 150 | 2 | 2 | 2 | -- |
| Fred'k Salady | 200 | 2 | 3 | 6 | -- |
| Wm. Denison | -- | 2 | 3 | 6 | -- |
| James Pugh | 100 | 2 | 2 | -- | -- |
| John Williams | 100 | 1 | 1 | -- | -- |
| Sam'l Wynn | 420 | 2 | 2 | -- | -- |
| Hockly & Potts | 80 | -- | -- | -- | -- |

Inmates

Tho's Meredith  
Sam'l Patrick  
Jam's Miller  
Nicolas Frely  
Dan'l Huffman  
Peter Emould  
Jacob Felty  
Simon Henko  
George Fulk  
Jacob Peholt  
Peter Chance  

Fredirick Painter  
Solomon Light  
Mich'l Swoop  
George Godfry  
Henry Michell  
Abra'm Moor  
John Brown  
Mich'l Meserly  
James Fisk  
Jam's Wynn  

Freemen

Levi Griffith  
Jno. Griffith  
Wm. Griffith  
Hugh Williams  
Jam's Miller  
John Blair  
James Evans  
John Lack  
David Davis  
William Ewing  
John Huffman  
Adam Peck  

Will'm Carson  
Stapbol Swoob  
Mathias Moyer  
Gasper Moyer  
Jacob Wiseberger  
Philip Rogers  
John Rogers  
Tho's Lighton  
Jacob Kergin  
Jacob Bartholomew  
Peter Sibbar  
Jno. Large  

Vincent Rate

| | Acres | Horses | Cattle | Sheep | Servants |
|---|---|---|---|---|---|
| Anthony Acre | 150 | 3 | 4 | 4 | -- |
| Abra'm Turner | 195 | 4 | 5 | 10 | 2 |
| Amos Davis | 150 | 2 | 4 | 12 | -- |
| Amos Thomas | 50 | -- | -- | -- | -- |
| Aaron Watkins | 150 | 3 | 3 | 5 | -- |
| Adam Miller, g.m. | 150 | 3 | 4 | 5 | 1 |
| Benj'n Brumback, tavern | 170 | 4 | 5 | 10 | 1 |
| Bastian Keely, s.m., g.m., tavern | 150 | 4 | 4 | 4 | -- |
| Casper Snider | 100 | 3 | 3 | 5 | -- |
| Conrod Shimer | 130 | 5 | 5 | 10 | 1 |

| Vincent | Acres | Horses | Cattle | Sheep | Servants |
|---|---|---|---|---|---|
| Chris'r Everhard | 100 | 2 | 3 | 4 | -- |
| David Thomas | 200 | 4 | 5 | 10 | 1 |
| David Thomas, tanner | 140 | 3 | 4 | 4 | 1 |
| David Jenkins | 250 | 2 | 4 | 6 | -- |
| David Davis | 70 | 3 | 4 | 6 | -- |
| Edw'd Parker, t.k., g.m. | 100 | 3 | 4 | -- | 1 |
| Enoch Meredith | 100 | 3 | 3 | 5 | -- |
| Enoch Watkin | 100 | 2 | 2 | 4 | -- |
| George Fitsimmons | 100 | 2 | 4 | 5 | -- |
| Geo'e Row | 150 | 3 | 4 | 3 | 1 |
| Geo'e Yeager | 200 | 3 | 4 | 4 | -- |
| Geo'e McFarlam | 100 | 2 | 3 | -- | -- |
| Geo'e Lewes, farmer | -- | 2 | 2 | -- | -- |
| George Dary | 200 | 3 | 2 | 4 | -- |
| Henry Dasher | 180 | 3 | 4 | 5 | -- |
| Henry Benner | 100 | 2 | 2 | 4 | -- |
| Hugh Williams | 100 | 2 | 2 | 4 | -- |
| Humphry Bell | 80 | 4 | 4 | 6 | -- |
| Henry Acre | 200 | 4 | 4 | 6 | -- |
| Henry Brumback | 180 | 3 | 4 | 6 | -- |
| Henry Christman | 190 | 3 | 3 | 3 | -- |
| Henry Miller | 100 | 3 | 3 | -- | -- |
| Henry Ditlow | 60 | 2 | 3 | 4 | -- |
| Henry Cnerr, weaver | 100 | 1 | 1 | 2 | -- |
| Henry Bearbower | -- | 2 | 2 | -- | -- |
| John Phillips | 50 | 1 | 2 | -- | -- |
| Jacob Munchour | 150 | 3 | 2 | -- | -- |
| John Paul | 200 | 5 | 5 | 6 | -- |
| Jno. James | 194 | 3 | 6 | 10 | 1 |
| Joseph Rogers | 200 | 4 | 5 | 12 | -- |
| Joseph Cox | 80 | 2 | 3 | 5 | -- |
| John Dotson | 60 | 2 | 2 | 5 | -- |
| John Hawse | 100 | 3 | 3 | 4 | -- |
| Jacob Shinhold | 190 | 3 | 4 | 3 | -- |
| Jacob Melsher, Jun'r | 80 | 2 | 2 | 4 | -- |
| John Melsher, Sr. | 130 | 3 | 3 | 6 | -- |
| John Martin | 50 | 1 | 2 | 5 | -- |
| John Bound | 100 | 3 | 3 | 5 | -- |
| John Lloyd | 180 | 3 | 4 | 5 | -- |
| Jonas Heck | 50 | 2 | 2 | -- | -- |
| Jacob Mower | 100 | 2 | 3 | -- | -- |
| Joseph Eddey | 50 | 2 | 2 | 4 | -- |
| Jacob Coleer | 120 | 1 | 1 | -- | -- |
| James Worthington | 50 | 2 | 2 | -- | -- |
| James Dugall | 50 | 1 | 1 | -- | -- |
| Joseph Bosler | 100 | 3 | 4 | 4 | -- |
| John Davis, taylor | 50 | -- | 1 | 4 | -- |
| James John, shoemaker | 150 | 3 | 4 | 10 | -- |
| John Thomas | 50 | 2 | 2 | 4 | -- |
| John John | 150 | 2 | 2 | 3 | -- |
| Joseph Hencock | 50 | 2 | 2 | 3 | -- |
| James Evans | 100 | 3 | 3 | 5 | -- |
| John McFarlan | 100 | 3 | 4 | 6 | -- |
| John Fitsimmons | 100 | 3 | 3 | 5 | -- |
| Joseph Davis | 100 | 4 | 3 | 4 | -- |

| Vincent | Acres | Horses | Cattle | Sheep | Servants |
|---|---|---|---|---|---|
| John Meredith | 200 | 3 | 6 | 10 | -- |
| John Jenkins | 100 | 2 | 2 | 5 | -- |
| John Jenkins, clog | 40 | 2 | 2 | 3 | -- |
| John Munshour | 64 | 2 | 2 | 5 | -- |
| John Arndorf | 200 | 3 | 3 | 4 | -- |
| James Roger | 100 | 2 | 2 | 3 | -- |
| Morgan Morgan | 50 | 2 | 3 | 5 | -- |
| Lawrence Hipple | 250 | 4 | 5 | 12 | -- |
| Michael Holman | 250 | 4 | 5 | 6 | -- |
| Michael Cypher | 200 | 4 | 4 | 6 | -- |
| Michael Chimer | 150 | 3 | 4 | 5 | -- |
| Michael Ragon | 100 | 2 | 2 | 4 | -- |
| Morris Evans | 100 | 3 | 2 | 10 | -- |
| Myrick Davis | 250 | 6 | 4 | -- | 1 |
| Mary Buchanan | 100 | 3 | 3 | 6 | -- |
| Nicholas Kiser | 200 | 2 | 2 | -- | -- |
| Owen Thomas | 200 | 4 | 4 | 10 | -- |
| Philip Arndorf | 70 | 1 | 2 | -- | -- |
| Paul Benner | 200 | 3 | 4 | 4 | -- |
| Peter Stager | 200 | 3 | 3 | 6 | -- |
| Peter Rhoades | 240 | 4 | 3 | 7 | -- |
| Peter Defrain | 190 | 4 | 5 | 5 | -- |
| Phelix Chrisman, blacksmith | 200 | 3 | 4 | 5 | -- |
| Philip Lewis | 130 | 2 | 2 | 4 | -- |
| Philip Leas | 50 | 1 | 2 | 4 | -- |
| Robert Ralston | 100 | 3 | 4 | 8 | -- |
| Rees Evans, taylor | 50 | 1 | 1 | -- | -- |
| Simon Shunk | 100 | 3 | 3 | 3 | -- |
| Sam'l Colberson | 70 | 2 | 4 | 6 | 1 |
| Peter Miller | 100 | 2 | 2 | 3 | -- |
| Tho's Wilson | 150 | 3 | 4 | 3 | -- |
| Tho's Davis | 100 | 3 | 3 | 6 | -- |
| Wm. Heterland | 200 | 3 | 4 | 3 | -- |
| Wm. Evans, tavern | 150 | 4 | 6 | 10 | -- |
| Wm. Bell | 50 | 2 | 2 | 3 | -- |
| Wm. Fullerton | 100 | 2 | 3 | 4 | -- |
| Wm. Gordon | 100 | 2 | 3 | 4 | -- |
| Wm. M'elshour, smith | -- | 1 | 2 | -- | -- |

Inmates

David Evans
Robert Blain
Peter Domerman
Conrad Herlman
Erasmus Loyd
John Thomas
Thomas Miller
Benj'n Jenkins
Alex'r Meglister
Alex'r Williams
Philip Strong
Nicholas Miller

Tho's Hunter
Tho's Bell
Jacob Rymey
John Bier
Andreas Keller
Michael Essick
Conemus Seller
Wm. West
John Rinehard
Tho's Metzger
George Keen
Gidean Voar

## Inmates

Frederick Bolinger
Frederick Brenhold
Henry Menges
John Julius

Henry Carl
Jam's Fitzsimmons
Anthony Housan

## Freemen

Jeremiah Jerman
Stophel Hetterling
Oliher Cradler
George Singloub
John Groff
James McClun
Frederick Shenliver
Adam Sheffer
James Shannon
John McNeal
David Morris
Joseph Treeby

Conrad Rouse
Samuel Rees
Thomas Batman
David Melchior
William Eddey
George Berkhiser
John Brade
Martin Holman
Adam Geter
John Ralson
Jno. Evans
Laughlin Laferty

## Tredyffrin Rate

|  | Acres | Horses | Cattle | Sheep | Servants |
|---|---|---|---|---|---|
| Will'm Currie | 242 | 4 | 3 | 5 | 2 |
| Sampson Davis | 200 | 4 | 3 | 6 | 1 |
| Samuel Havard | 200 | 2 | 1 | --- | 1 |
| David Havard | 300 | 4 | 6 | 10 | 2 |
| Ann Havard | 100 | --- | --- | --- | --- |
| John Simonton | 120 | 2 | 5 | 4 | 1 |
| John Rowland, g.m., miller | 133 | 4 | 4 | --- | --- |
| John Willson | 200 | 4 | 4 | 8 | 1 |
| Isaac Davis, Esq'r, s.m. | 300 | 5 | 8 | 10 | 1 |
| Thomas Calvert | 150 | 2 | 3 | 4 | 1 |
| Lydia Jones | 26 | --- | 1 | 3 | --- |
| Samuel John | 150 | 2 | 3 | 3 | 1 |
| John Meredith | 100 | 2 | 2 | --- | --- |
| Samuel Richards | 100 | 3 | 5 | 9 | --- |
| John Beaver | 280 | 2 | 6 | --- | --- |
| Daniel Walker | 30 | 2 | 3 | 6 | --- |
| Jacob Walker | 40 | 3 | 4 | --- | --- |
| Thomas Waters | 225 | 5 | 6 | 10 | 2 |
| Abijah Stephen | 200 | 2 | 2 | 10 | --- |
| Will'm Godfrey | 200 | 4 | 6 | 10 | 1 |
| Joseph Walker, s.m. | 200 | 4 | 6 | 6 | --- |
| James Davis, Jun'r | 400 | 4 | 6 | 10 | 1 |
| Levi Jones | 100 | 2 | 2 | --- | --- |
| Will'm Jones | 100 | --- | --- | --- | --- |
| David Davis | 150 | 3 | 6 | 10 | --- |
| John Gronow | 165 | 3 | 5 | 6 | 2 |
| David Jones | 55 | 2 | 2 | --- | 1 |
| John Maxwell | 190 | 3 | 5 | 7 | --- |
| Adam Ridebough | 175 | 2 | 5 | 6 | --- |
| James Duncan | 100 | 3 | 3 | 6 | --- |

Tredyffrin

| | Acres | Horses | Cattle | Sheep | Servants |
|---|---|---|---|---|---|
| Joseph Baker & Israel Davis | 124 | 3 | 4 | -- | -- |
| John Dunbar, f.m. | -- | 1 | -- | -- | -- |
| Jonathan Evans | 180 | 3 | 4 | 6 | -- |
| Elizabeth Davis | 100 | 2 | 2 | -- | -- |
| Jerman Walker | 100 | 4 | 4 | 8 | -- |
| Joel Evans | 100 | 2 | 2 | -- | -- |
| Joshua Evans | 160 | 3 | 5 | 8 | -- |
| David Howell, tavern, innkeeper | 140 | 3 | 4 | 12 | -- |
| Jacob Sharadon, g.m. | 190 | 3 | 2 | 6 | -- |
| Jacob Baugh | 194 | -- | -- | -- | -- |
| Emanuel Walker, miller | -- | 4 | 2 | -- | -- |
| David Evans, blacksmith | 105 | 2 | 2 | -- | -- |
| Whitehead Wetherby | 100 | 2 | 2 | -- | 1 |
| Jacob Huszard | 100 | 2 | 2 | -- | -- |
| Enoch Williams, farmer | 90 | 2 | 2 | -- | -- |
| Mary Sharp | 100 | -- | -- | -- | -- |
| Mary Richardson | 2 | -- | 1 | -- | -- |
| Benj'n Robison, weaver | 47 | 1 | -- | -- | -- |
| Samuel Weaver | 8 | 1 | 1 | -- | -- |
| Bostin Rink, shoemaker | 70 | 1 | 1 | -- | -- |
| Jno. Havard, Jun'r | 150 | 2 | 4 | 6 | 1 |
| John David | 50 | 1 | 1 | -- | -- |
| John Butler | 9 | 1 | 1 | -- | -- |
| Will'm McEntire | 22 | -- | 1 | -- | -- |
| Thomas Sharp, cooper | 7 | -- | 1 | -- | -- |
| Martin Conrad, carpenter | 15 | -- | 1 | -- | -- |
| Jacob Branamon | 30 | -- | -- | -- | -- |
| Will'm Pumroy, tinman | 14 | -- | -- | -- | -- |
| John Miller, wheelwright | 12 | 1 | 1 | -- | -- |
| Alex'r Logan | 100 | 3 | 5 | 5 | -- |
| George Davis, labourer | 100 | 2 | 1 | -- | -- |
| James Pursley | 50 | 2 | 2 | 2 | -- |
| John Briggs, shoemaker | 50 | 1 | 1 | 3 | -- |
| Sarah Cristie | 200 | 2 | 2 | -- | -- |
| Daniel James | 150 | 3 | 2 | 3 | -- |
| David John | 200 | 3 | 3 | -- | -- |
| John Kike | 260 | 2 | 2 | -- | -- |
| Ann Seringer | 200 | 2 | 2 | -- | -- |
| Edward Rees | 200 | 2 | 4 | -- | -- |
| Paul Sharadin, blacksmith | 94 | 2 | 3 | -- | -- |
| Jacob Delong | 78 | 1 | 2 | 7 | -- |
| Amos Jones, shoemaker | 34 | 1 | 2 | 6 | -- |
| Richard Miles | 8 | 1 | -- | -- | -- |
| Tho's James | 30 | 1 | 2 | -- | -- |
| George White, labourer | 20 | 2 | 2 | -- | -- |
| Chritian Workiser | 149 | 2 | 2 | 3 | -- |
| Thomas Nichols | 50 | 2 | 1 | -- | -- |
| Dennis McCahen, labourer | 50 | -- | 1 | -- | -- |
| Aquilla Potts, blacksmith | 15 | -- | 1 | -- | -- |
| Samuel Potts | 120 | -- | -- | -- | -- |
| Abel Freeman, labourer | 50 | 1 | 1 | -- | -- |
| Davis Jenkin, labourer | 22 | -- | 1 | -- | -- |
| Rob't Russell | 160 | -- | -- | -- | -- |

### Inmates

| | |
|---|---|
| Abel Rees | Peter Steegler |
| Thomas Watkin | Benj'n Evans |
| Morris Davis | John Evans |
| Conrad Coleman | Erratt Appler |
| Tho's Thompson | John Davis |
| David Peregrine | Tho's Morris |
| John Roberts | Philip John |
| Zachariah McCahen | Enoch James |
| Amos Jones | John John |
| John Lowrey | Matthew Bonner |
| James Miles | |

### Freeman

| | |
|---|---|
| David James | Joseph James |
| Abel Hammer | Jacob Thomas |
| Sam'l Davis | Enos Miles |
| Joseph Rowland | Benj'n Davis |
| Joseph Rowland, Se'r | Joseph Williams |
| John Fletcher | Joshua Evans, smith |
| Will'm Donachy | Matthew Hopkins |
| Benj'n Davis, carp'r | George Clifton |
| Charles Ramsey | James Miles |
| James Walker | Sam'l John |
| James Bailey | John Matthews |
| Peter Thomas | Rob't Parry |
| Lewis Gronow | |

### East Town Rate

| | Acres | Horses | Cattle | Sheep | Servants |
|---|---|---|---|---|---|
| James Aspin | 45 | 2 | 2 | 3 | -- |
| James Allison | 100 | 1 | 2 | 6 | -- |
| George Adams | 130 | 2 | 5 | -- | -- |
| Wm. Branaman, weaver | 50 | 2 | 3 | -- | -- |
| Jacob Conrad | 130 | 2 | 4 | 2 | -- |
| Samuel Davis | 150 | 2 | 4 | 8 | -- |
| Ann Ellis | 20 | -- | -- | -- | -- |
| Wm. Griffith | 100 | 2 | 3 | 6 | -- |
| Will'm Hunter | 360 | 5 | 7 | 10 | -- |
| Isaac Hughs | 115 | 2 | 4 | 3 | -- |
| David Hamilton | 10 | 1 | 1 | -- | -- |
| Benj'n Junken | 120 | 3 | 6 | 10 | -- |
| Joseph Junkin | 70 | 2 | 2 | -- | -- |
| Ann James | 100 | 2 | 2 | 2 | -- |
| Thomas John | 35 | 3 | 2 | 3 | -- |
| Will'm John | 50 | 2 | 2 | -- | -- |
| Tho's McKain | 633 | 4 | 6 | 6 | 1 |
| Mark Morris | 125 | 3 | 4 | -- | 1 |
| Mary Moore | -- | -- | -- | -- | -- |
| John Morris, s.m. | 300 | 2 | 4 | 8 | -- |

| East Town | Acres | Horses | Cattle | Sheep | Servants |
|---|---|---|---|---|---|
| Morris Morris | 40 | 1 | 1 | -- | -- |
| Joseph Massey, blacksmith | 70 | 2 | 2 | 7 | -- |
| Henry McQuaid | 150 | 1 | 2 | 2 | -- |
| Archibald McAlister | 30 | 2 | 2 | 4 | -- |
| Uphias McCormick | -- | -- | -- | -- | -- |
| Robert Miskelly | 50 | 2 | 2 | 5 | -- |
| Isaac Minshall | 10 | -- | -- | -- | -- |
| John Peek | 100 | 2 | 1 | 2 | -- |
| Andrew Steel | 75 | 3 | 4 | 7 | -- |
| John Steel | 140 | 3 | 4 | 6 | -- |
| John Smith | 75 | 2 | 4 | 4 | -- |
| Hugh Stuart | 150 | 2 | 4 | 6 | 1 |
| Robert Stephens | -- | 2 | 3 | 6 | -- |
| Thomas Tucker, carpenter | 105 | 3 | 5 | 15 | -- |
| George Turner | 60 | -- | -- | -- | -- |
| Isaac & Anthony Wayne, tanners, tanhouse, yard, &c. | 175 | 6 | 12 | 20 | 5 |
| Thomas Welsh | -- | 1 | 1 | -- | -- |
| Thomas Wilson | 125 | 1 | 3 | -- | -- |
| Jacob Woolman | 135 | 2 | 2 | -- | -- |
| Samuel Weatherby, tavernkeeper | 45 | 2 | 2 | -- | -- |
| Michael Wayne | 80 | -- | -- | -- | -- |
| Thomas Massey | 73 | -- | -- | -- | -- |
| Nathan Lewis | 20 | -- | -- | -- | -- |
| Will'm Bell | 70 | -- | -- | -- | -- |
| Rebeckah Lewellin | 100 | -- | -- | -- | -- |
| Whitehead Weatherby | 10 | -- | -- | -- | -- |

Inmates

Alex'r Boyd
Sarah Horner
Eneas Grimes
George Smiley

Robert McGugen
Alex'r Fulton
James Morris
James Taylor

Freemen

James Murdock
James Blair
Samuel Davis
John Griffith
Will'm Holaday
Benj'n Junken
Adam Junken
James Elliott
Edward Williams
Joshua Cliver
Lewis Morris

Arthur McQuaid
James McConnel
James Henry
Josiah Crawford
Isaac Norton
Hugh Wilson
Robert Holliday
George Thirlton
Isaac Lewis
James Mungomery
Robert Boreland

## Radnor Rate

|  | Acres | Horses | Cattle | Sheep | Servants |
|---|---|---|---|---|---|
| Enoch Abraham | 10 | -- | 2 | -- | -- |
| William Anderson | 50 | 2 | 3 | -- | -- |
| James Barry, tavernkeeper | 70 | 1 | 2 | 5 | -- |
| Lavallan Barry, tavernkeeper, tavern | 50 | 2 | 2 | 4 | -- |
| Frederick Bittle | 150 | 2 | 3 | -- | -- |
| John Bower | 140 | 2 | 4 | -- | -- |
| Henry Beare, taylor | 30 | 1 | 1 | -- | -- |
| David Cornick | 210 | 3 | 4 | 6 | -- |
| Sarah Chattin | 30 | -- | -- | -- | -- |
| Adam Cyter, tanner | 100 | 2 | 3 | 8 | -- |
| Andrew Cearns | 50 | 1 | 2 | -- | -- |
| Evan Davie | 180 | 2 | 6 | 8 | -- |
| John Davis, H | 35 | 2 | 2 | -- | -- |
| John Davis, C | 40 | 2 | 2 | 3 | -- |
| Evan Evans | 225 | 3 | 4 | 6 | -- |
| Elizabeth Evans | 150 | 3 | 4 | 6 | -- |
| Griffith Evans | 70 | 2 | 4 | 6 | -- |
| Griffith Evans, Jun'r | 70 | 2 | 2 | -- | -- |
| John Evans | 100 | 2 | 1 | 2 | -- |
| Mathuselah Evans, blacksmith | -- | 1 | 1 | -- | -- |
| Jane Evans | 200 | 2 | 3 | 4 | -- |
| Robert Elliott, weaver | 40 | 1 | 3 | -- | -- |
| George Fetterman | 32 | -- | -- | -- | -- |
| Jesse Guiger | 100 | 2 | 5 | 10 | -- |
| Jno. Roberts, miller | 45 | -- | -- | -- | -- |
| Hugh Griffiths | 20 | -- | 1 | -- | -- |
| Samuel Harry, Jun'r | 100 | -- | -- | -- | -- |
| Christopher Hoofman | -- | 2 | 2 | 2 | -- |
| Lewis Jerman | 120 | 2 | 4 | -- | 1 |
| Evans James | 200 | 2 | 3 | 10 | -- |
| John Jones | 170 | 4 | 6 | 8 | -- |
| John Jones, storekeeper | -- | 2 | 3 | -- | -- |
| Edward Jones | 233 | 4 | 8 | 10 | -- |
| David Jones | 90 | 3 | 4 | -- | -- |
| John Jacobs | -- | 1 | 2 | -- | -- |
| Elias James | 100 | 2 | 1 | -- | -- |
| David Lewis | 200 | 4 | 6 | 6 | -- |
| John Lewis, Jun'r & Evan Lewis | 250 | 2 | -- | -- | -- |
| John Lewis | 20 | -- | -- | -- | -- |
| Joseph Loyd | 37 | 1 | 2 | -- | -- |
| Benj'n Lewsley | 100 | 3 | 3 | 3 | -- |
| Hannah Loyd | 150 | 2 | 3 | -- | -- |
| Will'm Lee | 80 | 2 | 2 | -- | -- |
| Mordecai Morgan | 140 | 2 | 4 | 6 | 1 |
| Magdalen Morgan | 160 | 1 | 5 | 9 | 2 |
| David Morris | 24 | -- | -- | -- | -- |
| Earnest Miller | -- | 2 | 3 | 4 | -- |
| Joseph Miles, s.m. | 230 | 2 | 2 | 4 | -- |
| John Mathers | 100 | 2 | 3 | 4 | -- |
| Nathan Matlack | 178 | 3 | 6 | 6 | -- |
| Jacob Mower, labourer | 4 | -- | 1 | -- | -- |

| Radnor | Acres | Horses | Cattle | Sheep | Servants |
|---|---|---|---|---|---|
| Adam Ramsower, tavernkeeper, tavern | 90 | 2 | 3 | 4 | -- |
| George Ridoller, taylor | 60 | 1 | 2 | -- | -- |
| Jasher Roberts, storekeeper | 87 | 3 | 4 | -- | -- |
| Thomas Reed | 90 | 3 | 6 | 6 | -- |
| Michael Stradleman, tavernkeeper, tavern | 100 | 2 | 2 | -- | -- |
| John Stillwaggon | 100 | 2 | 2 | 4 | -- |
| Adam Smith, labourer | 140 | 2 | 2 | -- | -- |
| John Smith, mason | 50 | 1 | 1 | -- | -- |
| Thomas Thomas, g.m. | 192 | 2 | 4 | -- | -- |
| Michael Thomas | 143 | 3 | 2 | 8 | -- |
| John Thomas | 200 | 2 | 2 | 6 | -- |
| Owen Thomas | 90 | 2 | 3 | 3 | -- |
| Evan Thomas | 80 | 1 | 3 | 4 | -- |
| Elisha Thomas | 160 | -- | -- | -- | -- |
| Christ'r White | 76 | 2 | 2 | 6 | -- |
| Tho's Wilson, Sen'r, labourer | 100 | -- | 2 | -- | -- |
| Tho's Wilson | 90 | 2 | 4 | 6 | -- |
| Philip Waldhammer | 70 | 3 | 4 | 4 | -- |
| John Willson, farmer | 140 | 2 | 2 | -- | -- |
| John Krim | 10 | 2 | 1 | -- | -- |
| Enos Miles, carpenter | -- | 1 | -- | -- | -- |
| Morris Philips | 60 | 2 | 3 | -- | -- |
| Charles Humphreys | 10 | -- | -- | -- | -- |
| James Hunter | 80 | -- | -- | -- | -- |
| Abraham Cornock | 30 | -- | -- | -- | -- |
| Tho's Williams | -- | -- | -- | -- | -- |

Inmates

Joseph Smith
Joseph Evans
Joseph McVaugh
John Powel
Sam'l Pugh
Frederick Ernest

Will'm Gabb
David Rees
George Giger
Richard Richardson
Hugh Richards

Freeman

Levi Lewis
Isaac Davis
Henry Lewis
Casper Coyer
John Evans
Amos Evans
Rob't Mathers
John Mathers
Joseph Davis
Griffith James
John Ard
Owen Seelton

Evan Griffith
Samuel Vanleer
Christ'r Bergenstone
Henry Rydoller
Tho's Cunningham
John Dungen
Philip Evolt
Miles Thomas
Tho's Williams
Tho's Hazel
John Adair
Nail Odair

## East Whiteland Rate

|  | Acres | Horses | Cattle | Sheep | Servants |
|---|---|---|---|---|---|
| Henry Atherton, inkeeper | 300 | 4 | 6 | 20 | -- |
| Widow Ashton | 50 | 1 | 1 | -- | -- |
| Benj'n Bartholomew | 175 | 5 | 6 | 11 | 1 |
| Richard Kelly, labourer | 10 | -- | 1 | -- | -- |
| Thomas Bowen | 170 | 4 | 5 | 5 | 1 |
| Paul Bond | 100 | 3 | 3 | -- | -- |
| Benj'n Bond, weaver | 12 | 1 | 1 | -- | -- |
| Joshua Bean, blacksmith | 48 | 2 | 2 | 4 | -- |
| John Blackford | 300 | 2 | 6 | 10 | 1 |
| Gasper Beerbrower | 134 | 2 | 6 | -- | -- |
| John Cloyde | 130 | 3 | 7 | 15 | 2 |
| James Cloyde | 50 | 2 | 3 | 5 | 1 |
| Richard Dilworth, chairmaker | 130 | 4 | 4 | -- | -- |
| Daniel Derborow | 80 | 2 | 4 | -- | -- |
| William Garrett | 160 | 4 | 6 | 8 | 2 |
| Thomas Garrett | 80 | 1 | 2 | -- | -- |
| Thomas Harris | 195 | 4 | 8 | 10 | -- |
| Josiah Hibbard | 140 | 3 | 4 | 8 | 1 |
| Philip Hofman, labourer | 10 | 1 | -- | 5 | -- |
| Henry Jones | 200 | 4 | 2 | 4 | -- |
| Samuel Kennedy, physician | 52 | 3 | 3 | 6 | 1 |
| Jno. Kerlin, inkeeper | 150 | 3 | 2 | 8 | -- |
| Michael Lapp | 200 | -- | 2 | -- | -- |
| Joseph Lewis | 115 | 2 | 5 | 10 | -- |
| Randle Malin, lime burner, s.m. | 200 | 7 | 6 | 15 | 1 |
| William McGlaughlan | 200 | 2 | 2 | 5 | -- |
| John Maris | 70 | 3 | 3 | 8 | -- |
| Robert Powell, s.m. | 140 | 5 | 6 | 6 | 3 |
| Caleb Parry, innkeeper, tavern | 250 | 3 | 3 | 15 | -- |
| John Philips | 100 | 3 | 3 | 4 | -- |
| Heirs of Plumstead | 840 | -- | -- | -- | -- |
| Richard Richardson | 84 | 3 | 4 | 6 | -- |
| Estate of Kelly to Rich'd Richardson | 150 | -- | -- | -- | -- |
| John Smith, shopkeeper | 90 | 2 | 2 | 2 | -- |
| John Sloan | 150 | 3 | 4 | 8 | 1 |
| John Templeton | 160 | 3 | 6 | 10 | -- |
| Joseph Templeton, weaver | 7 | -- | 1 | -- | -- |
| Andrew Todd | 240 | 5 | 7 | 15 | 1 |
| Andrew Turk, sadler | -- | 1 | 1 | -- | -- |
| Will'm Thomas | 140 | 3 | 3 | 6 | -- |
| Michael Wayne, miller | 130 | 3 | 4 | 8 | -- |

### Inmates

Henry Bean  
Jacob Earnest  
Bryan Kelly  
Jno. McFall  
Tho's Reed  

Lodowick Spanager  
Michael Peters  
Caleb Atherton  
Patt McFall  
Owen Aston

## Freemen

| | |
|---|---|
| John Rose | Evan Evans |
| Edward Conner | Andrew Heaslip |
| James Hunter | James Magee |
| Alex'r McCaulley | James Baily |
| David Cloyde | John Knox |
| John Malan | John Parry |

## Newtown Rate

| | Acres | Horses | Cattle | Sheep | Servants |
|---|---|---|---|---|---|
| Nathan Lewis | 280 | 4 | 8 | -- | -- |
| James Hunter | 300 | 7 | 7 | 8 | 1 |
| Lewis Lewis | 280 | 1 | 2 | 4 | -- |
| John Williamson | 188 | 6 | 8 | 12 | 1 |
| David Thomas | 146 | 2 | 7 | 8 | -- |
| David Reece | 150 | 3 | 6 | 10 | -- |
| Aaron Vernon | 85 | 2 | 4 | 6 | -- |
| Nathaniel Newlin | 175 | 4 | 4 | 6 | -- |
| Hezekiah Thomas | 150 | 2 | 3 | 7 | -- |
| Will'm Lewis | 170 | 4 | 8 | 7 | -- |
| Samuel Kelly | 84 | 2 | 2 | 4 | -- |
| Richard Fawkes, s.m. | 280 | 7 | 8 | 20 | -- |
| Wm. Reese | 100 | 2 | 2 | 10 | -- |
| George Garrett | 220 | 3 | 6 | 4 | -- |
| John Hamilton | 150 | 7 | 8 | 10 | 2 |
| Abner Lewis | 54 | 4 | 2 | -- | -- |
| John Jordan | 200 | 4 | 6 | 6 | -- |
| James Scott | 150 | 5 | 8 | 6 | -- |
| John Scott | 150 | 4 | 8 | 8 | -- |
| Will'm Thomas, wheelwright | 52 | 1 | 3 | -- | -- |
| Jonathan Morris | 150 | 3 | 3 | 4 | -- |
| Jonathan Thomas | 50 | 2 | 2 | 3 | -- |
| Jonathan Hughs, smith's shop | 30 | 1 | 1 | -- | -- |
| Leonard Miller | 200 | 1 | 4 | 4 | -- |
| John McCutcheon | 30 | 1 | 1 | -- | -- |
| James Moore | 140 | 3 | 4 | 6 | -- |
| Christopher Slizman | 100 | 3 | 2 | 2 | -- |
| John Jervis, tavernkeeper, tavern | 30 | 1 | -- | -- | -- |
| James Maris | 45 | 2 | 1 | 9 | -- |
| Isaac Cochran | 120 | 3 | 5 | 4 | -- |
| Mary Hunter | -- | -- | -- | -- | -- |
| Isaac Harlan, cooper | 6 | 1 | 1 | -- | -- |
| James Jones | -- | 1 | 1 | -- | -- |
| Evan Lewis | -- | 2 | 4 | 8 | -- |
| Samuel Kelly | -- | 2 | 2 | 5 | -- |
| Philip Lynch, shopkeeper | -- | 1 | 1 | -- | -- |
| Daniel Hoopes | 69 | 1 | 1 | 2 | -- |
| Joshua Procter, hemp manu-facturer | 12 | 1 | 1 | -- | -- |
| Phelix Miller | 60 | 1 | 2 | 6 | -- |

| Newtown | Acres | Horses | Cattle | Sheep | Servants |
|---|---|---|---|---|---|
| Philip Dunn | 50 | 2 | 2 | -- | -- |
| George Dunn | 51 | 2 | -- | -- | -- |
| Samuel Hall | -- | -- | -- | -- | -- |
| Isaac Farr, shoemaker | -- | 1 | 1 | -- | -- |
| Phinehas Lewis | 45 | -- | -- | -- | -- |
| Thomas Courtney | 60 | -- | -- | -- | -- |
| Daniel Watkin, smith | -- | 1 | 1 | -- | -- |
| Elen Lewis | 193 | -- | -- | -- | -- |

Inmates

Abraham Vernon         James Hughes
John Skilton           John Moore

Freemen

Robert Peoples         Peter Evil
John Cochran           John Bradley
Abram Ferree           Onosyphorus Jones
John Fawkes            Will'm Thomas
Azariah Lewis          John Jones
James Hunter           Cochran Man, Alis Lions
Edward Baily           John Irwin
Michael McMullin       Joseph Lamb
John Miller            Nath'n Scott
Jacob Matson           John Forbes
James Moore

Goshen Rate

| | Acres | Horses | Cattle | Sheep | Servants |
|---|---|---|---|---|---|
| George Ashbridge, shopkeeper and dealer in flower, coopering, g.m., s.m. | 650 | 12 | 10 | 15 | 1 |
| Aaron Ashbridge | 300 | 5 | 11 | 19 | 1 |
| Jonathan Ashbridge, distiller | 117 | 3 | 3 | -- | -- |
| George Ashbridge, Jun'r, cooper, dealer in meal, g.m. | 308 | 6 | 8 | 12 | 1 |
| Will'm Bane | 215 | 6 | 5 | 8 | -- |
| Joseph Boggs, weaver | 130 | 4 | 3 | 10 | -- |
| John Chapman | 100 | 5 | 1 | -- | -- |
| John Butler | 214 | 4 | 4 | 7 | -- |
| Stephen Bakes | 17 | 1 | -- | 3 | -- |
| James Battin, chairmaker | 50 | 2 | 2 | 2 | -- |
| Jesse Canby | 90 | 3 | 3 | 4 | -- |
| Ellis Davis, fuller, f.m., s.m. | 253 | 7 | 8 | 20 | -- |
| Amos Davis, shopkeeper | 160 | 4 | 5 | 12 | -- |
| Will'm Eachus | 100 | 2 | 4 | 8 | -- |
| Enoch Eachus, weaver | 175 | 3 | 6 | 9 | -- |
| Phinehas Eachus, tavernkeeper, tavern | 150 | 4 | -- | -- | -- |

| Goshen | Acres | Horses | Cattle | Sheep | Servants |
|---|---|---|---|---|---|
| Lawrence Erberly | 140 | 2 | 2 | -- | -- |
| Ralph Forrester, schoolmaster | 100 | 2 | 3 | 8 | -- |
| Joseph Garrett, weaver | 500 | 6 | 11 | 12 | 1 |
| Jonathan Garret | -- | 2 | 4 | 6 | 1 |
| Tho's Goodwin | 130 | 3 | 4 | 8 | -- |
| Tho's Goodwin, Jun'r, weaver | 100 | 3 | 6 | 6 | -- |
| Richard Goodwin, joyner | 50 | 2 | 3 | -- | -- |
| Isaac Haines | -- | 2 | 4 | 10 | -- |
| Josiah Haines | 110 | 2 | 1 | 5 | -- |
| Isaac Haines, Jun'r, plowmaker | 150 | 4 | 4 | 6 | -- |
| Daniel Hoopes | 230 | 3 | 5 | 8 | -- |
| John Hoopes, distiller | 573 | 8 | 12 | 20 | -- |
| Tho's Hoopes | 340 | 6 | 7 | 10 | -- |
| George Hoopes, Jun'r | 200 | 5 | 7 | 6 | 1 |
| David Hoopes, Jun'r, tanner, tanhouse and tanyard | -- | -- | -- | -- | -- |
| Tho's Hoopes, Jun'r, shoemaker | 104 | 3 | 3 | 4 | -- |
| James Hemphill, malthouse and malster | 150 | 4 | 5 | 8 | -- |
| Joseph Hunt | 199 | 5 | 4 | 6 | -- |
| Jacob Hankee, wheelmaker | 100 | 2 | 2 | -- | -- |
| George Hoofman | 140 | 2 | 2 | -- | -- |
| Henry Hoofman | 50 | -- | -- | -- | -- |
| James Galbreath | 100 | 2 | 3 | 4 | -- |
| Will'm Jones | 230 | 3 | 6 | -- | -- |
| Will'm Johnson | 200 | 3 | 5 | 8 | -- |
| Hanse Killgeese | 80 | 2 | 1 | -- | -- |
| Joseph Lacey, tavernkeeper, tavern | 206 | 3 | 3 | 6 | -- |
| Jacob Lamey, taylor | 100 | 1 | 2 | -- | 1 |
| Tho's Lewis, taylor | 100 | 3 | 3 | 6 | -- |
| Jonathan Milleson | 230 | 4 | 5 | 7 | -- |
| Joseph Matlack | 290 | 5 | 6 | 2 | -- |
| Isaiah Matlack | 150 | 3 | 7 | 8 | -- |
| Nathan'l Moore, vendue cryer | 200 | 3 | 6 | 2 | -- |
| John Mechem | 139 | 5 | 5 | 3 | -- |
| Mary Mechem | -- | -- | -- | -- | -- |
| Samuel Oakes | -- | 2 | 1 | -- | -- |
| Samuel Oakes | -- | 2 | 1 | 4 | -- |
| Samuel Phipps, s.m. | 115 | 2 | 2 | 1 | -- |
| James Pierce | 150 | 4 | 4 | 4 | -- |
| Will'm Rattew | 220 | 5 | 7 | 8 | -- |
| Charles Ryan | 150 | 6 | 3 | 3 | 1 |
| Joseph Ray | 190 | 2 | 4 | 6 | -- |
| Aubrey Roberts, shopkeeper | 130 | 3 | 3 | 8 | -- |
| George Smith, cooper | 300 | 4 | 6 | 6 | -- |
| Thomas Speakman, taylor | 96 | 3 | 2 | -- | -- |
| Thomas Schoffield, blacksmith | 150 | 2 | 3 | 6 | -- |
| Will'm Tregoe | 65 | 1 | 1 | -- | -- |
| Joshua Thompson | 220 | 3 | 3 | 10 | -- |
| Will'm Eachus, Jun'r | 100 | 3 | 3 | 6 | -- |
| Benj'n Tregoe | 150 | 2 | 3 | 6 | -- |
| Thomas Russell | 200 | 4 | 6 | 10 | -- |
| Thomas Williamson | 100 | 3 | 4 | 6 | -- |
| Isaac Williams, mason | 180 | 5 | 5 | 6 | 1 |

| Goshen | Acres | Horses | Cattle | Sheep | Servants |
|---|---|---|---|---|---|
| James Travilla, shoemaker | 20 | 1 | 2 | -- | 1 |
| Samuel Wall, shoemaker | 60 | 2 | 2 | -- | -- |
| Lydia Williams | -- | 1 | 1 | -- | -- |
| Josiah Wilkinson | 160 | 2 | 2 | -- | -- |
| Thomas Reese | 115 | 2 | 4 | 5 | -- |
| Caleb Mercer | 100 | 2 | -- | -- | -- |
| Michael Lingor | 20 | 1 | 1 | -- | -- |

Inmates

Will'm Beazor
John Beachmont, smith
William Bale
John Brown
John Bane
Joseph Beaumont
Jacob Cook
George Dunavan
Will'm Dwire
Benjamin Ellis
Thomas Frames
John Goodwin
Paul Grundle
Samuel Hoopes
John Hemphill
Aaron Hoopes
Nathan Hoopes
Alexander Hemphill

Reese Jones
Robert Mercer
Joseph Moore
Amos Jones
John Patterson
William Patterson
Thomas Patterson
Thomas Malin
Jacob Malin
Thomas Reed
Frederick Smedley
John Robinson
John Underwood
Uriah White
Reese Williams
Lewis Williams
Henry Woodward
Richard Jones

Freemen

David Ashbridge
Thomas Butler
Enoch Battin
John Battin
Charles Carter
Ezekiel Forrester
Ralph Forrester
Jonathan Forrester
James Garrett
Joseph Garret
Christopher Goodwin
Peter Hill
John Hoopes
John Haines
Adam Taylor
James Stuart
Rob't Stuart
John Stuart
John Speakman
Tho's White

Will'm Johnson
John Johnson
Benjamin James
Patrick Kirl
Rob't McLoughlin
Thomas Morgan
Jonathan Matlack
Amos Matlack
Flower Oakes
Samuel Overthrew
Joseph Pritchard
Thomas Owen
John Patterson
Valentine Peaken
Ezekiel Griffith
Rob't Ruston
Will'm Smith
Joseph Wilkinson
James McClure
Thomas Lewis

## Willis Town Rate

| | Acres | Horses | Cattle | Sheep | Servants |
|---|---|---|---|---|---|
| Will'm Anderson | 83 | 2 | 2 | 3 | -- |
| Rowland Ellis | 80 | -- | -- | -- | -- |
| John Evans | 30 | 1 | 1 | -- | -- |
| Samuel Briggs, s.m. | 122 | 4 | 4 | 4 | -- |
| John Boggs | 123 | 4 | 5 | 2 | -- |
| Levi Bowen | 95 | 3 | 2 | 6 | -- |
| Ezekiel Bowen | 95 | 2 | 2 | 6 | -- |
| Will'm Bell | 148 | 2 | 10 | 8 | 1 |
| Andrew Buchanan, tanner | 25 | 1 | 1 | -- | -- |
| Daniel Cornog | 150 | 2 | 3 | 4 | -- |
| Abraham Crockson | 120 | 2 | 4 | 6 | -- |
| Moses David | 97 | 2 | 2 | -- | -- |
| Lewis David | 100 | 2 | 2 | -- | -- |
| Will'm Garrett | 200 | 4 | 7 | 8 | -- |
| Isaac Garret | 139 | 2 | 9 | 6 | -- |
| Josiah Garrett | 127 | 3 | 4 | 8 | -- |
| Jesse Garrett, shoemaker | 135 | 3 | 3 | 6 | -- |
| Thomas Garrett | 200 | 2 | 6 | 6 | -- |
| Samuel Grubb, g.m., s.m. | 147 | 3 | 4 | -- | 1 |
| Samuel Garrett | 127 | 3 | 6 | 6 | -- |
| Nathaniel Grubb, g.m., s.m. | 3 | -- | -- | -- | -- |
| Lewis Garrett | 150 | 1 | 4 | 6 | -- |
| Mary Griffith | 160 | 3 | 7 | 12 | -- |
| John Griffith | 127 | 3 | 4 | 5 | -- |
| Nathan Griffith | -- | 2 | 2 | 6 | -- |
| Benj'n Hibberd | 210 | 4 | 5 | 8 | -- |
| Samuel Hibberd | 150 | 2 | 5 | -- | 1 |
| Tho's Hall, Sen'r | 175 | 3 | 4 | 2 | -- |
| Thomas Hall, Jun'r | -- | 3 | 4 | 3 | -- |
| Phinebas Hibberd | 100 | 2 | 3 | -- | -- |
| Rachel Hampton | 160 | -- | -- | -- | -- |
| Joseph Hibberd | 100 | 3 | 3 | -- | -- |
| Caleb Hibberd, tanner | 40 | 1 | 1 | -- | -- |
| George Harris | 140 | 2 | 3 | 5 | -- |
| Richard Harris | 130 | 1 | 1 | -- | -- |
| Thomas Harris | 100 | -- | -- | -- | -- |
| Joseph James | 66 | 3 | 4 | 8 | -- |
| Griffith Jones | 152 | 2 | 5 | 12 | 1 |
| Robert Jones | 98 | 2 | 2 | -- | -- |
| Thomas Jones | 100 | 2 | 3 | -- | -- |
| David Jones | 42 | -- | -- | -- | -- |
| George King, shopkeeper | 150 | 3 | 4 | 6 | -- |
| Erasmus Loyd | 150 | 3 | 3 | 10 | -- |
| William Loyd | 90 | 2 | 2 | 3 | -- |
| Abra'm Lewis | 95 | 2 | 2 | 3 | -- |
| Jacob Lewis | 95 | 2 | 2 | 2 | -- |
| Joshua Lewis, glazier | 20 | 1 | -- | -- | -- |
| Thomas Massey | 88 | 2 | 4 | 4 | 1 |
| James Massey | 175 | 3 | 4 | 6 | -- |
| Thomas Moore | 140 | 1 | 2 | 4 | -- |
| Thomas Malin, Sen'r | 80 | 1 | 1 | -- | -- |
| Isaac Malin, shoemaker | 66 | 2 | 2 | 3 | -- |
| Samuel McCue | 100 | 2 | 3 | 5 | -- |
| Isaac Massey, sadler | 123 | 2 | 3 | 8 | -- |

| Willis Town | Acres | Horses | Cattle | Sheep | Servants |
|---|---|---|---|---|---|
| John Neal | 270 | 2 | 2 | -- | -- |
| Samuel Osbourn | 149 | 3 | 5 | 7 | -- |
| Samuel Powell | 295 | -- | -- | -- | -- |
| Joseph Pratt | 56 | -- | -- | -- | -- |
| Edward Pierce | 150 | 2 | 4 | 6 | -- |
| Caleb Reese | 97 | 2 | 2 | 6 | -- |
| William Reese, taylor | 40 | 1 | -- | -- | -- |
| John Smedley | 60 | 1 | 1 | -- | -- |
| George Smedley, fuller, f.m. | 170 | 2 | 3 | 10 | 2 |
| Francis Smedley, tavernkeeper, tavern | 140 | 5 | 8 | 9 | 1 |
| Thomas Smedley | 254 | 4 | 6 | 10 | -- |
| Joshua Smedley | 85 | -- | -- | -- | -- |
| Caleb Smedley | 218 | 2 | 4 | 7 | -- |
| James Sill | 130 | 1 | -- | -- | -- |
| Jacob Slaughter | 45 | 1 | 1 | -- | -- |
| Thomas White | 178 | 2 | 5 | 6 | -- |
| William Williamson | 300 | 3 | 5 | 12 | 1 |
| Isaac Wayne | 144 | -- | -- | -- | -- |
| Benjamin Walker | 187 | 3 | 3 | 8 | -- |
| Lewis Williams | 132 | 1 | 1 | -- | -- |
| Isaac Thomas, joyner & clockmaker, s.m. | 130 | 3 | 5 | 12 | -- |
| Joseph Thomas | 92 | 2 | 2 | 5 | -- |
| Samuel Thomas | 92 | 1 | 1 | -- | -- |
| John Yarnell | 117 | 2 | 2 | 6 | -- |
| Francis Yarnell, malthouse | 100 | 3 | 2 | 5 | -- |
| Amos Yarnall, Sen'r | 100 | 3 | 5 | 8 | -- |
| Moses Yarnell | 82 | 2 | 2 | -- | -- |
| Daniel Yarnell | 120 | 3 | 4 | 3 | -- |
| Amos Yarnell, Jun'r | 166 | 2 | 3 | 4 | -- |
| Enoch Yarnell | 45 | 4 | 4 | 12 | -- |
| George Yarnell | 100 | 1 | 1 | -- | -- |
| Thomas White | 4 | 1 | 1 | -- | -- |
| James Thompson | 20 | 1 | 1 | -- | -- |
| Alexander Tassey | 5 | -- | 2 | -- | -- |
| Crummel Pierce | 13 | -- | -- | -- | -- |
| Matthew Simpson | -- | -- | -- | -- | -- |
| Hugh Evans | -- | 1 | 1 | -- | -- |

Inmates

Nathan Moore
Phineas Massey
Joshua Yarnell
Daniel Reese
Aaron James

John Taylor
Tho's Wiggans
Arch'd McFall
Dudley McGee
John Oakes

Freemen

Thomas Jones
Caleb Yarnell
John Evans

Benj'n Weatherby
Benj'n Hibberd
Samuel Hibberd

Freemen

William Evans
Jonathan Evans
John Gabb
Sam'l Talbert
Ezekiel James
John Harris
Samuel Oliver

Benj'n Griffith
Joel Lewis
Enoch Lewis
George Grimes
Enoch Garrett
Nicholas Cook
Frederick Kellion

# INDEX

ABRAHAM Enoch 92
  James 84
ACKLES Charles 14
  Nathaniel 15
ACOFF Joseph 21
ACOFFE David 22
  Michael 22
ACRE Anthony 85
  Henry 86
ADAIR John 93
ADAMS George 90
  James 26, 33, 77
  Joseph 77, 81
  Robert 78
  Samuel 25
  William 77
AKEN James 23
ALDER John 42
ALES William 38
ALEXANDER Francis 70, 81
  Jacob 70, 72
  James 62
  John 23, 26, 62
  Samuel 63
  William 1, 61
ALFORD Thomas 70
ALLAWAYS William 30
ALLEN Benjamin 64
  David 74
  Isaac 12
  James 23, 26, 64, 78
  John 63
  Joseph 63
  Josiah 74
  Nathan 26
  Robert 14, 64
  Samuel 70
  William 12, 23, 66
ALLESON James 16
ALLEY John 46
ALLIN John 51
ALLISON Isaac 77
  James 77, 90
  Jarrat 47
  Robert 18, 33
ANDERSON Elizabeth 63
  Evan 13
  Henry 23
  Jacob 30
  James 25, 26, 47, 70
  Joseph 66
  Patrick 57
  Robert 81

  Stephen 32
  Thomas 38
  William 92, 99
ANDREW Widow 42
ANGEL John 83
APPLER Erratt 90
ARBECKLE James 38
ARCHER John 53
  William 53
ARD John 93
ARENTON Daniel 35
ARMENT John 50
  Thomas 51
ARMET William 51
ARMOR Samuel 55
ARMSTRONG Francis 17
  John 17
  Robert 15
  Thomas 72
  William 15, 44
ARNDORF John 87
  Philip 87
ARNOL Sarah 66
ARSKING John 59
ARTEER Robert 76
ARTHUR William 63
ARTHURS Joseph 14
  William 15
ASH Joseph 83
  Joshua 1(2)
ASHBRIDGE Aaron 96
  David 98
  George 96(2)
  Jonathan 96
  Joseph 2
ASHTON Abram 30
  Widow 94
  William 69
ASKEW John 46
  Joseph 46
ASKIN Henry 26
ASPIN James 90
ASTON Owen 94
ATHERTON Caleb 94
  Henry 94
  William 13
ATKINS William 22
ATKINSON Robert 44
ATTLEMAN Hance 81
AVERETT William 71
AVERY Daniel 32
AXELINE Adam 41

BABB Peter 81
  Thomas 81
BAIL David 13
BAILEY Isaac 22, 32(2), 64
  James 90
  Joel 32(2), 64, 66
  John 22, 32
  Josiah 32
  William 32, 64, 74
BAILIFF Daniel 9
BAILY Caleb 64
  Daniel 18
  Edward 96
  James 95
  Nathan 66
BAKER Aaron 32
  Aron 32, 49
  Jesse 9
  John 5, 32
  Joseph 6, 89
  Joshua 33
  Nehemiah 7, 49
  Richard 5, 66
  Samuel 32
BAKES Stephen 96
BALAH Alexander 57
BALDWIN Anthony 23
  John 50, 64, 78
  Joseph 53, 63
  Joshua 78
  Robert 63
  Sarah 12(2)
  Thomas 22, 68
  William 19, 47, 78
BALE John 50
  William 98
BALL George 51
  John 1
  Thomas 51
  William 67
BANE James 67
  John 67, 98
  William 27, 96
BARCLAY James 23
  Mary 55
BAREFIELD John 61
BARKER Henry 80
BARKLY John 26
BARNARD Jeremiah 32
  Richard 32
BARNETT Abraham 50
  Richard 22
  Thomas 32, 55
BARNHERD Anthony 40
BARNHILL John 55

INDEX

BARNS James 23
  Thomas 43
BARR Andrew 72
  John 1, 78
  Robert 19, 71
  William 70
BARRAN Edward 80
BARRETT Thomas 12, 73
BARRY Isaac 61
  James 92
  Lavallan 92
  Richard 44
BARTHOLOMEW Benjamin 94
  Edward 68
  Jacob 85
BARTLEY John 64
BARTLY John 65
BARTON James 2
  James 53
BARTRAM James 52
  John 37
BATEMAN John 40
BATMAN Thomas 88
BATTIN Enoch 98
  James 96
  John 98
BATTON John 66
BAUGH Jacob 89
BAYLEY James 74
BEACHMONT John 98
BEAGLY Dennis 80
BEAKER Joseph 50
BEAL William 12
BEALEY David 14
  Samuel 14
BEAN Henry 94
  Joshua 94
BEAR Henry 39
BEARBOWER Henry 86
BEARD John 23
  Thomas 59
BEARE Henry 92
BEARNS Robert 80
BEATES Richard 50
BEATEY Abraham 34
BEATON John 57
BEATS Richard 49
BEATTY James 3
  William 17
BEATY Abraham 35
  Arthur 33
  David 33
  James 70
  Joseph 78

  Robert 33
  William 35
BEAUMONS William 7
BEAUMONT Joseph 98
BEAVER John 88
BEAZOR William 98
BECKET George 26
BEERBROWER Gasper 94
BELL George 38
  Humphry 86
  John 77
  Joseph 36
  Robert 32
  Thomas 87
  William 87, 91, 99
BENNER Henry 39, 86
  Margaret 39
  Paul 87
BENNET Edward 64
BENNETT James 15, 19
  John 60
  Mary 5
  Titus 21
  William 78
BENSON James 33
  John 33
  Robert 35
  William 33
BENTLEY George 22
  Jeffery 14
  Jesse 22
  John 14
  Joseph 34
  Robert 22
BERGENSTONE Christopher 93
BERKHISER George 88
BERNARD Isabella 46
BERRETT Thomas 27
BERRY Christian 40
  Daniel 38
  Garret 13
  Jacob 44
  William 81
BETHEL Joseph 38
BEVEN Davis 2
BEVERLAND James 72
BEVERLY Samuel 65
BEZOR Jane 2
BIER John 87
BIGAM James 16
BIGHAM John 27
BIGHART James 72
BISHOP George 49
  John 72

  Joseph 81(2)
  Samuel 83
  Thomas 36, 49
BITTLE Frederick 92
BLACK Benjamin 55
  Charles 61
  James 5, 36
  John 50, 71, 73
  Joseph 49
  Sarah 12
  William 50
BLACKBORN Ephram 26
BLACKBURN John 25
  Mary 23
  Samuel 25
BLACKFORD John 94
BLACKLEG Lewes 31
BLAIN David 40
  Robert 87
  William 39
BLAIR Daniel 25
  Francis 74
  James 91
  Jane 23
  John 85
BLETTOCK James 14, 15
  William 15
BLEW Peter 76
BOBB Jacob 7
BOGE James 27
BOGENS Tobias 42
BOGG James 16
BOGGS Ezekil 9
  Francis 14
  John 27, 41, 99
  Joseph 96
BOGLE James 10
BOGS William 77
  William 78
BOGUE Abel 9
BOHANAN John 51
BOHANAN Mathew 71
BOHANNAN David 74
BOKER John 21
BOLINGER Frederick 88
BOLLING William 72
BOND Benjamin 94
  George 18
  Hugh 74
  Paul 94
  Samuel 13, 33
BONNER Matthew 90
BONSALL Abraham 1
  Benjamin 1
  David 1

INDEX

Enoch 1(2)
Jesse 37
Jonathan 1
Joseph 1, 19
Joshua 1
Obadiah 60
Sarah 37
BOOKTER Jacob 59
BOON Andrew 37(3)
Hance 37
Joseph 25, 37
William 53
BOOTH Charles 63
Jeremy 46(2)
John 47
Joseph 47
Robert 47
William 1, 30
BORELAND Robert 91
BORGY Jacob 71
BORLAND John 23
BOSLER George 44
Joseph 86
BOSSERD John 42
BOUGH Jacob 39
John 39
BOUHER Simon 42
BOUND John 86
BOWEN Ezekiel 99
Levi 99
Thomas 94
BOWER Jacob 13
John 92
BOWLE Adam 1
BOWMAN John 18
BOYD Alexander 91
Andrew 15
George 15
James 15
John 15
Matthew 15
Thomas 15, 81
BOYDE Alexander 26
Andrew 27
Francis 23
James 72
Nathan 29
William 11, 51
BOYER John 84
Michael 85
BOYLE Dorington 76
Thomas 21, 70
William 11
BOYS William 68
BRADE John 88

BRADEN James 26
BRADLEY Gilbert 11
John 96
BRAKENRIG Robert 81
BRANAMAN William 90
BRANAMON Jacob 89
BRANNAN Benjamin 1
BRATTN James 47
BRATTON James 47
John 64
William 55
BREACHLEY Joakim 25
BREEDEN William 72
BREICENRIDGE David 74
BRENEMAN Benjamin 17
BRENEMON Samuel 15
BRENHOLD Frederick 88
BRENNAN John 1
BRIGGS John 7, 89
Richard 36
Samuel 99
Thomas 36
BRINTON Caleb 7, 60
David 61
Edward 60
George 7, 60
James 19
John 7, 19, 50
BRISBAN Eliza 29
BRISLAND William 29
BRISON John 11
BROADLEY Barney 78
BROADY John 1
BROCKDEN Susannah 56
BROMALL Daniel 49
BROOK Isaac 37
BROOKE Thomas 1
BROOKES John 1
BROOKS David 76
Matthew 44
BROOM Thomas 48
BROOMER David 43
BROOMIL Daniel 31
BROWER Abraham 40
Christian 39
Daniel 39
Henry 38
John 39
BROWN Daniel 27, 33, 46, 48, 57
David 27, 74
Elias 58
Elisha 23
Elnor 23
George 19, 26, 76

Isaac 23, 35
Jacob 21, 23(2)
James 13, 22, 66
Jeremiah 29
John 21, 22, 23, 43, 55, 57, 70, 85, 98
Jonathan 66
Joseph 23, 23, 45
Mary 23, 69
Mathew 69, 80
Messer 27
Nathaniel 46
Olrick 42
Peter 55
Robert 19, 26, 71
Samuel 23
Solomon 57
Thomas 23, 68
Timothy 27
William 23, 27, 66, 82, 83, 84
BRUCE James 67
William 70
BRUMBACK Benjamin 85
Henry 86
BRUMBAKER Peter 39
BRUTON John 61
BRYAN Andrew 29
John 54
BUCHANAN Andrew 99
Gilbert 27
Mary 87
William 26
BUCKANAN William 23
BUCKRAM Elizabeth 37
BUCKWALTER John 41, 57
BUFFINGTON Curtis 68
John 33, 57, 66
Jonathan 22
Joseph 55
Richard 67, 68, 78
Robert 67
Thomas 22
William 67
BUFFINTON Joseph 11
BUHANNAH Andrew 69
BUHANNAN Mathew 69
Samuel 69
BUKER John 7
BULL Richard 13
Thomas 13
BULLA Thomas 15
BULLAR James 26
John 22(2)
Richard 22

# INDEX.

BULLOCK Isaac 50
  John 51
  Timothy 5
BUNDLE Jacob 17
BUNTIN William 43, 77
BUNTING Josiah 37
  Samuel 37
  Sarah 37
  William 73
BURBOWER Herman 42
BURGETT Peter 15
BURGINDINE Peter 80
BURGSIGN Hannah 9
BURK Rowland 5
BURNETT John 50
BURNIT Joseph 7
BURNS Patrick 3, 64
  Robert 77
  William 52, 55
BURNSIDE Andrew 81
BUSSARD Frederick 57
BUTCHER Hannah 27
BUTLER Benjamin 35
  Enoch 33
  John 33, 89, 96
  Noble 33(2)
  Thomas 40, 98
  William 33
BUTTERFIELD John 23
BYER Phillip 39
BYERS Andrew 27
  Benjamin 57
  Samuel 78
  William 33, 80

CADWALADER Nathan 35
CAIN Robert 63
CALDWELL Andrew 63
  John 3
  John 48
  Sarah 52
  William 71
CALHOON William 25
CALLER Nicholas 39
CALLWELL Joseph 44
CALVEL Joseph 74
CALVERT Daniel 49
  John 36, 65
  Nathaniel 36
  Thomas 88
CALWELL James 45
CAMBEL John 50
CAMBELL Charles 83
  George 17, 83
  Hugh 18

  Jacob 69
  James 23
  John 18, 26, 81
  Josiah 81
  William 24
CAMBLE John 76
CAMEL James 43
CAMERON Daniel 52
  Dugall 47
  Finley 48
  William 1
CAMERRON John 47
CAMMEL Alexander 75
  Robert 72
CAMP Fredirick 9
  Hezekiah 48
CAMPBELL Alexander 58
  James 33
  John 58, 69
  Josiah 3
  William 19
CANBY Jesse 96
CANNON John 30
  Joshua 29
  Patrick 25
CANT Mark 71
CARE Thomas 55
CAREY Charles 48
CARL Charles 14
  Henry 88
CARLES Josiah 41
CARLINTON Thomas 19
CARLISLE William 73
CARMICHALL John 23
CARMICKLE John 80
CARPENTER Frederick 23
  John 67
  Samuel 5
  Thomas 12
CARR John 13
  Joseph 71
  Robert 14
  William 30
CARRINGTON Thomas 65
CARSON Andrew 51
  Archabald 72
  David 35
  Francis 64
  John 14
  Patrick 14
  Robert 33, 81
  William 30, 85
CARSWELL James 71, 75
  John 75
  Samuel 75

CARTER Abraham 3
  Charles 98
  Edward 3, 5
  George 9
  John 10
  Martin 46
  Nicolas 42
  Thomas 40
CARUTHERS Alexander 78
  James 76
  John 76
  Samuel 70
CAVEAT Patrick 33
CAVENAUGH Timothy 65
CAYME Stephen 42
CAYS William 12
CEARNS Andrew 92
CHAFF Phillip 22
CHALFANT Henry 32
  Isaac 66
  James 67
  John 67
  Jonathan 33
  Martha 60
  Robert 22(2), 68
  Thomas 60
  William 32
CHALTON Henry 64
CHAMBERIN William 6
CHAMBERLAIN Robert 60
CHAMBERLIN Isaac 31
  John 31, 51
  Joseph 31, 50
  Joshua 15
CHAMBERS John 61
CHANCE Peter 85
CHANDLER Emmor 60
  George 12
  James 60
  John 65
  Joseph 19
  Moses 64
  Samuel 21
  Thomas 60
  William 63
CHANDLEY Benjamin 27
CHAPMAN Isaac 11
  John 96
  William 61
CHARLES Jacob 45
CHARLTON Samuel 70
  Thomas 75
CHATTIN Sarah 92
CHECK John Sarah 53
CHERREY Robert 3

INDEX

CHERRY Benjamin 37
  James 53
  Samuel 12
CHEYNEY Ann 8
  John 8
  Joseph 8
  Richard 8, 31
  Thomas 8
CHIMER Michael 87
CHISM John 5
CHRISMAN Phelix 87
CHRISTIE Samuel 72
  Simon 61
CHRISTMAN George 41
  Henry 86
CHRISTY William 42
CHURCHMAN Edward 49
  George 27, 73
  John 27
  Thomas 27
  William 27
CISOR Paul 39
CLARK Jacob 23
  James 10, 51
  John 13, 16, 19, 68, 78
  Joseph 30, 68, 81
  Michael 42
  Thomas 81
  William 67, 68
CLAXTON James 3
CLAYTON Adam 55
  John 67
  Joseph 55
  Joshua 67
  Richard 55
  William 67
CLELLAND Samuel 75
CLENDENAN Thomas 25
CLENDENEN Alexander 15
  William 16
CLENDENON John 27
CLIFTON George 90
CLIMES Phillip 53
CLIMSON Thomas 15
CLINE John 42
CLINGAN William 81
CLINTON William 63
CLIVER Joshua 91
CLOUD Abner 65
  Jason 69
  Jeremiah 19
  Jeremy 65
  Jesse 66
  Joel 66

  John 55
  Joseph 50(2), 57
  Mordecai 57
  Mordica 30, 45, 65, 78
  William 19, 65
CLOYD Thomas 72
CLOYDE David 95
  James 94
  John 94
CNERR Henry 86
COATES Aaron 44
  Benjamin 58
  Jonathan 58
  Moses 58, 78
  Thomas 78
COBOURN David 4
  Jacob 55
  John 55
  Joseph 3, 55
  Robert 3, 57
  Thomas 53, 55
  William 55
COBURN Caleb 3
COCHRAN David 76
  Isaac 95
  Jacob 71
  James 71, 77, 83
  John 96
  Stephen 77(2)
COCK Benjamin 7(2)
  JN
  Moses 8
COCKRAN Alexander 25
COHRAN James 52
COLBERSON Samuel 87
COLBERT Daniel 66
COLE John 26
  Robert 83
  William 23
COLEER Jacob 86
COLEMAN Conrad 90
COLLENS Joseph 5
COLLINS Joseph 35
  Thomas 23
COLTSON John 23
  Joseph 23
  Thomas 23
COLVEN Robert 27
COLVIN Robert 55
  Samuel 29, 55
CONLY Terence 69
CONN Hugh 55
CONNELL William 55
CONNELLY John 62

CONNER Edward 95
  William 9
CONNOR Manasah 38
CONRAD Jacob 90
  John 57
  Joseph 59
  Martin 89
CONRADTICE Hance 38
CONTENHOSER Rynord 39
COOK Jacob 98
  James 9
  John 46
  Joseph 18
  Nicholas 101
  Rebecca 63
  Stephen 63
COOKE John 3
COOKSON Thomas 49
COOPER Adam 73
  James 73
  John 17, 74
  Robert 15, 19, 81
  Samuel 16
  Thomas 73(2)
  William 17, 67
COPE John 10
  Joseph 10
  Joshua 69
  Michael 53
  Nathan 10
  Samuel 10
COPPER Job 1
COPPOCK John 4, 52
CORNELIUS Stephen 72
CORNICK David 92
CORNOCK Abraham 44, 93
  Thomas 44
CORNOG Daniel 99
CORODON Philip 54
CORREY Moses 75
COSMAN Jacob 71
COUCHANOUR John 39
COUGHRAN George 76
COURTNEY Thomas 96
COWAN Joseph 15
  William 53
COWDAN Robert 77
COWDEN James 23, 27
COWEN David 17
  Hugh 15
  Matthew 17
  Robert 15, 22
  William 15, 42
COWPLAND David 3(2)
  George 76

INDEX

Jonathan 4
Joshua 3
COX Andrew 78
  John 3
  Joseph 86
  Lawrence 55, 78
  Richard 81
COYER Casper 93
COYLE Michael 3
CRABB William 55
CRADLER Oliher 88
CRAFORD John 23
CRAGE Walter 19
  Walter 19
CRAIG Alexander 70
  James 30
  John 53
CRAIGE George 3
CRATOR Andrew 21
CRAVEN James 59
CRAWFORD Catherine 61
  Hugh 68
  James 30, 61
  John 27, 55
  Josiah 27, 91
  Robert 4
  William 81(2)
CREADLER Jacob 40
CREAG Victor 25
CREMER John 68
CRESWELL Elijah 74
  James 26
  Joseph 74
CRETAM John 78
CRIBERSON Nicolas 33
CRISTIE Andrew 69
  Sarah 89
CRISWELL James 72
  Robert 72
  Samuel 74
CROCKSON Abraham 99
CROMPTON John 25
CRONEY John 37
CROOKS Edward 63
CROOKSHANK Charles 44
CROOS Samuel 75
CROSBY Samuel 5, 75
  William 75
CROSE William 47
CROSGROVE John 23
CROSWELL Benjamin 76
  Robert 23
CROW George 62
  John 78
  Moses 61

William 40
CROWD John 30
CROXEN Randal 1
CROZBY John 53
  Richard 53(2)
CROZIER James 1, 47
  Robert 1
CRUMBRAKER Abraham 39
CRUMPTON Samuel 64
CRUSWELL George 73
CRY John 60
CULBERSON Andrew 81
CULBERTSON Abigal 78
  Jane 21
  John 63, 78
  Samuel 80
CULBREATH John 73
CULIN Andrew 37
  Daniel 53, 55
  John 53
CULING Swan 53
CULLEM Patrick 35
CULLEPHER William 11
CUMMENS William 75
CUMMINGS Alice 3
CUMMINS Agnes 23
  George 83
  John 11
  Joseph 26, 83
  William 18, 76
CUNEY Daniel 62
CUNINGHAM Allen 12
  Mark 23
CUNNINGHAM Barnabas 5
  John 5
  Joseph 4
  Samuel 69
  Thomas 93
  William 71
CUNTMAN Martin 42
CURL James 26
  John 12
CURREY George 18
  James 71
  Robert 28
CURRIE William 88
CURRY David 17
  James 51
  Mathew 69
CURTAIN Joseph 9
CUSTARD Richard 39
CUSTULOVE Paul 37
CUTHBERT John 13(2)
  Thomas 13

CYPHER Michael 87
CYTER Adam 92

DAILEY Timothy 10
DAILY Charles 9
DANALSON John 80
DANALY Owen 80
DANFETTGER Jacob 41
DARBY Richard 60
DARLING Nathan 71
DARLINGTON Abraham 60(2)
  John 81
  Joshua 71
  Robert 71, 78
DARLINTON John 10
  Thomas 10
DARRAGH Robert 27
DARY George 86
DASHER Henry 86
DAVID Ann 3
  Griffith 45
  Jenkin 58
  Jeremiah 58
  John 58(2), 89
  Lewis 99
  Moses 99
  Peter 1
  Zepheniah 59
DAVIDSON Alexander 81
  William 81
DAVIE Evan 92
DAVIS Abram 11
  Amos 85, 96
  Assa 1
  Benjamin 35, 90(2)
  Caleb 55
  Daniel 9, 11, 34
  David 58, 58, 85, 86, 88
  Elizabeth 89
  Ellis 96
  George 89
  Isaac 8, 44, 48, 88, 93
  Israel 89
  James 1, 10, 88
  Jermon 34
  Jesse 44
  John 1(2), 9, 10, 35, 39, 41, 44, 86, 90, 92(2)
  Joseph 32, 86, 93
  Lewellyn 58
  Lewes 44

INDEX

Lewis 47, 53
Miles 34
Morris 90
Myrick 87
Nathan 52
Neal 43
Nehemiah 5
Sampson 88
Samuel 90(2), 91
Susannah 10
Thomas 1, 15, 87
Walter 76
William 1, 33
DAVLIN Patrick 78
DAWSON Jacob 83
  Thomas 81(2)
DAY James 3, 5
  John 27, 30, 36
  Silvenes 21
  Thomas 30
DAYBEL Leonard 42
DEAL Nicolas 54
  Godfrey 58
DEFRAIN Peter 87
DELAP John 21
DELONG Jacob 89
DEMPSEY Alexander 59
DENCEY Samuel 81
DENIN William 31
DENISON William 85
DENMILLER Peter 42
DENNEY John 80
  William 33
DENNY Walter 25
DERBOROW Daniel 94
DERMOND John 17
DERRAH John 31
DERRICK Thomas 56
  Zachariah 55
DERROUGH John 46
DEVING Felix 83
DIBLIN Charles 66
DICK Archibald 56
DICKEY James 30
  John 15, 24, 64
  Samuel 27(2)
  William 15, 74
DICKS James 43
  John 48, 53
  Joseph 53
  Roger 43, 53
DICKSON Andrew 27
DICKY Samuel 73
DILLEN John 13
DILLON Hannah 27

DILWORTH Charles 61
  James 60
  Richard 94
  William 61
DIMOND Andrew 53
DIMSON William 21
DINGEE Christopher 45
  Jacob 45, 46
DINSMORE Adam 62
DISART William 73
DITLAW George 40
DITLOW Henry 86
DIX James 44
  Job 43
  Joseph 43
  Sarah 43
DIXSON Enock 19
  Henry 19
  John 24
  Rebecca 12
  William 12, 71
DOBBINS James 37
  John 48
  Thomas 42
DOHERTY George 12
  James 45
  John 12
DOMERMAN Peter 87
DONACHY William 90
DONALDSON Thomas 17
  William 72
DONALLY John 78
DONALSON Charles 1
DONAUGHEY John 17
DONAULY Philip 30
DONLAY John 75
DONOUGHY William 72
DORAN Patrick 55
DOTSON John 86
DOUDALL John 65
DOUGHERTY Hugh 78
  James 24
  Patrick 17
  Phillip 17
DOUGLASS George 27
  James 27
  Thomas 29(2)
DOWNEY William 83
DOWNING James 5
  John 57, 68, 78
  Joseph 12, 78
  Richard 33, 67, 68, 78
  William 5
DOYLE Mathew 42
DRENNON David 22

DRENON Joseph 27
DREW David 73
DRUITT John 56
DUGALL James 86
DUNAVAN George 98
DUNBAR John 89
DUNBARR John 1
DUNCAN Alexander 14
  David 56
  James 88
DUNCIN Aron 61
DUNFELTON Wintle 84
DUNGEN John 93
DUNINGHOUR Godfry 39
DUNLAP Alexander 76
  Alexander 78
  David 78
DUNN George 96
  Jacob 36
  James 78
  John 77
  Philip 96
  Thomas 15
  William 36
DUNWODDLE John 71
DUNWODDY William 70
DUNWOODEY David 13
DUNWOODY James 13
  Robert 71
DURNALL John 37
DUTTON Ann 46
  David 5
  John 46
  Richard 31, 46
  Samuel 46
  Thomas 31
DWIRE John 60
  William 98
DYMON Patrick 84
DYSART James 73

EACHOFF William 23
EACHUS Enoch 96
  Phinehas 96
  William 96, 97
EAKINS Samuel 61
EARL John 45
  Robert 51
EARLY Edward 81
  John 71
EARNEST Jacob 94
  James 80
  John 78
EAVENSON Elizabeth 8
  Seth 8

INDEX

EAVES John 19
EBISON Elizabeth 6
ECHUFF David 66
EDDEY Joseph 86
  William 88
EDGE John 78
EDMONDSON David 25
EDMUNDSON David 24, 26
  Margaret 24
EDMUNSTON William 72
EDWARD James 35
EDWARDS Amos 60
  Elisha 59
  John 6, 19, 43
  Jonathan 24
  Joseph 5, 43
  Joshua 33
  Moses 32
  Nathan 5
  Robert 53
  Thomas 46(2)
  William 33, 53
EFFIBIT George 11
EFFINGER Henry 52
ELDER Robert 19
  Thomas 77
ELDRIDGE Jonathan 10, 13
ELIOT James 51
ELLIOT Christopher 53
  Enoch 37
  John 12, 14, 37
  Martha 37
  Peter 37, 53
  Robert 80
  William 31
ELLIOTT Andrew 80
  James 91
  Robert 92
  Samuel 27
  Thomas 69
  William 3, 12
ELLIS Ann 90
  Benjamin 98
  David 45
  Everard 37
  James 12
  Jeremiah 44
  Jesse 45
  Jonathan 45
  Rowland 99
  Thomas 44
ELY Sarah 43
EMBLEN William 55
EMERY George 41

EMOULD Peter 85
ENGLAND Daniel 24
  David 63
  John 64
  Samuel 28
  William 9
ENGLE Fredirick 5
ENGLIS David 60
ENTERKIN Samuel 7
  Samuel 11
ENTREKIN George 9
ENTRIKIN Samuel 82
ERBERLY Lawrence 97
ERNEST Frederick 93
ERVIN Godson 16
  Josiah 16
ERWIN Archibald 79
  David 68
  James 79, 81
  John 27, 77, 79
  Robert 27, 79
  Theophelus 78
  William 21
ESERY Jonathan 50
ESSICK Michael 87
ESSY John 5
EVANS Abner 83
  Amos 93
  Aresiah 13
  Benjamin 90
  Cadwalader 49
  Daniel 13, 34
  David 34, 87, 89
  Elihu 84
  Elizabeth 92
  Evan 1, 61, 92, 95
  George Elihu 84
  Griffith 92(2)
  Hugh 100
  James 24, 41, 85, 86
  Jane 92
  Joel 89
  John 35, 88, 90, 92, 93, 99, 100
  Jonathan 1, 89, 101
  Joseph 93
  Joshua 89, 90
  Mathuselah 92
  Morris 87
  Phillip 30
  Rees 87
  Richard 34
  Robert 49
  Samuel 30

  Thomas 13, 34, 50(2)
  William 3, 87, 101
EVENSON Geo. 8
  Thomas 9
EVERHARD Christopher 86
EVERS James 78
EVERSON Richard 8
EVIL Frederick 40
  Peter 96
EVOLT Philip 93
EWING Alexander 73
  Henry 27, 73, 74
  James 73
  Robert 27
  Samuel 24
  Thomas 27
  William 85
EYERE Lewis 46
  Robert 45
EYERS William 47
EYRE Isaac 3
EYRES John 3
  Lewis 47

FAGAN Barnabas 32
FAIRLAMB Frederick 5
  Nicholas 5
FARAH John 31
  Oliver 31
FARLOW William 33
FARON James 33
FARR Edward 49
  Isaac 96
FARREL Lewis 5
FARRIER Robert 6
  William 1
FARRILL Michael 10
FAULES James 30
FAWKES John 96
  Richard 95
FEAR Samuel 13
FEGAN William 33
FELL Edward 48
  William 43, 47
FELTON Thomas 4
FELTY Jacob 85
FEMBLE Jacob 45
FERGUSON Mathew 82
  William 70
FERREE Abram 96
  John 53
FETTERMAN George 92
FEW James 10
  Joseph 57

# INDEX

FIELD Ginnings 80
  William 52
FILE John 3
  Robert 5
FILSON Davidson 14(2)
  Robert 14
FINGER Mathias 13
FINNEY John 19
  Robert 17(2)
  Thomas 17
  Widow 17
FISHER Custin 69
  David 53
  Francis 32
  George 68
  Robert 21
  Samuel 79
  Thomas 33, 79
FISK James 85
FISSILER George 42
FITSIMMONS George 86
  John 86
FITTING Gaspar 41
FITZGARRAL John 19
FITZSIMMONS James 88
FLATCHER John 75
FLEEMAN John 42
FLEMING Alexander 79
  Ann 79
  Archibald 74
  David 73
  Hance 74
  James 15, 72
  John 17, 74(2) 82
  Joseph 79
  Peter 79
  William 82
FLEMMIN Archabald 78
FLEMMING Benjamin 55
FLETCHER John 90
  Robert 66
FLING Abigail 9
  Lawrence 21
  Nicholas 51
FLOWER Hannah 46, 56
  James 30
  John 56
  Richard 63
  William 57
FLOYD Samuel 18
FOOS Nicholas 58
  Vallentine 42
FORBES John 96
FORBUS Andrew 81

FORD Abraham 67
  Benjamin 57
  John 46, 47, 67
  Margaret 53
FORDOM Joseph 37
FOREMAN Alexander 9
  Elizabeth 45
FORGY James 56
FORKER Charles 26
FORREST William 47
FORRESTER Ezekiel 98
  Jonathan 98
  Matthew 11
  Ralph 97, 98
FORSTER Simon 7, 9
  Thomas 72
FOSSET George 68
FOSSTER Francis 63
FOULK Eneas 47
  John 47
FOWLER Morris 45
FOWLES Archibald 72
FOX John 36
FRAME John 61
  Nathan 60
  William 71
FRAMES Thomas 98
FRANCIS John 41, 58
FRANK Isaac 9
  Sebastian 84
FRAZIER Moses 63
  Persifor 8
FREAD Joseph 11
FRED John 19
FREDRICK Lawrence 37
FREEMAN Abel 89
FRELY Nicolas 85
FREW Alexander 29, 30
FRICH Daniel 56
FRIER George 8
  Thomas 8
FRISHEOM Leonard 40
FRITH William 51
FRYER William 62
FULK George 85
FULLER Christopher 84
FULLERTON William 87
FULTON Alexander 75, 91
  John 27, 72
  Samuel 74
  Thomas 18
  William 27
FUREY James 68
FURRY Elizabeth 17
  Joseph 17

FUSSELL William 58
FUTHEY Robert 78
  Samuel 77

GABB John 101
  William 93
GABEY James 82
GAFF Patrick 55
  Robert 65
GALASPEY William 19
GALBREATH James 97
GALESPY Andrew 17
  John 17
GALLY Jacob 53
GAMBEL Patrick 50
GAMBELL Andrew 17
GAMBLE Hambleton 72
GANGER George 51
GANTER Jacob 41
GARBISON Jane 76
GARDNER Francis 71
  James 60
  John 69, 72
  Joseph 78
GARICK George 39
GARINGER Jacob 39
GARMAN James 71
GARRET Isaac 99
  John 13
  Jonathan 97
  Joseph 98
GARRETT Enoch 101
  George 95
  James 98
  Jesse 99
  John 1
  Joseph 97
  Josiah 99
  Lewis 99
  Nathan 1(2)
  Samuel 99
  Thomas 94, 99
  William 1, 94, 99
GATCHELL Jeremiah 30
GATLES Reece 34
GATTREY Adam 69
GAUTT James 27
GEERHART Frederick 58
GEETY William 74
GELESPY Roger 59
GEORGE David 55
GERICK George 84
GETER Adam 88
GETINGER Jacob 39, 40
GEVOAD Geratt 15

INDEX

GHEEN Joseph 68
  Thomas 67
GIBB Hugh 82
  James 82
GIBBINS Joseph 47
GIBBONS James 7
  Joseph 7
  Thomas 10
  William 8, 60
GIBBS Gilbert 83
GIBSON Alexander 74
  Andrew 76
  George 78
  Isaac 71
  James 77
  John 73, 78
  Thomas 19
  William 27
GIFFEN William 62
GIFFIN Robert 18
GIGER George 93
GILBREATH John 29
GILFELLIN Robert 68
GILKEY Jonas 15
  Robert 82
GILKIE William 71
GILL Michael 3
GILLALEN James 77
GILLELAND James 75
  John 79
GILMORE Robert 17, 18, 69
  Thomas 17
GILPIN George 57, 60
  Gideon 60
  Israel 19
GINNEY Timothy 25
GITCHELL Elisha 27
  Joseph 27
GIVEN Robert 24
GLANSEY Peter 61
GLASCO John 27
GLASGOW John 24, 26
  Samuel 24
GLEN Hugh 79
  William 72
GLENDENNING James 77
GLOVER Archabald 27
GODFREY George 85
  William 88
GOLLINGHER Francis 5
GOODLOOP John 12
GOODWIN Christopher 98
  John 98

Richard 97
  Thomas 97(2)
GORDON Harry 60
  John 61
  William 87
GORMAN Richard 36
GORMINGLY James 21
GORMLEY Thomas 21
GOTHERP Thomas 27
GOTTAS Widow 18
GOTTRY John 73
GOUDY James 80
GOULD Alexander 71
  William 71
GRAHAM Arthur 69
  Eleanor 3
  Henry 71
  Henry H. 3
  James 69
  Jane 69
  John 69
  Michael 69
  Patrick 76
  Robert 27, 76
  William 58
  Zedekiah 5
GRANGEE Joseph 56
GRANT John 36(2)
  Nicholas 59
  William 14
GRANTHAM Charles 53
  Margaret 53
GRANTUM Charles 37
GRASY Samuel 53
GRAVEW Jacob 34
  James 5
GRAY Enoch 11
  George 21
  Gilbert 72
  James 14(2) 77
  John 23
  Sterret 62
GREACY John 44
GREAMES Henry 30
GREEN Abel 49
  Edward 8
  Isaac 79
  John 5
  Joseph 79
  Robert 50(2) 60
  Thomas 9, 71, 79
GREENFIELD James 63
GREENLAND Flower 26

GREER Ivan 27
  Robert 14
  Thomas 74
GREGORY Levy 46
GRENT Isaac 1
GREY John 10, 73
  Robert 71
GRIBBLE Joseph 56
GRIEST John 23
GRIFFITH Abel 67, 69
  Benjamin 101
  Dan 84
  David 40
  Evan 83, 93
  Ezekiel 98
  James 38
  John 58, 84, 85, 91, 99
  Levi 85
  Mary 99
  Nathan 99
  Susannah 49
  William 12, 34(2), 45, 84(2), 85, 90
GRIFFITHS Hugh 92
GRIFFITS William 31
GRIGG Benjamin 19
  Enoch 12
  Joseph 19
  Michael 19
  Stephen 21
GRIM Conrod 39
GRIMES Eneas 91
  George 101
  John 49
  Peter 79
  William 75
GRISELL Thomas 49
GRISSELL Edward 8
GRIST George 33, 56
  Samuel 56
GRIVE Matthew 27
GROFF John 88
GRONOW John 88
  Lewis 90
GROUCE George 39
GRUBB Abra. 39
  Adam 3
  family 57
  Hary 5
  Henry 39
  John 39
  Mary 10
  Nathaniel 99
  Samuel 19, 99

# INDEX

GRUBER John 37
GRUNDLE Paul 98
GUBBY Peter 18
GUEST Daniel 9
  Henry 8
  James 35, 84
  John 35
  Phebe 50
  Thomas 34
  William 47
GUI Isabel 72
GUIGER Jesse 92
GUTREY James 83
GUTTRY James 74
  John 72
GUY Archibald 76

HACKLEY James 39
HADDON Thomas 54
HAGUE William 21
HAILEY John 23
HAILMAN Peter 42
HAINES Ellis 13
  Isaac 97(2)
  John 98
  Josiah 97
HAINS Joseph 24
  William 24
HALL Andrew 60
  Charles 11
  David 52
  George 36
  Hezekiah 31
  James 51
  John 47, 50, 57, 80
  Joseph 75
  Robert 50
  Samuel 96
  Stephen 50
  Thomas 60, 99(2)
  Walter 75
  William 75
HALLBRIGHT Jacob 9
HALYARD Phillip 11
HAMBLE Archibald 76
HAMBLETON James 14, 70, 71
  John 70, 72
  Patrick 28
  Robert 26
  William 82
HAMEL Robert 77
HAMILTON David 90
  John 95
HAMMER Abel 90

HAMORS Thomas 76
HAMPTON Rachel 99
  Simon 8
  Thomas 47
  Walter 9
HANCE Benjamin 3
  James 19
HANCOCK Hiram 3
  James 58
  William 58
HANKEE Jacob 97
HANKER Henry 42
HANKIN Peter 41
HANLEY Barney 80
  John 3
HANNAH Francis 22
  James 69
  John 14, 72
  William 14, 23, 35
HANNUM John 10, 50
  Thomas 60
HANNUMS John 67
HARBISON James 18, 24
HARDEN William 8
HARDY James 66
  Joshua 44
HARE James 69
HARISON George 82
HARLAN Caleb 21, 63
  David 63
  George 32, 33
  Henry 64
  Isaac 95
  James 33
  Jesse 21
  Joel 22
  Jonathan 33
  Joshua 20
  Michael 32, 64
  Soloman 63
  Stephen 64, 67
  William 14, 32(2)
HARLIN George 50
  Joseph 19
  Samuel 19
HARNS Rudolph 34
HARPER John 8, 13, 61
HARRACK John 11
HARRIS Daniel 51
  George 99
  James 74
  John 101
  Joseph 30
  Richard 26, 99

  Thomas 94, 99
  William 24
HARRISON Alexander 76
  Caleb 5
HARRY Amos 19
  Evan 19
  Jesse 21
  Samuel 92
  Silas 66
  Thomas 21
  William 65
HART Barnabas 35
  John 82
  Samuel 83
  Thomas 80
HARTLEY Elisha 56
HARTMAN John 41
  Peter 42
HARTSHORN George 55
HARTZ Adam 41
HARVEY James 19
  Job 59
  John 23, 59
  Robert 27, 30
  Samuel 58
  Thomas 30
  William 19, 60
HASTAND John 79
HASTINGS David 76
HASTON William 45
HATHORN John 28(2)
HATTEN James 51
HATTON John 21, 35
  Nehemiah 64
  Peter 50
HAVARD Ann 88
  David 88
  John 89
  Samuel 88
HAVERSACK John 5
HAWES John 1
HAWLEY Benjamin 9, 61
  Joseph 67
  William 51
HAWS Michael 84
HAWSE John 86
HAYCOCK Joseph 48
  Josiah 52
  Nathan 6
HAYES Caleb 22
  David 73
  Hannah 22, 32
  Henry 22
  John 1, 21, 29
  Joseph 1, 22

INDEX

Mary 14
Mordica 65
Nathan 32
Samuel 65
Stephen 19
Thomas 14
William 21
HAYNES Isaac 24
  Jacob 24
  Job 24
HAYNEY James 7
HAZEL Thomas 93
HAZLETT William 77
HEACOCK John 5
  Jonathan 44
  Joseph 43
HEADDIN John 68
HEALD John 19
  Joseph 21
  Samuel 20
HEASLIP Andrew 95
HEATH Daniel 40
HECK Jonas 86
HEDLESTON James 17
HELBSBY Ralph 35
HELMES William 37
HELVEY Jacob 41
HEMPHILL Alexander 98
  James 97
  John 8, 98
  Samuel 33
HENCOCK Joseph 86
HENDERSON Alexander 71
  Daniel 16, 70
  Edward 63
  James 82
  John 18, 60, 70
  Joseph 17
  Matthew 28
  Robert 74
  Samuel 55, 70
  Widow 18
  William 16, 18, 56
HENDRICKSON Isaac 53
  John 55
  Susannah 53
HENGE John 41
HENKO Simon 85
HENON James 16
HENRY James 91
  John 16
  Joseph 19
  Widow 42
  William 56, 82
HERKIN Dennis 83

HERKINS Edward 42
HERLMAN Conrad 87
HERNICK Nicholas 39
HERREGE Robert 19
HERRING William 37
HESLIP Francis 15
HETERLAND William 87
HETERLING William 39
HETh Andrew 39
HETHERINGTON Henry 33
HETTERLING Stophel 88
HEW Richard 47
HEWING James 1
HIBBARD Joseph 7
  Josiah 94
HIBBERD Benjamin 99, 100
  Caleb 99
  Isaac 1
  John 1
  Joseph 99
  Phinebas 99
  Samuel 99, 100
HIBBIN John 7
HICK Andrew 42
HICKEY James 79
HICKMAN Facis 7
  John 9
  Joseph 7
  Thomas 9
HIE Daniel 84
HIGGINS Peter 53
HIGH Jacob 85
  John 39
HILL John 5, 83
  Jonathan 30
  Margarett 28
  Moses 5
  Peter 98
  Robert 30
  Samuel 28
  Thomas 28
  William 71
HILLES William 27
HILLHOUSE James 71
HIMBLERIFE Samuel 39
HIMES Casper 42
HINDMAN John 63
  Robert 24, 68
HINDS Vallentine 42
HINES Joseph 20
HINKEAD John 72
HINKSON John 43
HIPPLE Henry 41
  Jacob 41
  Lawrence 87

HIVO Godfrey 31
HOBSON Joseph 11, 63
HOCKLEY James 83
HODGE Samuel 13
HOFFER George 37
HOFMAN Philip 94
HOGAN John 55
HOGG David 28
  James 19
  Robert 72
HOLADAY William 91
HOLDEN John 23
HOLDERMAN Christopher 39
  Michael 39
  Nicholas 58(2)
HOLDMAN Charles 63
HOLLAND Nathaniel 52
HOLLIDAY Robert 91
  Samuel 34
HOLLINSWORTH Enoch 20
HOLLIS Henry 68
HOLMAN Adam 41
  Martin 88
  Michael 87
HOLMES Abraham 48
  Francis 35
  William 78
HOLSTON John 49
HOLTON Isaac 32
HOMES John 26
HOOD James 83
  Walter 74
HOOFMAN Christopher 92
  George 97
  Henry 97
HOOK John 61
HOOPES Aaron 98
  Daniel 95, 97
  David 97
  George 97
  John 97, 98
  Joshua 10
  Nathan 10, 98
  Samuel 98
  Thomas 97(2)
HOOPS Abraham 7, 49
  Amos 7
  Isaac 50
  John 49
  Joshua 7, 8
  William 68, 80
HOPE Adam 83
  Amos 19
  Richard 82

# INDEX

Robert 16
Thomas 16, 19
HOPKINS Matthew 90
 William 72
HOPMAN Adam 71
HOPPERGET Jacob 5
HORN Elizabeth 1
 John 38, 84
 William 37, 38
HORNER Sarah 91
HORSSFALL Thomas 3
HOSKINS John 34
 Joseph 3
 William 1
HOUK Frederick 40
HOUSAN Anthony 88
HOUSE Amos 20, 60
HOWARD Hugh 28
 James 49
 John 49
 Law'e 52
 Thomas 28
HOWEL David 13
HOWELL David 89
 family 57
 Jacob 3, 5, 46, 56
 Mary 56
 Thomas 9
HOYER Jacob 40
HUCHESON Robert 75
HUDDERS James 28
HUETT William 72
HUFFMAN Adam 59
 Daniel 85
 Henry 13
 John 85
HUGHES Charles 61
 Edward 52
 Edward 52
 Elisha 27
 Isaac 53
 James 17
 James 96
 Samuel 31
 Timothy 18
HUGHS Isaac 90
 James 7
 Jonathan 95
HULDERMAN Christopher 59
HULFORD Joseph 11
 Samuel 11
HUMPHREY Charles 44
 Edward 44
 John 38

Richard 37
Samuel 44
HUMPHREYS Charles 93
 Daniel 37
 David 58
 John 59
 Jonathan 59
 Joshua 59
HUNT John 7, 37
 Joseph 7, 97
 Peter 68, 79
 Samuel 68, 79
 William 7, 81
HUNTER Andrew 47
 George 8, 49, 71
 James 47, 93, 95(2), 96
 Jonathan 49
 Mary 95
 Peter 71
 Thomas 8, 72, 87
 William 83, 90
HURFORD John 11
HUSS Johanas 24
HUSTON James 43, 46
 John 74
 Thomas 21
HUSZARD Jacob 89
HUTCHENSON David 19
 James 17
 John 17
 Samuel 19
HUTCHESON George 25
 Thomas 56
 William 62
HUTSON Richard 13
HUTTON Benjamin 11
 Joseph 12
 Thomas 11
HUTTONBACK Peter 42
HUTTONSTONE Peter 40

IDDINGS Henry 70
 John 71
ILES William 13
INGLAR Jacob 39
INGRAM John 5
 Lethrim 11
 Will 13
INHUFF John 39
IRWIN George 69
 Jerrard 69
 John 69, 96
 Thomas 77
 William 71

ISBURN Thomas 83
IVES Thomas 58

JACK Allen 39
 Andrew 32
 Charles 79
 James 79, 80
 John 70, 82
 Robert 45
JACKSON Caleb 65
 Catherine 56
 David 5
 George 65
 Isaac 11(2)
 James 11
 Jesse 65
 John 63, 65, 67
 Jonathan 65
 Joshua 12, 63
 Josiah 63
 Samuel 73
 Thomas 35, 80
 William 63
JACOBS Isaac 78
 John 13, 92
 Richard 63
JAMES Aaron 100
 Ann 90
 Benjamin 98
 Caleb 5, 36
 Daniel 89
 David 90
 Elias 92
 Enoch 90
 Evans 92
 Ezekiel 101
 George 24
 Griffith 93
 Isaac 7
 Jacob 7
 John 86
 Joseph 7(2), 61, 90, 99
 Mankin 40
 Micajah 24
 Mordica 28
 Thomas 6, 89
 William 83
JAY John 26
JEFFERIS Amer 9
 Benjamin 67
 James 10
 Lidia 10
 Nathan 11
 Nathaniel 10

INDEX

Richard 7
Samuel 65
Thomas 11
William 10(2)
JEMESON David 21
William 21
JENKIN Davis 89
JENKINS Benjamin 87
David 11, 78, 86
Evan 69
John 34, 84, 87(2)
Samuel 16
Thomas 84
JERMAN Jeremiah 88
Lewis 92
JERVIS John 95
JOB Daniel 24
JOBB Archabald 28
Benjamin 37
JOBSON Joseph 36
JOHN Daniel 34
David 58, 60, 89
Griffith 34
Isaac 39
James 35, 86
John 59, 84, 86, 90
Joshua 41
Philip 90
Reese 59
Reuben 35
Samuel 35, 84, 88, 90
Thomas 35(2) 90
William 34, 90
JOHNSON Abraham 1
Alexander 17
Andrew 36
Benjamin 9
Caleb 65
Closs 44
David 56
Humphrey 3
James 62, 81
John 24, 36, 44, 55, 82, 98
Ruth 24
Samuel 44, 81
Thomas 10, 21, 55, 62
William 8, 26, 60, 64, 97, 98
JOHNSTON George 31
Isaac 62
Jacob 45

James 28, 51
John 36, 84
JOLLY John 13
JONES Amos 89, 90, 98
Benjamin 9
Cadwalader 34
David 88, 92, 99
Edward 11, 35, 60, 92
Elisha 43, 48
Evan 9, 34
Griffith 58, 99
Henry 94
James 95
John 10, 13, 35, 66, 92(2), 96
Joseph 5, 41
Levi 88
Levy 35
Lydia 88
Malica 35
Nathaniel 35
Onosyphorus 96
Reese 98
Richard 10, 98
Robert 34, 99
Silas 38
Thomas 99, 100
Will 61
William 7, 33, 48, 60, 63, 88, 97
JONSTON Thomas 28
JORDAN John 50, 62, 95
Thomas 62(2)
JORDEN Rachel 73
JULIUS John 88
JUNKEN Adam 91
Benjamin 90, 91
JUNKIN David 28
Joseph 90
JUSTISON Andrew 55
John 55

KALAHAN Patrick 62
KARR James 69
Joseph 69
KAY Zacchus 20
KEARN John 45
KEARNS Joseph 22
Simon 23
KEELY Bastian 85
KEEN George 87
KEEPERS William 31
KEER Jacob 42

KEETCH Nathaniel 66
Samuel 66
William 68
KEITH George 3
KELL John 32, 33
KELLER Andreas 87
KELLION Frederick 101
KELLVY John 37
KELLY Bryan 94
James 82
Richard 94
Samuel 95(2)
KELTON James 63
KENNEDY David 75
Hugh 48
James 62, 71, 73
Mondgory 75
Samuel 94
Thomas 70, 82
William 62, 70(2)
KENNEY James 10
KENNY John 47
KERGIN Jacob 85
KERLIN John 94
Joseph 50
William 60
KERNS Hugh 30
Robert 83
KERR James 71
John 42
Thomas 77
William 75
KESLIP Thomas 14
KETCHER Jacob 84
KEY Allen 9
KEYS James 82, 83
KIDD John 42
KIKE John 89
KILKEY Charles 16
KILLGEESE Hanse 97
KILPATRICK John 26
Samuel 17
KIMBER Predick 51
KIMBLER John 60
KINCADE John 30
Robert 79, 82
Samuel 82
KINDE John 38
KING Charles 6
George 99
Michael 41
KINKAD David 75
KINKEAD Charles 16
James 17
KIRGIN Hugh 31
Will 22

INDEX

KIRK Caleb 79
  Elizabeth 24
  Isaac 1
  Jacob 41
  John 1
  Joseph 1
  Joshua 36
  Mary 24, 28
  Samuel 1
  Timothy 24, 28, 42
  William 84
KIRKPATRICK Andrew 76
  Edward 63
  John 24(2), 46, 77
KIRL Patrick 98
KIRLIN Mathias 46
KISER Nicholas 87
KITHCART John 74
KITSELMAN Christopher 45
KITZ Jacob 54
KLUGER John 41
KNIGHT William 12, 24
KNOWER Christopher 83
KNOWLS John 37, 53
KNOX Andrew 81
  John 31, 95
KRANK John 42
KRIM John 93
KYLES John 78

LABACH John 41
LACEY Joseph 97
LACK John 85
LACKEY George 76
LADLY Richard 23
LADWIGG Balser 42
LAFERTY Laughlin 88
LAMB Joseph 96
LAMBORN Robert 20
  William 20
LAMBOURN Francis 63
  Josiah 63
  Thomas 63
LAMBURN John 20
LAMEY Jacob 97
LAMPLUGH Jacob 46
  William 45
LAMPLY Samuel 56
LANCASTER Joseph 35
LANCER Samuel 45
LANE William 3
LAPP Michael 94
LARDNER John 54
  Linford 83

LARGE John 85
LARKAN Isaac 47
  John 47
  Joseph 47
LARMAN Hugh 63
LASHEY John 69
LASHLEY George 18
LASK Robert 69
LASSLEY William 68
LATMER Edward 78
LAUGHLIN James 77
LAW James 75
  Robert 73
  Thomas 16, 82
LAWRENCE Catherine 56
  Edward 11
  Henry 52
  John 10
  Thomas 45
  William 44
LAWSON John 28
LEAPER Andrew 24
LEAS Philip 87
LEAVIS Samuel 20
  William 20
LEE Richard 77
  William 92
LEECH Thomas 52
LEGGITT William 26
LEIP George 58
LEMART Lodowick 63
LEMMAN John 18
LENDERMAN John 37
  Justice 39
LEONARD Benjamin 65
  Daniel 21
  Ezekel 21
  Peter 46
  Richard 56
  William 15
LERL Bartley 35
LEVIS Isaac 54
  John 48
  Joseph 1
  Samuel 1(2), 48, 54
  Thomas 48
LEWDEN John 24
LEWELLIN Rebeckah 91
LEWES Abraham 1(2)
  Alexander 82
  Anthony 1
  Curtis 79
  David 83
  Enoch 83
  George 86

  Henry 79
  Jesse 83
  John 54, 81
  Lewes 81
  Phineas 79
  Samuel 1
LEWIS Abner 95
  Abraham 44(2) 99
  Azariah 96
  David 8, 92
  Elen 96
  Enoch 101
  Evan 92, 95
  Harvey 55
  Henry 93
  Isaac 34(2) 91
  Jacob 99
  James 58
  Joel 101
  John 34, 44, 92
  Joseph 94
  Joshua 99
  Josiah 49
  Levi 93
  Lewis 95
  Nathan 91, 95
  Philip 87
  Phinehas 96
  Samuel 13, 55, 58
  Thomas 1, 97, 98
  William 42, 95
LEWLYN David 44
LEWSLEY Benjamin 92
LIGET James 74
LIGETT William 73
LIGGIT Lodowick 79
LIGHT Jacob 39
  John 39
  Solomon 85
LIGHTFOOT Samuel 3
  Thomas 42, 82
  William 42
LIGHTON Thomas 85
LIGHTS Michael 48
LIGOTT David 76
  Elizabeth 67
LIKING Frederick 37
LILLEY Walter 13
LINDSEY Alexander 60
  James 30
  Samuel 31
  William 1
LINDSY James 5
LINGOR Michael 98
LINLEY Jonathan 63

INDEX

LINN Andrew 36
  Charles 35, 51
LINSAY John 31
LINSEY David 58
  James 31
  Robert 44
  Thomas 44
  William 34, 43, 45
LINSFIELD Margret 63
LINVILL Edward 45
LINVILLE William 2
LINWILL William 37
LIONS Cochran 96
LIRISH George 41
LISK Morrice 38
LITTLER Will 79
LITZENBERG Simon 44
LLEWELLIN William 60
LLOYD Hugh 54
  John 86
LLOYDE Joseph 47
LOBB Benjamin 1(2)
  Isaac 1
  Jacob 58
LOCKARD Alexander 50
  James 72
  Robert 79
LODGE Abel 1
LODWIG Philip 41
LOGAN Alexander 89
  James 52
  Samuel 12, 69
  Will 70
  William 72
LOGMIRE John 44
LONG David 72
  George 28
  John 44, 83
  Joseph 70
  William 82
LONGACRE Andrew 54
  Israel 54
  Jacob 39
LONGMORE James 83
LONGSTREATH Benjamin 58
  John 58
LOUGE Patrick 64
LOVE John 77
  Samuel 24
  William 75
LOW Henry 58
LOWNES Alice 48
  George 48
LOWNS James 48

LOWRY James 74
  John 90
  William 71, 74
LOYD Erasmus 87, 99
  Hannah 92
  Hugh 59
  Joseph 92
  Thomas 84
  William 99
LOYDE David 35
  Humphrey 34, 35
  Hugh 37
  Isaac 37(2)
  John 84
  Phillip 39
LUCKEY Hugh 72
  William 74
LUNN Thomas 62
LUTHER George 58
LYNCH James 23
  Philip 95
LYNN Charles 52
LYON William 82

M'ELSHOUR William 87
MACKEY David 17
  James 75
  John 70
  William 14, 28
MADARY John 40
MADDOCK Benjamin 54
  James 48
  William 48
MADSON Aaron 50
  Morris 31
  Peter 37
MAESE John 8
MAGEE James 95
MAHAFFY Joseph 28
MAHANY Timothy 21
MAHONY Cain 80
MAIRS Samuel 18
MALAN John 95
MALEY James 28
MALIN Gideon 36
  Isaac 99
  Jacob 98
  Randle 94
  Thomas 98, 99
  William 36
MAN John 81
MANLY Thomas 54
MARCH John 41
MARIS Ann 48
  Caleb 1

  Isaac 52
  James 95
  Jesse 4, 48
  John 33, 48(2), 94
  Jonathan 52
  Richard 52
MARK Lucas Nether 54
MARLOE Joseph 3
  Will 3
MARSH Henry 16
  James 65
  William 16
MARSHAL Benjamin 50
MARSHALL Humphry 67
  Isaac 67
  James 59, 67
  John 2, 21, 56, 64, 67, 83
  Samuel 67
  Thomas 2, 8, 31
  William 16(20
MARSHMAN John 25
MARTIN Abraham 31
  Alexander 71
  Caleb 67
  George 61, 67(2), 68
  James 58
  Joel 58
  John 22, 65, 82, 86
  Jonathan 6
  Joseph 67, 69
  Mathias 58
  Roger 58
  Samuel 16
  Thomas 34
  William 58
MARY Black 4
MASON John 52
MASON William 43
MASSEY Isaac 99
  James 99
  Joseph 91
  Phineas 100
  Thomas 91, 99
MASTER James 11
MATHER James 3, 54
  John 3
MATHERS John 92, 93
  Peter 60
  Robert 93
MATHEWS John 78
MATHIAS David 58
MATLACK Amos 98
  Isaiah 97
  Jonathan 98

# INDEX

Joseph 97
Nathan 92
MATSON Jacob 96
  John 31
MATTHEWS David 63
  George 76
  John 90
  Jonathan 64
  Robert 69
MATTHIAS David 58
MAXFIELD Helvert 21
  John 16, 30
MAXTON George 41
MAXWELL Hugh 36
  James 24
  John 88
  Nathaniel 83
  Robert 28
  Will 73
  William 24, 52
MAY David 61
Mc'LEHOE Robert 60
McADAMS Henry 75
McAFEE Daniel 50
  William 49
McAFERSON Stephen 12
McALISTER Archibald 91
  Duncin 83
  John 74
McANALLY Daniel 18
McANTEER Thomas 79
McBATH Andrew 17
McBRIDE Edward 8
  Samuel 45
McCAHEN Dennis 89
  Zachariah 90
McCALISTER Duncan 14
  William 74
McCALL Thomas 50
McCALLAH Alexander 59
McCALLEY Charles 21
McCALLION James 5
McCANNEY Cain 21
McCARAKAN William 81
McCARTNEY Thomas 24
McCARTY Benjamin 79
  John 11, 21, 35
  Neal 13
McCASKEY Samuel 72
McCAULLEY Alexander 95
McCAY William 50
McCEALVY Patrick 35
McCLAIN Daniel 75
McCLAIR John 75
McCLANAHAN Elisha 75

McCLANE James 32, 80
McCLANTICK John 75
McCLEAN Alexander 71
  Michael 79
  William 79
McCLEANE James 28
McCLEARY Thomas 26
McCLELAND James 6
  Robert 6
  Samuel 16
McCLELLAND Andrew 62
  William 44
McCLENAN Henry 48
  William 2
McCLENAUGHEN John 14
McCLENICHEN John 73
McCLEOSS James 37
McCLERNON John 28
McCLERY Alexander 76
McCLOSKEY James 31
McCLUER Arthur 17
McCLUN James 88
McCLUNG James 26
McCLURE David 16, 35
  James 35, 98
  John 34
  Samuel 12
McCOCHRAN James 70
McCOLOUGH George 73
  James 36
  William 21
McCONALLY Lawrence 51
McCONAUGHEY David 72
McCONAUGHY Robert 70
McCONAWAY Cornelius 66
  David 70
McCONLEY John 28
McCONNALL Mathew 20
  Thomas 20
McCONNEL Dennis 64
  James 91
McCONELL1 William 12, 80
McCONOUGHY Robert 84
McCOOLL Samuel 20
McCORD John 35
  Robert 37, 38
McCORMACK Henry 29
  John 55, 66, 67
  Joseph 11
  Samuel 21
McCORMICK James 28
  Robert 77
  Uphias 91
McCOWAN Benjamin 21

McCOWN Andrew 26
  Isaac 25
McCOY Andrew 12
  Dennis 8
  John 56
  William 80
McCRACKAN James 44
McCRACKIN James 76
  John 38
McCRAKEN Joshua 75
McCROSKEY James 69
McCUE Samuel 99
McCULLACK John 68
McCUNE Bryan 80
McCURDY Daniel 72
McCURTY Patrick 68
McCUTCHEON John 95
McDADE John 66
McDANIEL Cornelius 8
  Darby 13
McDERMONT Patrick 72
McDEVOR Joseph 8
McDOWEL George 17
  James 73
  Joshua 62
McDOWELL Andrew 24
  Robert 24
  William 18
McDUFF Samuel 71
McENTIRE Andrew 12
  John 13
  William 89
McFADDIN Thomas 66
McFAILEY Barney 80
McFALAM John 21
McFALL Archibald 100
  John 94
  Patrick 43
  Patt 94
McFARLAM George 86
McFARLAN James 79
  John 86
  William 22, 79
McFARREN John 79
McFERSON Alexander 16, 82
  Robert 16
  William 14
McFETRIDGE Mathew 32
McGEE Dudley 100
  James 80
  Patrick 33
McGILTON John 38
McGINNIS Barnibas 31

## INDEX

McGLAUGHLAN Charles 78
  William 94
McGLAUGHLIN Cornelius 47
McGLOUGHLEN Benjamin 68
McGOMERY Moses 65
McGORMAN David 47
McGOWEN John 72
McGRAW Thomas 82
McGREGOR Hugh 62
  Samuel 62
McGREW Finley 28
  Robert 30
McGUGEN Robert 91
McGUIRE Cornelius 67
  John 11, 46
  Patrick 35
  Thomas 75
McHANEY George 58
McHURD John 33
McILROY James 15
McILVAIN Ann 82
  Hugh 54
  John 54
  William 14
McILVAINE Andrew 55
McINTIRE Andrew 57
  Henry 68
  John 24
  Robert 68
McKAIN Thomas 90
McKAN Daniel 26
McKAY Francis 59
McKEE Jane 28
  Martha 24
McKELVY James 79
McKETRICK John 72
McKIM David 15
  James 14
  William 14
McKINLEY Charles 72
  Daniel 9
  Joseph 84
McKINLY Alexander 41
  John 41
  William 79
McKISCOCK Arthur 73
McKISOCK John 74
McKLEHENY James 41
  John 42
McKNEE John 82
McKNIGHT Hugh 26
  John 84
McKUSICK John 74

McL'EHANEY William 77
McLAUGHLIN Amos 33
  Matthew 56
  Patrick 77
  William 28
McLEES Manasah 13
McLEHANEY John 78
McLOUGHLIN Robert 98
McLOY Dennis 9
  Patrick 24
McMAHON Samuel 80
McMASTER James 65
  William 24
McMASTERS James 68
McMICKOLL John 54
McMIN Andrew 31
  John 31(2)
  Robert 33
  Samuel 31
McMITCHELL Archibald 46
McMULLAN James 26
McMULLEN Alexander 82
  James 25
  John 24
McMULLIN Michael 96
McNAB Andrew 83
McNEAL Alexander 74
  Archibald 32
  Hector 32
  John 88
  Samuel 73
McNEASE Josiah 8
McNEIL John 66
McNIGHT Paul 70
McNUTT Robert 23
McQUAID Arthur 91
  Henry 91
McREYNOLDS James 26
  Joseph 24
McSPARROW Duncan 55
McVAUGH Jonathan 35
  Joseph 93
McVICKER John 82
McWHIRLER Moses 30
MEAL John 56
MEARS John 28
MEASE Thomas 73
MECHEM John 97
  Mary 97
MEGLISTER Alexander 87
MEHAFFEY Thomas 75
MELAN David 52
MELCHIOR David 88
MELSHER Jacob 86
  John 86

MELTON Timothy 21
MENAN Cornelius 26
MENDENHALL Benjamin 20(2), 51
  Griffith 79
  Isaac 20
  Jesse 20
  Joshua 79
  Moses 20, 51
  Nathan 9
  Philip 51
  Robert 50
  Samuel 50
MENGES Henry 88
MENION Joseph 55
MENOUGH Murtough 62
MENTS Christopher 41
MERCER Caleb 98
  Daniel 65
  David 20
  Joseph 8
  Nathaniel 49
  Robert 60, 77, 98
  Solomon 66
  Thomas 7
  William 10
MERCHANT James 24
MEREDITH Enoch 86
  John 87, 88
  Thomas 85
  William 80
MERIDETH John 13
  Moses 49
  Simon 84
  William 80
MERSEY Levy 51
MERTLE William 30
MESSERLY Michael 85
METZGER Thomas 87
MICHEL Andrew 75
  Hugh 75
MICHELL Henry 85
MIDKIFF Curtis 24
MILEMAN John 5
MILES Enos 90, 93
  James 90(2)
  John 81
  Joseph 92
  Richard 89
MILHOUSE John 41
  Thomas 42
MILL George 31
MILLEKIN William 70
MILLER Adam 24, 84, 85
  Benedict 42

# INDEX

Conrad 41
Earnest 92
George 35
Henry 58, 86
Hugh 72
Isaac 11
Jacob 60, 69
James 11, 16, 85(2)
Jesse 11, 20
John 11, 28, 55, 62, 82, 89, 96
Joseph 44, 81
Leonard 95
Mary 75
Michael 79
Nicholas 87
Peter 87
Phelix 95
Phillip 39
Robert 6, 35
Samuel 11
Thomas 87
Tobias 39
Warrick 79
Will 11
William 6(2), 11
MILLESON James 67
  Jonathan 97
MILLHOUSE James 12
  Robert 34
  Thomas 42
  William 42
MILLINER Nathan 44
MILLISON John 71
MILLS William 81
MILNER Joseph 20
MINARD Thomas 17
MINSHALL Aaron 43
  Isaac 91
  Jacob 6
  John 6
  Thomas 5
MIRE George 8
MISKELLY Robert 91
MITCHEL Andrew 20
  George 28
  John 3, 5, 76
  William 75
MITCHELL Andrew 33, 50
MOAD William 14
MODARY Jacob 39
MODRELL Francis 72
MODRIL Francis 75
MOLLON William 6
MONAGAN Michael 51

MONEY Joseph 21
MONKE Thomas 21
MONOUGH John 17
MONTGOMERY John 14
  Samuel 72
MOODEY Robert 16
MOOK Peter 39
MOOR David 24, 53, 76
  James 21, 24, 64, 70
  John 16, 71
  Joseph 18, 63
  Nicholas 66
  Robert 24
  Sampson 28
  Samuel 36, 63
  Trustram 32
  William 16, 74
MOORE Abraham 85
  Daniel 71
  Elizabeth 52
  Francis 55
  Isaac 8
  James 2, 36, 71, 95, 96
  John 2, 19, 71, 96
  Joseph 98
  Mary 56, 90
  Nathan 100
  Nathaniel 97
  Richard 57
  Thomas 99
  William 58, 82
MORETON Erasmus 3
  John 56
MORGAN Ann 24
  Benjamin 48
  Lewis 58
  Magdalen 92
  Mordecai 92
  Morgan 87
  Thomas 62, 84, 98
  William 42
MORISON Mary 50
MORREL Robert 13
MORRIS David 88, 92
  James 91
  John 48, 52, 90
  Jonathan 65, 95
  Joseph 13
  Lewis 91
  Mark 90
  Mary 52
  Mordica 52
  Morris 91
  Thomas 90

MORRISON Alexander 17
  David 51
  Ephraim 19
  Guyan 28
  Hugh 19
  James 74
  John 30
  Joseph 19
  Joshua 51
  Nathaniel 51
  William 18
MORRISSON John 4
MORROW Alexander 37
  John 21
MORTLIN Robert 47
MORTON Daniel 54
  George 37
  Israel 38
  John 54, 55
  Martin 31
  Morton 37, 54
  Samuel 63
  Thomas 24, 63
  Tobiah 37
  William 63
MOSELEY Richard 56
MOSES Jacob 42
  Peter 84
MOSS James 18
  John 75
MOSSES Adam 41
MOTE John 61
MOULDER Benjamin 56
  Robert 56, 57
MOUNTGOMERY Isaac 18
  James 20, 28
  John 35, 81
  Michael 17
  Robert 18
  Widow 18
  William 28, 75
MOWER Jacob 86
  Jacob 92
MOYER Gasper 85
  Mathias 85
MUHAIC John 90
MULL Joseph 63
MULOY Bryan 78
MUMFORD George 4
MUNCHOUR Jacob 86
MUNGOMERY James 91
MUNROW George 74
MUNSHOUR John 87
  Nicolas 40
MUNTON Robert 74

121

INDEX

MURDOCK James 91
MURIS Allin 56
MURPHY Darby 60
  James 25
  John 82
  William 12
MURREY Jacob 84
MURTLIN Robert 31
MUSGROVE Aaron 20
  Abraham 1(2)
  Joseph 12, 20
MYERS Christopher 23
  Peter 22
MYRE Henry 50
  Jacob 84

NAIL William 75
NAILOR Hance 34
  Jacob 35
NANHOLT Vellentine 45
NANNY Isaac 72
NEAL Elias 60
  Henry 16, 65
  John 11, 100
  William 66
NEALLY William 71
NEEZM Thomas 43
  John
NELSON Patrick 25
  Robert 22
NESBITT John 31
NETHERINGTON John 78
NEWLIN John 13
  Nathaniel 95
  Nicolas 45
NEWMAN Thomas 65
NICHOLS John 20
  Thomas 89
  William 22
NICKLIN John 50
NICKOLS John 21
  William 22
NICLIN Joseph 50
NICOLSON John 52
NIECE George 81
NIESBIT James 79
  Joseph 25
NITFALLUS Arthur 37
  Mathiak 37
NIXON Robert 55
NOBLE Andrew 76
NOBLET Joseph 31
  Samuel 6
  William 6
NOBLIT John 6
NORMAN Joseph 66

NORRIS Charles 57, 67
  John 63
  Mary 4
  Mary 7
  Robert 18
  William 5
NORRY John 6, 8
NORTON Isaac 91
NORY John 47
  William 47
NUBROUGH John 20
NUBY John 75
NUFER Christopher 8
NUGIN William 76
NULIN Nathaniel 50
  Nicholas 50
NULLARD Phillip 14
NUTT Isaac 35
NUZUN Thomas 36

O'DANIEL Peter 68
O'NEAL Arthur 31
  Francis 58
  Hugh 57
  John 44, 59
  Robert 57
OAKES Flower 98
  John 100
  Samuel 97(2)
OAKFORD Aron 37
OBRIAN Patrick 76
ODAIR Nail 93
OFFICER Thomas 77
OGDEN David 3
  Hannah 48
OGHALTREE James 76
OGILBY John 28
OLDHAM John 28
  Robert 30
OLIPHANT Andrew 14
OLIVER Alexander 52
  Andrew 18
  John 3
  Richard 5
  Samuel 43, 101
  Thomas 3
ORAM Thomas 62
ORAN Benjamin 19
ORNER Martin 39
  Vallentine 42
ORR James 26
OSBORN Peter 7
  Samuel 7
OSBOURN Samuel 10, 100
OTLEY John 49

OVERLY Michael 2
OVERTHREW Samuel 98
OWEN David 34, 80
  George 21
  John 35, 39
  Thomas 98
  William 3, 34

PACKER James 79
  Moses 44
PAINTER Fredirick 85
  James 11
  Samuel 10
  Sarah 61
PALMER John 38, 51(3)
  Moses 50
  William 60
PANCAST Seth 48
PANCOST Seth 52
PANTER Richard 5
PARK Arthur 76
  John 77
  Joseph 82
  Obiah 79
  Robert 79
PARKE Samuel 48
PARKER Edward 28, 86
  John 81
  William 37
PARKHILL William 15
PARKS John 74
  Joseph 10
  Richard 8
PARR Stephen 62
PARRY Caleb 94
  John 95
  Robert 90
PARSONS Thomas 4
PARTE Will 78
PARVIN Benjamin 82
PASCHALL Benjamin 38
  John 38(2)
  Stephen 58
PASMOORE George 28
PASMORE Enoch 20
  George 20, 32
  John 32
PASTE William 48
PATERSON Robert 76
PATON John 43
PATRICK Samuel 85
PATTERSON James 28
  John 98(2)
  Thomas 98
  William 11, 98

# INDEX

PATTIN William 1
PATTON Abraham 16
  David 25
  James 25
  Michael 25
  Thomas 26
PAUL John 86
PAWLIN John 2
PEAKEN Valentine 98
PEAN George 59
PEARMAN Gyles 45
PEARSALL Abraham 70
  Dinah 69
  Jacob 69
  Jeremiah 69
  Richard 71
PEARSON Elias 49
  Francis 79
  Gideon 80
  Hannah 38
  Isaac 38
  John 38
  Joseph 38, 65
  William 10
PECHEEN Peter 44
PECK Adam 85
PEDRICK Thomas 4(2)
PEEK John 91
PEFOUTZ Jacob 40
PEHOLT Borick 84
  Jacob 85
PEIRCE Caleb 8, 50, 65
  George 22
  Henry 51
  Isaac 65
  James 82
  John 8, 50
  Joseph 60
  Joshua 65
  Lewis 60
  William 51
PEMBERTON Israel 14
  Israel & James 80
PENNALL Hayes 52
  Isaac 46
  Joshua 52, 53
PENNELL Mary 4
  Robert 6
  William 6(2)
PENNINGTON Edward 54
  Isaac 77
PENNOCK Joseph 32
  Levis 32
  Nathaniel 32, 48

PENOCK Joseph 65
  Moses 65
  Nathaniel 63
PEOPLES John 17
  Robert 96
  William 14
PEPPER Michael 65
PEREGRINE David 90
  Nicholas 60
PERKINS Caleb 51
  John 8
  Thomas 57
PERRY James 30
  Jane 28
PETER William 47
PETERS Michael 94
  Reese 30
  William 30, 51
PETERSON William 15
PEUGH David 34
  James 34
PEW John 28
  William 20
PHEENIX Thomas 48
PHILIP David 34
PHILIPS John 94
  Morris 93
  Thomas 26
PHILLIPS Elizabeth 2
  Griffith 1
  John 35, 47, 70, 86
  Joseph 34
  Stephen 34
  Thomas 56
PHIPPS Aaron 34
  Caleb 54
  George 34
  John 34
  Joseph 34, 79
  Joshua 35
  Nathan 34
  Samuel 97
PICKET Thomas 26
PICKING Samuel 79
PIERCE Crummel 100
  Edward 100
  James 97
  Joshua 22
PILKENTON
  Edward 56
PILKERTON Joseph 6
  Levy 6
  Thomas 6
PIMM Hannah 79
  Thomas 79

PINKERTON John 74
  William 72
PIPER John 51
PLAISTER Michael 12
PLANKENTON Peter 51
PLAT Henry 4
PLUMMER Thomas 32
PLUMSTEAD Heirs of 94
PLUSTEAD William 7
POAK David 25
POAKE James 25
  William 25
POE John 77
POGUE James 33
POLES John 7
POLIN Joseph 38
PONWARD Michael 9
POOK Thomas 26
POOR Patrick 28(2)
PORT Joseph 61
PORTER James 61, 72, 81
  John 62, 74, 82
  Joseph 76
  Nathan 69
  Patrick 82
  Robert 80
  Samuel 62
  Will 69
  William 55, 73
PORTERFIELD Josiah 28
POSLEY Charles 15
POSTON Robert 72
POTTS Aquilla 89
  Hockly & 85
  John 39, 83
  Samuel 58, 89
  William 60
POWEL David 14
  James 23, 52
  John 43, 93
  Joseph 15, 52
POWELL David 68
  John 67, 68
  Joseph 53
  Robert 94
  Samuel 100
  Thomas 53
  William 16
POWER John 4, 56
PRATT Abraham 50
  Joseph 49, 100
PRESTON Jonas 3
  Thomas 66

# INDEX

PRICE Adam 57
  Daniel 54
  David 28
  Elisha 3, 57
  John 56
  Rees 62
PRICHARD Thomas 50
  William 50
PRICHAT Thomas 36
PRICHETT William 49
PRIM Thomas 55
  William 55
PRISLER John Hendrick 38
PRITCHARD Anthony 58
  Joseph 98
PROAD William 8
PROCTER Joshua 95
PRYOR Syles 51
PUGH James 85
  John 84
  Jonathan 84
  Joshua 28
  Samuel 93
PUMROY William 89
PURDY William 81
PURNELL John 5
PURSEL Peter 83
PURSLEY James 89
PURTLE James 18
PURVAIN James 72
PUSEY David 65
  Ellis 76
  John 64
  Joshua 64
  Thomas 65
  William 32
PYATT Abraham 48
  James 2
PYKE Jacob 30
PYLE Abraham 10
  Caleb 21, 51
  Isaac 32, 47
  Israel 9
  Jacob 8
  James 68
  John 20(2) 21, 60, 68
  Joseph 32, 65
  Levy 9
  Phillip 21
  Robert 47
  Samuel 21
  William 8, 67

QUAINTANCE George 80
  William 79
QUAY Archibald 14
QUIN William 52

RAGON Michael 87
RAINE Mary 56
  Samuel 57
RALPH William 21
RALSON John 88
RALSTON John 54
  Joseph 62
  Robert 74, 87
  William 80
RAMMAGE James 11
RAMOND Isaac 30
RAMSEY Charles 90
  David 75
  James 67
  John 30, 75
  Samuel 75
  William 28
RAMSOWER Adam 93
RANDLE Abraham 51
  Joseph 58
  Michael 30
  Nicolas 38
RANKIN Alexander 62
  David 28
  John 11, 62
  Robert 31
RASMORE Phillip 40
RATCLIFFE Thomas 82
RATEW John 31(2)
RATTEW William 97
RAWSON Moses 56
RAY James 64, 83
  Joseph 97
  Patrick 25
  Samuel 13
READ Andrew 21
  William 11
REAGON Patrick 26
REAK Andrew 26
REECE Andrew 21
  David 25, 95
  John 13
REED Andrew 76
  Charles 35
  James 18, 33, 62, 74, 81, 82
  John 25, 31, 62, 64
  Thomas 93, 94, 98
  Will 19
  William 62, 77, 81

REEL John 38
REES David 45, 93
  Edward 89
  Samuel 88
  William 45
REESE Abel 90
  Caleb 100
  Daniel 48, 100
  Thomas 98
  William 95, 100
REGESTER John 49
  William 49
REILEY James 68
REYM Peter 42
REYNOLD John 55
REYNOLDS Benjamin 25, 45
  David 33
  Henry 25, 26
  Isaac 26
  Jacob 25
  John 26, 51, 56
  Samuel 25, 46, 56
  Sarah 46
  Thomas 33
  William 25
RHADS James 36
RHEA John 82
RHOADES Peter 87
RICE Daniel 38
  James 25
  John 42
  Philip 42
  Zachariah 42
RICH Joseph 25
RICHARD Jacob 46
RICHARDS Adam 80
  David 45
  Hugh 93
  Isaac 11
  Jacob 31, 46
  Jonathan 31
  Margaret 30
  Nathaniel 11
  Rowland 42
  Samuel 88
  William 11, 84
RICHARDSON Daniel 82
  Francis 4
  James 13
  John 20
  Mary 89
  Richard 93, 94(2)
RICHEY John 74, 75
  Robert 35
  William 74

# INDEX

RICHIE Andrew 72
RICHLY David 76
RICHMOND George 17
RIDDLE Humphry 29
  Samuel 12
RIDDLEMAN Jacob 42
RIDEBOUGH Adam 88
RIDGE William 40(2)
RIDGWAY Job 4
RIDOLLER George 93
RIFE Christian 39
RIFFITT Nicholas 59
RIGBY James 56
RIGG Clement 34
  Robert 42
RIGHTER George 38
  Michael 10
RILEY Richard 56
  Thomas 60
RINCHARD Fredirick 39
  John 39
  Uldrick 40
RINCHERT Peter 40
RINEHARD John 87
RING Benjamin 61
  Elizabeth 21, 32(2)
  Nathaniel 61
  Nathiel 32
  William 13
RINK Bostin 89
RIX Christopher 66
ROAD Michael 42
ROADS Isaac 52
  James 52
  Joseph 35, 52
  Martin 84
ROB William 78
ROBB Samuel 72
  William 72
ROBENETT Allen 56
ROBERTS Aubrey 97
  Jasher 93
  John 90, 92
  Joshua 34
  Reubin 44
  Thomas 2, 59(2)
  Walter 48
  Will 78
ROBESON Anthony 16
  George 16
  John 17
ROBINS Joseph 49
ROBINSOIN Estate
  Thomas 46

ROBINSON Ephraim 70
  James 10
  John 70, 98
  Mathew 70
  Ralph 81
  Robert 71
  Samuel 4, 84
  Thomas 57, 59
  William 72
ROBISON Benjamin 89
RODDAN Philip 77
RODGERS Alexander 82
  David 83
  Robert 82
ROGER James 87
ROGERS David 62
  Isaac 74
  John 4, 29, 59, 85
  Joseph 26, 86
  Philip 85
  Robert 5, 6, 78
  Rowland 29
  Thomas 25, 28
  William 29(2) 70, 72
ROLSTON William 69
ROMMANS Rachael 80
ROMMONS John 80
ROMOND Phillip 30
ROOD James 5
ROSE John 95
ROSS Andrew 81
  James 54
  John 62, 64, 73
  William 12, 72
ROSSITER Daniel 81
  Thomas 67, 79
ROUSE Conrad 88
ROW George 86
  William 11
ROWAN James 11, 56
  Martha 56
  Michael 75
  Moses 12
ROWLAND Hugh 25
  Jane 25
  John 88
  Joseph 90
ROWLE Will 51
ROWLES John 61
ROWLS Hezekiah 29
RUDOLPH Jacob 38
  John 38
  Joseph 38
  Thomas 1
RUDROUGH Jonas 39

RUMMOND Jacob 4
  Thomas 31
RUSHTON William 54
RUSK Humphrey 17
  Robert 14
RUSSEL Joseph 71
RUSSELL Edward 4
  Hugh 72
  James 1, 49, 61
  John 51, 64
  Robert 89
  Thomas 97
  William 49(2)
RUSTON Job 72
  Robert 98
RUTH Francis 4, 57
  James 5
RUTHERFORD John 30
RYAN Charles 97
  Patrick 54
  Thomas 6
RYDOLLER Henry 93
RYMEY Jacob 87

SALADY Frederick 85
SALKELD William 4
SALKIELD Isaac 4
  John 4
SALMON Robert 30
SAM Black 4
SAMPLE John 23
SANDERSON Richard 51
SANKEY Giles 47
SAUNDERS John 40
SCANTLING John 4
SCARLET John 12
  Joseph 12
  Nathaniel 12
SCHOFFIELD Thomas 97
SCOFFIELD George 59
SCOTT Abraham 34
  Andrew 14, 17
  James 25, 70, 95
  Jane 29
  John 16, 17, 26, 81, 95
  Joseph 62
  Joshua 20
  Mary 46
  Moses 62(2)
  Mosses 80
  Nathan 96
  Patrick 29
  Philip 29
  Robert 71

INDEX

Samuel 25
Thomas 14, 18, 25, 29, 35, 62
William 62(2)
SEAL William 61
SEELTON Owen 93
SELCUS Paul 61
SELECT Thomas 52
SELENOR Conrod 42
SELLER Conemus 87
 Peter 42
SELLERS John 2
 Samuel 2, 67, 68
SERGEANT Robert 62
SERINGER Ann 89
SHANKEL Henry 40
SHANKLIN William 8
SHANNON James 88
SHARADIN Paul 89
SHARADON Jacob 89
SHARKPATRICK James 78
SHARP Benjamin 12
 George 12
 James 16
 John 16
 Mary 89
 Samuel 64
 Thomas 29, 89
SHARPLESS Abraham 31
 Benjamin 6
 Daniel 4, 6, 43, 54
 Jacob 8, 31
 James 43
 Job 44
 John 4, 7, 43, 54
 Joseph 6(2) 31
 Samuel 6
 Thomas 4, 6, 54
SHARRON John 33
SHAW Charles 16
 Edward 54
 Mary 4
 Samuel 3(2), 4
SHEARRE Conrad 41
SHEERER Archibald 46
 William 69
SHEFFER Adam 88
SHEIFFER Henry 59
SHELDEN Joseph 52
SHELLEY James 45
SHENLIVER Frederick 88
SHEPARD Robert 59
SHEPHARD Robert 29
 William 29
SHERER William 19

SHERRON Thomas 82
SHEWARD James 81
 Thomas 67
SHIELDS James 14, 22
 John 64
 Joseph 64
 Martha 75
 Mathew 63
 Peter 80
 Robert 12
SHILDEN William 53
SHIMER Conrad 41
 Conrod 85
 Fredirick 41
SHINHOLD Jacob 86
SHINHOLT Martin 59
SHINTZ John 59
SHIRLEY Thomas 80
SHIVERLY Andrew 65
SHIVERY Michael 21
SHLIR Henry 42
SHOEMAKER Thomas 48
SHOOSTER Jacob 84
SHULL Fredrick 40
SHUMAN Peter 42
SHUNK Simon 87
SIBBAR Peter 85
SIDESTRIKER Philip 40
SIDWELL Abraham 25
 Henry 25
 Hugh 29
 Jacob 25, 26
 Richard 29
SILL James 49, 100
 John 50
 Michael 6
 Richard 6
SIMCOCK James 11
 Samuel 11
SIMCOCKS Benjamin 1
SIMERAL Thomas 17
SIMERALL Alexander 16
 James 16
 John 16
SIMMER Daniel 40
SIMMONDS William 16
SIMON Thomas 45
SIMONSON Edward 61
 William 61
SIMONTON John 88
SIMPLIN William 40
SIMPSON Henry 74
 James 73
 Matthew 100
SIMS William 26

SIMSON Allen 73
 David 74
SINCLAIR Conrod 52
SINGLETON Thomas 62
SINGLOUB George 88
SINK Michael 40
SINKLER John 82
 William 82
SIVILL Joseph 46
SKEEN James 69
 Joseph 81
SKELTON Alexander 66
SKETCHLEY John 4
SKETCHLY Mary 54
SKILTON John 96
SLATER Thomas 6
SLATTON William 43
SLAUGHTER Jacob 100
 John 6
SLEAR Jacob 41
SLIZMAN Christopher 95
SLOAN John 94
SLONE Robert 75
SMALL Barney 33
 John 18
SMEDLEY Caleb 100
 Elizabeth 6
 Francis 100
 Frederick 98
 George 100
 John 100
 Joshua 6, 100
 Thomas 6, 100
SMEDLY Ambrose 6
 Mary 36
SMILEY George 91
SMITH Abraham 82
 Adam 93
 Barney 16
 George 2, 44, 97
 Hugh 62
 James 22, 29, 30, 46, 55, 60, 61, 71, 77
 John 2, 4(2), 13, 18(2), 21, 22, 29, 36, 40, 70, 73, 74(2), 80, 91, 93, 94
 Joseph 17, 30, 93
 Joshua 7
 Jost 59
 Leonard 41
 Patrick 38
 Richard 43

# INDEX

Robert 34, 73, 74
Samuel 2, 29(2), 74
Thomas 54
Trustrum 5
Vallentine 42
William 2, 51, 54, 61, 71, 74, 98
SNIDER Casper 85
John 41
Leonard 40
Thomas 42
SNOWDER Magnus 81
SOLE Francis 41
SOLELY Alexander 45
SOLSUS George 61
SOMMERFIELD John 71
SOOK John 70
SORRELL John 2
SOWDER John 40
SPANAGER Lodowick 94
SPAVIN James 35
SPEAKEMAN Thomas 10
SPEAKMAN Hugh 64
John 98
Thomas 97
SPEAR William 62
SPECKMAN Isaac 68
SPEER George 4
SPENCE Andrew 70
Colin 71
SPICKMAN Micajah 51
SPIKEMAN Ebenezer 22
SPIKER Wyant 60
SPOTSWOOD James 60
SQUIB Nathaniel 4
Robert 4
SQUIBB Caleb 5
STAFFON Philip 41
STAGER Peter 87
STALKER George 67
Jonathan 81
Thomas 80
STANFIELD William 35
STANLEY James 70
STAR Moses 12
STARKER Christian 61
Frederick 61
STARR Alexander 64
James 10, 41
Jeremiah 4, 18
John 21, 70
Joseph 59(2)
William 4, 43
STARRAT Robert 69
STARRATT John 70

STARRETT James 71
STAURT John 60
STEAL Alexander 21
Andrew 25
James 25
William 71
STEARN George 21
STEEGLER Peter 90
STEEL Andrew 91
David 84
James 2, 29, 30, 75, 80
John 33, 91
Ringen 76
Robert 47
William 18
STEELL Peter 4
STEEN John 51
STEPHEN Abijah 88
STEPHENS David 84
Isaac 11
John 84
Joshua 84
Robert 91
Thomas 11
William 68
STEPHENSON Daniel 44
John 15
STERN Paul 56
STERRETT John 84
William 74, 84
STEVENSON Robert 36
STEWARD Archibald 46
David 17, 18
John 51, 73
Robert 55, 84
STICKLE Christopher 59
Jacob 59
STILLWAGGON John 93
STINSON John 11
Joseph 30
STOCKMAN James 73
STONE Lodowick 5
STORK Jacob 54
STORY Robert 66
STOW Joseph 56
William 57
STRADLEMAN Michael 93
STRAWBRIDGE David 30
James 76
John 29
Joseph 75
Thomas 75
STRETCH Joseph 71
STRINGER William 77
STRITHERS John 29

STRODE Isaac 61
Thomas 61
STRONG John 71
Philip 87
STROUD Caleb 9
George 9
Richard 61
STROWD John 11
STUARD Eleck 21
STUART Andrew 16
Hugh 91
James 17, 98
John 98
Robert 98
STUFFLE Henry 40
STURGEON John 18
STYATT Edward 62
SUGAR Thomas 65
SUGARS Zacarius 33
SUIT Thomas 20
SULLAVAN Dennis 20
SULLEN John 51
SULLENDER Jacob 38
SUMPTION Anthony 56
SUNLIGTER George 40
SUPER Philip 45
SUSANNER Peter 40
SUTOR John 33
SUTTON Bartholomew 6
SWAFAR Joseph 36
SWAFFER John 5
Joseph 4
William 4
SWAGGER Barnabas 14
SWAIN Francis 20
SWAN John 64
SWANE Edward 32
SWANGOR Abraham 47
SWARNER John 40
SWAYNE Isaac 65
Jesse 33, 66
Jonathan 64
Samuel 65
Thomas 54
William 65, 66
SWIL Samuel 36
SWISLER Uldrick 40
SWITYER Daniel 40
SWITZAR John 40
SWITZER Daniel 40
SWOOP Michael 85
Stapbol 85
SYNG George 4

INDEX

TAGART Archibald 73
TAGGART Jacob 65
TAGGART John 34, 55
TALBERT Joseph 46
  Samuel 101
TALBOT Jeremiah 40
  John 46
  Joseph 6(2)
TALKINTON Samuel 51
TANNER Phillip 29
TANYERS Joseph 48
TARBET Hugh 73
TARTAN Andrew 55
TASSEY Alexander 100
TATE Jacob 81
  Samuel 77
TAYLOR Abiah 9
  Abraham 9, 20
  Adam 98
  Ann 52
  Benjamin 20(2), 53
  Caleb 20
  Deborah 9
  Elisha 45
  Elizabeth 8
  Frederick 6
  George 33
  Isaac 8, 9, 20, 36
  Israel 31
  Jacob 51
  James 9, 62(2), 91
  Jesse 22
  John 4, 20, 22, 36, 54, 65, 100
  Joseph 20, 33, 54
  Mathew 80
  Michael 42
  Nathan 36
  Peter 36
  Robert 68, 78
  Samuel 43
  Stephen 8, 9
  Thomas 4, 7, 8, 48
  William 11
TEENE Christopher 42
  Michael 41
TEIS John 42
TEMPLE Abraham 80
  John 81
  Thomas 20, 80
  William 20, 81
TEMPLETON John 94
  Joseph 94
TENNANT John 48
THARLOW William 49

THASHER Nicolas 7
THATCHER Edith 51
  John 61
  Jonathan 61
  Thomas 8
THIRLTON George 91
THOMAS Amos 85
  Ann 71
  Benjamin 41, 54
  David 86, 86, 95
  Elisha 93
  Evan 93
  George 13
  Hezekiah 95
  Isaac 100
  Jacob 40, 90
  James 59
  John 2 44, 59(2), 86, 87, 93
  Jonathan 95
  Joseph 4, 53, 100
  Joshua 15, 38
  Lewis 55
  Mary 59
  Michael 93
  Miles 93
  Morris 62, 81
  Owen 87, 93
  Peter 90
  Reuben 84
  Richard 13
  Samuel 100
  Seth 2
  Thomas 59, 93
  William 42, 84, 94, 95, 96
THOMPSON Ann 75
  Archibald 71
  Daniel 36, 49
  Henry 81
  Hugh 29
  James 45, 80, 100
  John 26, 31, 48, 67, 69, 70, 76
  Joseph 31
  Joshua 1, 97
  Moses 52
  Nathan 48
  Robert 49
  Thomas 76, 77, 90
  William 22, 30, 31, 75
THOMSON James 66
  John 20
THORNBERY Edward 7
  Richard 7

THORNBOROUGH Joseph 68
  William 68
THORNTON Robert 67
  Samuel 68
THYLE Joseph 77
TIBBS John 26
TIDBALL Elizabeth 25
  William 25
TIMS Bartholomew 14
  Henry 13
TMPLIN Richard 84
TODD Andrew 94
  James 29
  John 18
TOMKIN Ann 59
TORBERT Catherine 73
TOUCHSTONE Sampson 30
TOWNSEND Benjamin 9
  Francis 9, 10
  John 10
  Richard 67
  William 45
TRAPNAL John 38
TRAVALLEY Price 15
TRAVERSE Hugh 43
TRAVILLA James 98
  Thomas 32
TRAYHORN Mary 38
TREAT Christian 34
TREEBY Joseph 88
TREGOE Benjamin 97
  Joseph 71
  William 69, 97
TRIMBLE Daniel 13
  Henry 54
  James 32, 67, 68
  John 51
  Joseph 29
  Lewes 54
  Samuel 6, 51
  Thomas 6
  William 8, 13(2)
TROUTON Richard 66
TRUEMAN John 16
  Thomas 16
TUCKER Thomas 91
TURK Andrew 59, 94
  John 14
  William 60
TURNER Abraham 41, 85
  Daniel 29
  George 91
  James 74
  John 16, 74
  Thomas 29

INDEX

TUSSY Alexander 46
TUSTON Jacob 45

UNDERHILL John 68
UNDERWOOD Jeremy 64
  John 61, 98
  Samuel 80
  Thomas 64
URIN Andrew 38
  Benjamin 38
URMS John 41

VALENTINE Jonathan 80
VAlINTINE Robert 80
VALOE Peter 57
VANBOUGHT Isaac 31
VANCE John 29
VANDORIN John 54
VANHORN Bernard 59
VANLEER Branson 4
  Samuel 53
  Samuel 93
VANLIER Bernard 52
VARLEY John 59
VAUGHAN Thomas 2, 45
VAUGHEN Isaac 44
VERNAN Elias 43
  Jonathan 43
  Moses 43
  Nathan 43
VERNON Aaron 95
  Abraham 96
  Edward 82
  Elizabeth 9
  Gedion 43
  Jacob 9
  John 83
  Mordica 65
  William 51
VERNUM Aron 52
  Job 44
VERNUN Abigal 43
  Edward 43
  Jonathan 44
  M. 43
  Mary 43
  Nathan 43
  Nathaniel 43
VILEY David 18
VOAR Gidean 87
VOGDES Jacob 35
VOLEY Dennis 5

WADDLE David 61
  James 69
  William 72

WADE John 57
WADLE David 31
WAGGONER Bastian 59
  John 83
WAGONER John 41
  Peter 41
  Philip 41
WAIT Moses 80
WAITING John 45
WALDHAMMER Philip 93
WALKER Alexander 64
  Andrew 17, 72
  Benjamin 21, 100
  Daniel 88
  David 80(2)
  Emanuel 89
  Jacob 88
  James 90
  Jerman 89
  John 15, 80
  Joseph 88
  Michael 54
  Nathaniel 76
  Robert 74
  Samuel 45, 46
  William 23
WALL Absolam 68
  John 57
  Samuel 98
WALLACE Francis 68
  Guyan 70
  Hugh 71
  John 72, 73(2), 83
  Josiah 83
  Oliver 80
  Robert 70
  Thomas 73
  William 26, 76
WALLAR William 26
WALLIS George 74
WALTER Gebril 9
  James 21
  John 7, 31, 41, 47
  Joseph 20
  William 42, 51
WALTERS Thomas 31
WALTS Jacob 11
WANGER Peter 40
WARD Job 76
  John 64, 71
WARNER George 83
  John 21
  Thomas 1, 83
WARNOCK John 29
  Samuel 74

WARSON Matthew 61
  Samuel 64
WATERS James 59
  Thomas 88
WATKIN Daniel 96
  Enoch 86
  Evan 44
  Thomas 90
WATKINS Aaron 85
WATSON John 5, 22, 77
  William 5
WATT David 73
  John 29
WAUGH John 64
WAY Caleb 82
  Jacob 20, 21
  John 20
  Joshua 78
  Mary 82
  Robert 21
  Samuel 61
WAYAND Philip 42
WAYNE Anthony 91
  Isaac 59, 91, 100
  Michael 91, 94
WEATHERBY Benjamin 100
  Samuel 91
  Whitehead 91
WEAVER Isaac 43
  Samuel 89
  Valentine 4, 51
WEBB Daniel 20, 51
  Isaac 80
  James 80
  Joshua 81
  Richard 51
  Stephen 20
  William 20
WEBBER Jacob 38
WEBSTER John 65
WEER James 57
WELDEN Moses 21
WELLS Jonathan 59
  Susannah 40
WELSH Thomas 20, 66, 91
WELTS Abraham 59
WEST George 40
  Thomas 35, 54
  William 2, 21, 87
WESTENBERGER George 40
WESTON John 11, 68
WETHERBY Whitehead 89
WHAN John 62
WHEALIN Dennis 34, 46
  John 34

## INDEX

WHERREY David 29
  James 29
WHILEY John 15
WHIPO George 64
WHIPPO John 68
WHITAKER Edward 46
  John 83
WHITE Christopher 93
  David 30
  Francis 26
  George 33, 89
  James 26, 59
  John 29(3), 59, 73, 81
  Jonathan 29
  Joseph 7
  Nathaniel 83
  Richard 60
  Samuel 66, 80
  Thomas 16, 73, 80, 98, 100(2)
  Uriah 98
  William 20, 21, 59, 68
WHITECRAFT James 18
WHITEY Mary 4
WHITHEAD John 4
WHITTON Benjamin 62
  John 18, 62
WICKERSHAM Abel 66
  Elinor 21
  Enoch 66
  James 65, 66
  Jesse 66
  Peter 22
  William 22(2)
WICKWERE Ezekiel 55
WICTDEN Obediah 44
WIDDAS John 76
WIDEFORD George 40
WIELDY Obediah 45
WIGGANS Thomas 100
WIKERSHAM John 76
WILCOX James 36
  Mark 51
  Thomas 51
WILEY Alexander 71
  Caleb 21
  David 64
  Joshua 21
  William 15, 21
WILKIN John 17
  Leonard 80
  Robert 17
WILKINS William 16

WILKINSON Francis 80
  John 38
  Joseph 48, 98
  Josiah 98
  Thomas 43, 80
WILKS Fredrick 54
WILLIAM David 60
  Evan 83
  Hugh 59
  James 59, 60
  John 59(2)
  Joseph 59
  Owen 35
  Thomas 59, 60
WILLIAMS Alexander 87
  Amos 42
  David 34
  Edward 91
  Enoch 89
  Hugh 85, 86
  Isaac 22, 97
  Jacob 84
  James 16(2)
  John 62, 85
  Joseph 16, 33, 90
  Lewis 98, 100
  Lydia 98
  Mordica 42
  Reese 98
  Samuel 57
  Thomas 93(2)
  William 66
WILLIAMSON Daniel 50
  John 57, 64, 66, 95
  Thomas 97
  William 100
WILLIS Elizabeth 57
  Joel 48
  Richard 40(2)
  Thomas 55
WILLS Thomas 6
WILLSON Andrew 70
  James 62, 70
  John 88, 93
  Joseph 34
WILSON Andrew 26(2), 43, 70
  Benjamin 29
  Caleb 22
  Charles 22
  Christopher 54
  Daniel 59
  Flemming 29
  Francis 71
  George 35, 80
  Hugh 91
  James 26, 29, 30, 77, 83

  John 12, 30, 31, 64, 66, 77
  Joshua 15, 77
  Matthew 17
  Peter 64
  Richard 68
  Robert 29, 33, 35, 68, 77, 83
  Samuel 29, 64, 77
  Thomas 22(2), 25, 83, 87, 91, 93(2)
  William 68, 72, 73, 80
WILSTON John 21
  Matthew 21
WINDER Christian 70
WINDLE Francis 65
  John 66
  Thomas 80
  William 66
WINGER Jacob 40
WINN Jonathan 84
WISE Rudolph 40
WISEBERGER Jacob 85
WISELEY William 50
WISLER Christian 40
WITCRAFT John 66
WITHERS Samuel 64
WITHROW Robert 83
  Samuel 47, 83
  William 31, 83
WOCCHTER Sebastian 40
WOLDE Joseph 40
  William 40
WOLFINTON Abraham 15
WOLLERTON James 10
  John 10
WOLLIS Nathaniel 64
WOLLY John 53
WOMSLEY Jonathan 38
WOOD Cornelius 7
  Hannah 38
  Isaac 56
  Jonathan 38
  Peter 38
  William 64
WOODROW Isaac 21
  John 25
  Joseph 21
  Joshua 68
WOODS Joseph 25
  William 73
WOODSIDE Archibald 18

## INDEX

WOODWARD Amos 11
  Henry 9
  James 68(2)
  John 9, 61, 68
  Joseph 68
  Nayle 66
  Richard 10
  Robert 68
  Thomas 26, 32, 64, 66
  William 67; 68(2)
WOODWORD Henry 98
WOOLEY Thomas 53
WOOLF Andrew 40(2)
  John 40
  Martin 40
WOOLMAN Jacob 91
WOOLSON Jacob 76
WORKISER Chritian 89
WORLEY David 29
WORRAL Peter 6
WORRALL Adam 36
  Elijah 55
  Elisha 52, 53, 55
  Jacob 54
  James 52(2)
  John 6, 54
  Jonathan 52
  Joseph 53, 54
  Peter 52
  Phebe 52
  Thomas 6, 43
  William 54
WORREL Benjamin 36
  Edward 36
  Isaiah 36
  Joseph 35
  Owen 36
  Peter 36
  Samuel 36
WORRELL John 49
  Joshua 31
WORRIL Jacob 56
WORTH John 68
  Samuel 68
  Thomas 10
WORTHINGTON James 86
WRIGHT Jacob 66
  John 1, 26
  Richard 55
  Robert 8
WROTH Ebenezer 11
WYNN Isaac 70
  James 85
  Samuel 85

YARNAL Nathan 6
YARNALL Amos 100
  Caleb 49
  David 49, 84
  Jacob 49
  Job 49
  Mary 49
  Nathan 31, 49, 52
  William 49
YARNELL Amos 100
  Caleb 100
  Daniel 100
  Enoch 100
  Francis 100
  George 100
  John 100
  Joshua 100
  Moses 100
YARNILL Daniel 48
YEAGER George 86
YEARSLEY Isaac 9
  Susannah 9
YEARSLY Thomas 7
YORK John 22
YOULE Thomas 29
YOUNG Archibald 68(2)
  Daniel 31
  Elenor 15
  James 57
  John 68, 77
  Joseph 17
  Mathew 76
  Thomas 9
YOUNGBLOOD John 59

ZIMPHER Jacob 21

**Other Heritage Books by F. Edward Wright:**

*Abstracts of Bucks County, Pennsylvania Wills, 1685–1785*
*Abstracts of Cumberland County, Pennsylvania Wills, 1750–1785*
*Abstracts of Cumberland County, Pennsylvania Wills, 1785–1825*
*Abstracts of Philadelphia County Wills, 1726–1747*
*Abstracts of Philadelphia County Wills, 1748–1763*
*Abstracts of Philadelphia County Wills, 1763–1784*
*Abstracts of Philadelphia County Wills, 1777–1790*
*Abstracts of Philadelphia County Wills, 1790–1802*
*Abstracts of Philadelphia County Wills, 1802–1809*
*Abstracts of Philadelphia County Wills, 1810–1815*
*Abstracts of Philadelphia County Wills, 1815–1819*
*Abstracts of Philadelphia County Wills, 1820–1825*
*Abstracts of Philadelphia County, Pennsylvania Wills, 1682–1726*
*Abstracts of South Central Pennsylvania Newspapers, Volume 1, 1785–1790*
*Abstracts of South Central Pennsylvania Newspapers, Volume 3, 1796–1800*
*Abstracts of the Newspapers of Georgetown and the Federal City, 1789–99*
*Abstracts of York County, Pennsylvania Wills, 1749–1819*
*Bucks County, Pennsylvania Church Records of the 17th and 18th Centuries
Volume 2: Quaker Records: Falls and Middletown Monthly Meetings*
Anna Miller Watring and F. Edward Wright
*Caroline County, Maryland Marriages, Births and Deaths, 1850–1880*
*Citizens of the Eastern Shore of Maryland, 1659–1750*
*Cumberland County, Pennsylvania Church Records of the 18th Century*
*Delaware Newspaper Abstracts, Volume 1: 1786–1795*
*Early Charles County, Maryland Settlers, 1658–1745*
Marlene Strawser Bates and F. Edward Wright
*Early Church Records of Alexandria City and Fairfax County, Virginia*
F. Edward Wright and Wesley E. Pippenger
*Early Church Records of New Castle County, Delaware, Volume 1, 1701–1800*
*Frederick County Militia in the War of 1812*
Sallie A. Mallick and F. Edward Wright
*Inhabitants of Baltimore County, 1692–1763*
*Land Records of Sussex County, Delaware, 1769–1782*
*Land Records of Sussex County, Delaware, 1782–1789*
Elaine Hastings Mason and F. Edward Wright
*Marriage Licenses of Washington, District of Columbia, 1811–1830*
*Marriages and Deaths from the Newspapers of Allegany and
Washington Counties, Maryland, 1820–1830*
*Marriages and Deaths from The York Recorder, 1821–1830*
*Marriages and Deaths in the Newspapers of Frederick and
Montgomery Counties, Maryland, 1820–1830*

*Marriages and Deaths in the Newspapers of Lancaster County, Pennsylvania, 1821–1830*
*Marriages and Deaths in the Newspapers of Lancaster County, Pennsylvania, 1831–1840*
*Marriages and Deaths of Cumberland County, [Pennsylvania], 1821–1830*
*Maryland Calendar of Wills Volume 9: 1744–1749*
*Maryland Calendar of Wills Volume 10: 1748–1753*
*Maryland Calendar of Wills Volume 11: 1753–1760*
*Maryland Calendar of Wills Volume 12: 1759–1764*
*Maryland Calendar of Wills Volume 13: 1764–1767*
*Maryland Calendar of Wills Volume 14: 1767–1772*
*Maryland Calendar of Wills Volume 15: 1772–1774*
*Maryland Calendar of Wills Volume 16: 1774–1777*
*Maryland Eastern Shore Newspaper Abstracts, Volume 1: 1790–1805*
*Maryland Eastern Shore Newspaper Abstracts, Volume 2: 1806–1812*
*Maryland Eastern Shore Newspaper Abstracts, Volume 3: 1813–1818*
*Maryland Eastern Shore Newspaper Abstracts, Volume 4: 1819–1824*
*Maryland Eastern Shore Newspaper Abstracts, Volume 5: Northern Counties, 1825–1829*
F. Edward Wright and Irma Harper
*Maryland Eastern Shore Newspaper Abstracts, Volume 6: Southern Counties, 1825–1829*
*Maryland Eastern Shore Newspaper Abstracts, Volume 7: Northern Counties, 1830–1834*
Irma Harper and F. Edward Wright
*Maryland Eastern Shore Newspaper Abstracts, Volume 8: Southern Counties, 1830–1834*
*Maryland Militia in the Revolutionary War*
S. Eugene Clements and F. Edward Wright
*Newspaper Abstracts of Allegany and Washington Counties, Maryland, 1811–1815*
*Newspaper Abstracts of Cecil and Harford Counties, Maryland, 1822–1830*
*Newspaper Abstracts of Frederick County, Maryland, 1816–1819*
*Newspaper Abstracts of Frederick County, Maryland, 1811–1815*
*Sketches of Maryland Eastern Shoremen*
*Tax List of Chester County, Pennsylvania 1768*
*Tax List of York County, Pennsylvania 1779*
*Washington County Church Records of the 18th Century, 1768–1800*
*Western Maryland Newspaper Abstracts, Volume 1: 1786–1798*
*Western Maryland Newspaper Abstracts, Volume 2: 1799–1805*
*Western Maryland Newspaper Abstracts, Volume 3: 1806–1810*
*Wills of Chester County, Pennsylvania, 1766–1778*

www.ingramcontent.com/pod-product-compliance
Lightning Source LLC
Chambersburg PA
CBHW070454090426
42735CB00012B/2545